Narrative Design for Mobile and Live Games

This is a comprehensive guidebook for long-term storytelling in mobile games and games-as-a-service (also known as live games). This book formalizes creative techniques of game writing and narrative design for a platform (and revenue model) that has shown drastic growth and changes over the past few years. The unique challenges of mobile games and live games are also increasingly relevant across the whole games industry. With hybrid consoles such as the Nintendo Switch, cloud gaming, and cross-platform titles, the lines between mobile and console have begun to blur. Additionally, many games now offer live support to extend player engagement.

This book starts with an introduction to narrative design and the world of mobile games, followed by a deep dive into open-ended and seasonal storytelling. Besides the creative aspect of development, it covers areas of production such as documentation, collaboration, and monetization. To illustrate its solutions, it uses examples from video games and other media, specifically screenwriting for TV shows.

This book will be of great interest to all game narrative and writing professionals working on mobile and live games.

Valentina Tamer is a narrative designer and game writer with several years of experience in the games industry, throughout which she's crafted engaging stories for a wide range of videogames, from mobile games to narrative adventures. Val currently works as a senior narrative designer for Ubisoft Paris Mobile.

Narrative Design for Mobile and Live Games

Valentina Tamer

CRC Press
Taylor & Francis Group
Boca Raton London New York

CRC Press is an imprint of the
Taylor & Francis Group, an **informa** business

Cover Image Designer: SCJ

First edition published 2024
by CRC Press
2385 Executive Center Drive, Suite 320, Boca Raton, FL 33431

and by CRC Press
4 Park Square, Milton Park, Abingdon, Oxon, OX14 4RN

CRC Press is an imprint of Taylor & Francis Group, LLC

© 2024 Valentina Tamer

Library of Congress Cataloging-in-Publication Data
Names: Tamer, Valentina, author.
Title: Narrative design for mobile and live games / Valentina Tamer.
Description: First edition. | Boca Raton, FL : CRC Press, 2024. | Includes
bibliographical references and index.
Identifiers: LCCN 2023024151 (print) | LCCN 2023024152 (ebook) |
ISBN 9781032286044 (hardback) | ISBN 9781032285948 (paperback) |
ISBN 9781003297628 (ebook)
Subjects: LCSH: Mobile games—Design. | Storytelling. | Mobile games
industry. | iPhone (Smartphone)
Classification: LCC GV1469.15 .T36 2024 (print) | LCC GV1469.15 (ebook) |
DDC 794.8/1525—dc23/eng/20230602
LC record available at https://lccn.loc.gov/2023024151
LC ebook record available at https://lccn.loc.gov/2023024152

ISBN: 9781032286044 (hbk)
ISBN: 9781032285948 (pbk)
ISBN: 9781003297628 (ebk)

DOI: 10.1201/9781003297628

Typeset in Times
by codeMantra

Contents

PART II   Interactive Storytelling

PART III Live Game Storytelling

Acknowledgments

For their support and inspiration, I'd like to thank: Marina Hennig, Bettina Tamer, Matt Kempke, Kevin Mentz, Kenny Shea Dinkin, Abigail Rindo, Jana Sloan van Geest, Barnabé Anglade, Lucy Morris, and Michael Bhatty.

Part I

Introduction

Introduction

Picture this: You've just finished a videogame you had a great time with. The characters have started to feel like good friends, and by the time you have saved the world together (or whatever the plot amounted to), you want to keep them in your life just a little longer. You talk to other fans to exchange your theories and opinions, and you all agree that you can't wait for the sequel. But after the initial honeymoon phase, your attention is suddenly caught by the next blockbuster game. Perhaps your passion for that finished game will be reignited when the next installment comes around, maybe sooner or maybe not at all. Anyway, you would have had more passion to spare, if there had been only more content to engage with.

Now, think of the biggest pop culture franchises of today. Those which release something new all the time. Think Pokémon, Marvel, and Disney – with a new game, TV show, comic, and merchandise drop right around the corner at any given time, there's no need to stop being an active fan. These properties are transmedia giants, each with a unique starting point but videogames in their line-ups. It's a game company's dream: Keeping fans loyal to your property and regularly providing new content for them to purchase and consume. Brands make money, make marketing easier, and can grow audiences indefinitely (supposedly). There's a reason why so many creative industries aim to create brands, series, and cinematic universes nowadays – and games are not exempt from that trend. The dream is to stay relevant indefinitely and take over pop culture. If you want to be ambitious, that is.

Imagine a videogame that does this all by itself – not as a franchise in sequels and spin-offs, but as one single game. This is what the games-as-a-service model aspires to do. This release structure, also called live games, is defined by persistent new releases of permanent updates and time-limited content, keeping a game alive and growing over a long period of time. Many live games have already tried this ambitious feat, but only few have managed to keep it going over the years. Massive multiplayer online (MMO) games are among the oldest examples, but usually reserved for a specific niche target audience. But what if I told you that these types of "endless" games could exist for all target audiences, all game genres, and all kinds of stories?

There's a catch of course: You have to write them. Or get lucky that somebody else does. But if you've picked up this book and have read thus far into the introduction, then this is probably something you're interested in doing. The fact of the matter is that it's hard to pull off. It's not a project for beginners or a humble budget. They're ambitious, expensive, and need a lot of foresight and planning – with a good portion of luck on top.

But it's not only enough to understand how to make a game with regular updates – you need to understand how to make players *care* about it for that long. This is where narrative design comes into play: Writing that never-ending story that will keep players engaged for years on end.

DOI: 10.1201/9781003297628-2

To make things more complicated, a lot of those live games are launched on the most accessible, content-flooded platform of them all: Smartphones. Therefore, to understand how to make good live games, it's important to understand the platform as well – and there's a high chance it'll be for mobile, or have monetization and design strategies inspired by mobile games.

However, storytelling in mobile games has often been treated like the black sheep, under-appreciated, underused, and underestimated. Narrative is often the first game aspect to be reduced or cut entirely. Alas, in recent years, we've seen more and more narrative-driven mobile and live games. There are narrative games (like Chapters or Episodes) where narrative is the core gameplay, multiplayer games with heroes that have a deep backstory and a unique voice (like Overwatch or League of Legends), and of course, the MMO genre is still thriving with games like World of Warcraft or GTA Online. There is an increasing awareness that narrative isn't only window-dressing – it's essential for player motivation, brand loyalty, and the enjoyment of the final product. And this applies to all platforms, smartphones included.

Many live games have done interesting things, and managed to stay live for years or failed spectacularly – but there's still much to explore. The idea of a premium live game that is as captivating as an whole media franchise has been reserved for MMOs for the longest time, and only recently, we've seen more varied experiences for this type of release structure. There's still untapped potential for a videogame that promises players to captivate them for a long time to come, both in terms of gameplay, and with the story they're telling. And with live games, it's possible to offer a new experience of long-form interactive narrative that no other medium can pull off in the same way.

THE STATUS QUO OF MOBILE AND LIVE GAMES

Videogames are a fairly young but rapidly evolving medium. The year 1947 saw the invention of what is now assumed to be the first interactive electronic game, the Cathode Ray Tube Amusement Device by Thomas T. Goldsmith Jr.[1] But it wouldn't be until the 1970s before we got a first commercial arcade machine (Computer Space, 1971), followed by a home console with the Magnavox Odyssey (1972).[2] So within just over half a decade of mass marketed videogames, we went from simple toys with 8-bit pixel graphics to sprawling worlds in 4K HD. From arcade-style mini games with a simple premise (like Pong, Space Invaders, etc.) to vast open worlds in hyper-realistic detail and endless freedom to experience a virtual world (like Cyberpunk 2077, Assassin's Creed Odyssey, etc.) – sometimes even in Virtual Reality.

Each technological advancement has brought new trends and monetization strategies, which, in turn, influence how games are designed and distributed. As much as games are art, most games are also consumer products and reflective of technological status quos – even indie titles are a result of available and accessible game engines. And nowadays, more and more games are released as live games, even if the same idea wouldn't have been 10 years ago. The reason for that is, naturally, technological developments, consumer behavior, and shifting monetization strategies in an attempt to be where money can be made and the future is taking the industry.

Mobile games have been taking over the videogame market, and this trend is likely to continue. With smartphone capabilities rapidly increasing, and an increasing rate of smartphone ownership all across the world, they are the most accessible gaming device ever.[3] Most people don't buy it for gaming but for all its other features, so even those who would never invest in a gaming console suddenly have one at their disposal. And since countless mobile games nowadays are free-to-play, downloading a good-looking game is as easy as the tap of a button. You can delete it if you don't like it and lose no money over it. This means the entry barrier to a new game is much lower, but also that the competition is fierce, simply based on the sheer amount of options. The skyrocketing revenue of mobile games has left the rest of the games industry salivating, with a total revenue of $92.2 billion in the year 2022, which is 50% of the global gaming market earnings.[4] Their raging success is arguably a combination of device accessibility, low required time investment, low financial entry level, and a diversification of target audiences – in combination with in-app purchases and subscription models as monetization methods that allow players to spend as little or as much as they want.

In something akin to a free-to-play gold rush, non-mobile game developers have recognized that there is potential to learn something from monetization in mobile games. The most financially successful mobile games have been published as live games, adding new features, content, and updates over an extended period of time, instead of releasing sequels (or at least only rarely). Motivating players to stay with one game longer, instead of buying many individual games, is becoming an increasingly popular development strategy. The longer a player stays with one game, the more social relevance the game can stand to gain, and the more in-game purchases or advertisement money can be made. Create a great foundation, keep players around, and benefit for years to come.

A lot of console and PC developers are now releasing live games or premium games with live support, may that be as a multiplayer game (or a single-player game with extensive multiplayer modes) striving to be the next eSport (like Call of Duty: Modern Warfare), or a single-player premium game with a roadmap of regular new content for a year or longer (like Far Cry 6). Consequently, a lot of mobile release and monetization strategies have crept into non-mobile games. We can also see more cross-platform games with a release on mobile and non-mobile, making these games simultaneously available on more than one platform (like Pokémon UNITE or Genshin Impact).

This is why this book will take a look at both of these increasingly overlapping topics: Live games and mobile games – for if you work on a mobile game, there's a high chance it will be a live game, and if you're working on a live game, there's a high chance mobile game tools can give you some valuable inspiration. With mobile games becoming more and more ambitious in terms of quality and graphics, and console/PC games being released as games-as-a-service that take inspiration from mobile games, these mediums can't really be separated when it comes to learning how to design and write engaging narratives for them.

To better understand why things have gone in this direction, it's enlightening to know what technological advancements led to these trends. We can assume that these **technological developments** have played a role in this:

- Smartphones have seen drastic **technological improvements**, allowing them to handle more ambitious games.
- **Mobile internet plans** for smartphones offer **higher monthly capacities** and are making gaming on the go increasingly feasible, even with high download packages.
- The amount of **people owning smartphones** worldwide is constantly on the rise, making it an accessible gaming device.
- Mobile games have been booming, making up **50% of the annual revenue of the games industry** (in 2022).
- Game developers seek to **increase their profit** by creating cross-platform titles (mobile/non-mobile), live games, and games with free-to-play monetization strategies, inspired by the mobile industry's success.

While it may sound rather business-oriented to say that design follows technology and monetization, but this is neither new nor does it mean that it can't be creatively interesting to do so. TV shows changed their production strategies when streaming had become more viable than TV broadcasting – now we often get entire (albeit shorter) seasons for binge-watching instead of only one episode per week banking on re-runs (although there's a revival of that structure in some cases). Technology, distribution, and monetization change the way media is made, it always has. As a member of the industry, it's up to us to figure out how to make it enjoyable for the consumer, pushing the medium's ever-changing forms and creative potential.

WHO IS THIS BOOK FOR?

Despite the skyrocketing industry relevance of live and mobile games, it's not easy finding resources on long-form storytelling specifically for them, especially with modern design sensibilities. This book seeks to change that fact and deliver a comprehensive toolbox for any developer facing this challenge. It strives to provide a comprehensive guidebook for narrative design and long-form storytelling in videogames, with a particular spotlight on live games. To achieve this, I will present established narrative design methods and expand them with learnings from my experience working in the games industry (as a narrative designer and game writer who's been involved in the development of several mobile and live games), as well as analysis of existing live games and other long-running media. This book is conceived as a structured course, to learn in your own time, and as a helpful toolbox to reference during active work on a project. With it, I hope to equip narrative designers, writers, and any other creative with the tools they need to create better, more effective long-form stories in videogames – giving the medium the narrative revolution it rightly deserves.

This book is for you if…

- You're a narrative designer who wants to learn about narrative design for live and mobile games.
- You're a narrative designer who wants to learn how to write seasonal or long-running stories.
- You're a game writer who wants to break into narrative design.

- You're a writer who wants to break into videogame storytelling or narrative design.
- You're a student who wants to break into narrative design.
- You're a game developer who wants to better understand narrative design to infuse it into your craft.

WHO IS THIS BOOK *NOT* FOR?

This book is not meant as an introduction to game writing and dramatic writing as whole. It assumes that you have a basic understanding of dramaturgy and storytelling already, and if you don't, that you will make use of additional resources to fill the gaps. There is no need to do homework before you start reading, however, as we will cover the basics as they become relevant – we just won't go into their depths. This book is meant to function as an advanced training for narrative design and live game storytelling, and not meant as a sole educative tool for beginners of creative writing. However, if you are a game writer who doesn't know anything about narrative design yet, you'll be fine – we will cover this aspect in detail.

This book is not for you if…

- You're looking for an introduction to creative writing and game writing. This book's focus is on narrative design and long-term storytelling for live games.
- You have *no* previous knowledge about video games, neither personally nor professionally. This book assumes that you have a basic understanding of video games and game development.

HOW TO USE THIS BOOK?

There are several ways how to use this book: Either as a chronological course, read in the order of chapters, or as a package of individual educational units. If read in order, chapters build upon each other, going from a general exploration of narrative design, to interactive narrative design, up to live game narrative design – and then ends on additional narrative topics relevant to live games (such as transmedia storytelling and monetization methods). If you're already on a project and seek information on a specific aspect, you can browse the table of contents and see where you can find your answer.

REFERENCES

1 D.S. Cohen, "Cathode-Ray Tube Amusement Device: The First Electronic Game," Lifewire, March 14, 2019, https://www.lifewire.com/cathode-ray-tube-amusement-device-729579.
2 "The Father of the Video Game: The Ralph Baer Prototypes and Electronic Games: Video Game History," Smithsonian, accessed April 20, 2023, https://www.si.edu/spotlight/the-father-of-the-video-game-the-ralph-baer-prototypes-and-electronic-games/video-game-history.
3 "Global Mobile Market Report," Newzoo, 2021, https://newzoo.com/resources/trend-reports/newzoo-global-mobile-market-report-2021-free-version.
4 Tom Wijman, "The Games Market in 2022: The Year in Numbers," Newzoo, December 21, 2022, https://newzoo.com/insights/articles/the-games-market-in-2022-the-year-in-numbers.

1 What is Narrative Design?

GAME WRITING VS. WRITING FOR OTHER MEDIA

Think about your favorite movie and your favorite novel, and why you like them. Some of those reasons are likely to overlap, such as a certain topic, engaging characters, or suspenseful storytelling. But chances are that there are some things that only apply to one or the other, too. While your favorite novel may have prose describing the rich inner lives of characters, the movie doesn't. While your favorite movie may have amazing visuals and great acting performances, the novel doesn't. After all, they're different mediums and have their own unique means of storytelling, strengths, and limitations. Even though fiction generally shares some common principles of drama and storytelling, it doesn't mean that every writer is *automatically* equipped to create masterpieces in *every* medium. A novelist isn't necessarily a good screenwriter – and the other way around – because each medium has its own way of telling a story. To be able to use the full potential of a fictional medium, one must understand *how* it tells stories, and this also applies to videogames. They're not simply playable movies – they're their own thing.

In cinema – similar to games due to their shared audiovisual basis – the audience takes on an observer role, watching a linear experience with a predefined camera and timeline. The sequences may be nonchronological, but the timeline of experience is determined by the filmmaker. The audience's experience is shaped by interpretation, rather than interaction. The interaction is purely psychological and doesn't influence the movie itself, just the audience's perception of it.

In games, however, audiences are active participants who exert agency over their navigation of an interactive and potentially nonlinear experience. The camera depends on player input, just as the timeline of the story does, and even the exact nature of the events themselves. The player's experience is shaped by their own actions, the game's reactions, and the player's interpretation of these loops of causality. They become an active part of the story, even if they play a predefined fictional role on a pre-determined path inside the game world.

This implies that the meaning of authorship shifts ever so slightly. The "authors" of a movie (namely the screenwriters and directors) decide what the audience will see, in what order, and on what timeline. On the other hand, the "authors" of a game (namely the creative directors, game writers, and narrative designers) and the development team create a space for a player-driven experience, where the game's rules, virtual spaces, and systems create a directed and purposeful experience that allows freedom to take things at their own pace, stray from the golden path, or even experience alternative story developments. Players become co-authors of their own experience, to the extent that the developers allow. Games guide the action of the player in a way that creates story, but the story isn't pre-authored in all its minute details – even if it's a linear action adventure. There is still room for player stories, emergent gameplay, and exploration – and players get to play a part in shaping their experience.

DOI: 10.1201/9781003297628-3

To create a narrative experience like this implies a skill set that goes beyond screenwriting, based on the unique storytelling methods of the medium. And *this* is where the narrative designer comes in.

NARRATIVE DESIGNER VS. GAME WRITER

The job title "narrative designer" is much younger than that of the game writer, which is one reason why they've often been used as synonymous. But there has been an increasing differentiation between one and the other, so that now they can be treated as two separate but closely related crafts with some shared responsibilities. This is especially true for projects with larger narrative teams, where both job titles exist and are more likely to be strictly separated. In smaller projects, there is often a stronger overlap. For the sake of clarity, we will try to differentiate the crafts as much as possible, which will also help us understand the full narrative potential of games beyond plot and texts.

Generally, the definition of a game writer's job seems intuitive. They structure the plot, write the lore, cutscenes, and further in-game texts. But in order to understand what a narrative designer does, it's crucial to clear up some misunderstandings of how storytelling for videogames works. It's a widespread misconception that it only consists of writing these previously mentioned elements. Just based on that alone, it's no surprise that the difference between a narrative designer and a game writer can be a source of confusion – don't they both write the game's story? This is rooted in the ignorance of narrative methods unique to videogames – those that go beyond the aspects that would also be present in, for example, a movie screenplay. Namely, expressing a story through gameplay, systems, and the creative direction of all of a game's aspects.

Some might also conflate being a storyteller working in games with the solitary author myth – someone who types away on their computer all day to create a story that is then somehow added to the project – either delivered *before* or *after* the complete development of the game. Not to say that such work arrangements can't happen in real life, but they're far from the ideal. If anything, separating a writer from the rest of the team can result in a lot of friction between game and story, wasted narrative potential, and an overall worse product. Things won't fit together, like a jumbled mess of separate elements thrown together at random, and not actually trying to tell the same story.

Another aggravating factor is the assumption that narrative specialists don't work with the game engine, like a programmer or game designer would, and just focus on writing. In reality, narrative designers often work directly in the game engine to implement and balance the narrative features they created, to test and polish them, and to see whether they have their intended effect.

A narrative designer usually puts a high focus on the **medium's unique narrative methods** (like interactive narrative systems), **implementation**, and **collaboration with the rest of the team**. They don't sit alone in their office and just write a story; they seek conversations with other team members to figure out how to express the game's story with *their* craft as well.

Videogames are...

- A medium with a unique language that conveys narrative through all its aspects – not only using lore, plot, dialogue, and texts but also gameplay, narrative systems, and creative direction.
- A collaborative team effort of many different crafts, which need to communicate and work together for the best results.

To separate the game writer from a narrative designer, one can say that a game **writer creates the narrative backbone** of a game and **writes player-facing texts**, whereas a **narrative designer** designs the **holistic narrative experience** of the player using every tool a videogame has to offer, from gameplay and game systems to creative direction – either by designing solutions themselves or by collaborating with team members. This often includes aiding narrative implementation, testing, and balancing. But depending on the project, narrative designers may also take over some or all responsibilities of a game writer.

GAME WRITER

Generally speaking, a **game writer** is likely to focus exclusively on the lore and story of a game and how to express that story through dramaturgy, dialogue, and texts. They are creating the narrative basis that the rest of the team can then use for inspiration for their own work with lore documents, character profiles, timelines, and other documentation. They also help define the plot points that the players will experience throughout the game, write dialogues, and other in-game texts needed to express them.

COMMON RESPONSIBILITIES OF A GAME WRITER

- Story vision documents (defining which story to tell)
- Narrative guidelines
- Localization guidelines
- Lore documents (worldbuilding, character profiles, timelines, etc.)
- Plot outlines
- Dialogues
- Barks
- Quest stories
- Descriptions (weapons, skills, attacks, items, enemies, etc.)
- Additional in-game texts
- Directing voice actors during recordings

NARRATIVE DESIGNER

On the other hand, being a **narrative designer** means that you're designing a player's narrative experience using all elements of the game, including gameplay, narrative systems, and creative direction. A special focus lies on narrative features and narrative system design – which define how a story is *presented* to the player. A narrative designer's responsibilities possibly include aiding in the implementation of narrative features too, testing and balancing them for maximum effect and optimal pacing. Narrative designers don't only think about what story to tell, but *how* they want to tell it: What are the narrative units, how are they structured, how will they be triggered, can they be influenced, and how do they relate to gameplay? To further shape the player's narrative experience, they collaborate with other crafts to find opportunities to reveal the game's narrative in their craft too – so that the whole narrative experience tries to tell the player the same thing.

Another main challenge of a narrative designer is authoring a story space for players, allowing movement for agency and decisions while still providing a well-paced playthrough, no matter how players decide to play. It's a cross-functional, decision-heavy profession where a basic understanding of all aspects of game development is crucial for making the best of the medium. Narrative design is more than dramatic writing; it's about finding the best narrative solutions for all game aspects and then overseeing the correct implementation (if they aren't doing the implementation themselves).

Common Responsibilities of a Narrative Designer

- Narrative vision document (defining which story to tell – and how)
- Narrative guidelines
- Localization guidelines
- Narrative system design (format, triggers, and pacing of narrative units)
- Creative direction and cross-functional collaboration, to express a story with all aspects of the game
- In-game texts (including functional interface texts)
- Implementation and balancing of narrative features inside the game engine
- Playtesting and balancing narrative features
- Directing voice actors during recordings

However, depending on the project, narrative designers may also have **some or even all responsibilities** of the game writer, as previously mentioned. They may also write the lore, dialogue and in-game texts, on top of their unique narrative design tasks.

In short, a game writer focuses on *what story to tell*, whereas a narrative designer focuses on *how the story is told* – sometimes in addition to some or all of a game writer's tasks.

JOB DEFINITIONS IN THE INDUSTRY

In the real world, things are often not as clear-cut. These two job titles often overlap and are sometimes even used interchangeably, even though they are technically different specializations. The practical definition of a narrative designer's responsibilities will differ from company to company and project to project, usually depending on the project's needs and team size.

The smaller a project is, the more likely a person will cover both responsibilities (using either of the job titles). The bigger a project is, the more likely you will have specialized job descriptions that separate the two more strictly. In other words, if you're hired as a narrative designer for a small indie team, chances are you'll also cover responsibilities of a game writer. If you're hired as a narrative designer for a big AAA project with a narrative team that contains both, narrative designers and game writers, you're more likely to find a clearer separation between responsibilities. In that case, a narrative designer may not even write any in-game text at all, but focus on narrative systems, creative direction, and implementation of narrative features. But maybe one or the other type of text will fall under their responsibilities after all. It really depends on each unique situation.

The definitions given in this book are meant to create an awareness of the terminology in its more distinctive form, while still acknowledging the common shared responsibilities of game writing in a narrative designer's repertoire. Therefore, this book will provide lessons for any creative working with any of the tools of a game writer *and* narrative designer.

SUMMARY

- **Writing for games** requires **another skill set** than writing for other media.
- In **traditional media, readers are the observer**, watching a linear, pre-authored story.
- In **games, players are an actor** in an interactive and potentially non-linear medium.
- Narrative designer and game writer are **not the same job**, but they overlap.
- **Narrative designers** create the **player's narrative experience** using **all elements of the game**, including interactivity, game design, game systems, and creative direction.
- **Game writers** are usually more focused on **worldbuilding, lore, dramaturgy, and writing**.
- Narrative designers may have additional responsibilities of a game writer (this depends on the project and company).

2 An Overview of Narrative Design

A narrative designer has many tools at their disposal when it comes to storytelling in videogames. Some of those tools are player-facing and will be visible in the final product, while others are internal documents meant to guide the game's creative decisions during the creation of player-facing content. Before we dive deeper, let's get an an overview of those internal and external tools. This list is meant as a reference and initial introduction, rather than a deep dive – for more in-depth explanations, *see Chapter 11.* Also, please note that each of the following documents might have another name in your project, depending on established studio terms.

INTERNAL DOCUMENTS

The following list lays out the narrative tools that are used during pre-production and production, used to plan and structure the game's narrative. They are internal and thus designed to be seen by team members, not the players.

- **Story Vision:** A document to capture the overall story premise of the game. This is usually the earliest document and part of a pitch phase, but it remains important throughout development, in order to keep the game's initial goal in mind and the team on the same page. It usually outlines the game's basic story concept, including the key conflict, central characters, setting, and plot summary.
- **Narrative Pillars:** An overview of the most important narrative features of the game, and *how* the story will be told. A game's narrative pillars can be, for example, obligatory main missions and optional side missions, in addition to milestone cutscenes and documents that can be discovered across levels. It's usually best to have three to five pillars as your main focus.
- **Narrative Guidelines:** A document that is meant to formalize any narrative restrictions, such as tone (→*see Tone Document*), player perspective, how to address the player, stylistic choices, or any idiosyncratic phrasing within the game's universe. This is also the document to define restrictions such as the word count limits for various narrative units, intended length of narrative units, sentence structures for aspects of the game (such as skill descriptions), or any other matters of restrictions and guidelines.
- **Tone Document:** This document focuses on the tone alone, outlining the game's intention in terms of genre, style, mood and age rating. This often includes comparison to other games or movies, as well as some examples. This can be part of the narrative guidelines.

DOI: 10.1201/9781003297628-4

- **Localization Guidelines:** Another version of the narrative guidelines document is the one created for localization teams. It usually contains any information that can be useful for their localization efforts, such as a game overview, story summary, plot outline, and character profiles but also the required word count of specific narrative units (to make sure they fit the interface in all languages), questions of tone, characterization, idiosyncratic speech and dialects. This is the place to describe your intention with your characters and various narrative aspects of the game, in order to clarify any intention that might not be easily understandable from the texts alone, but which you want to be present in translations as well.
- **Narrative System Design:** A design document for the narrative systems of a game, defining all narrative tools and their individual purpose, format, triggers, and dependencies. Based on the narrative pillars, this document goes into the details of every single type of narrative tool, building the framework of the game's narrative before production starts. This includes defining the logic flows of any narrative systems.
- **Glossary:** A comprehensive list of all relevant in-game terms, meant as a reference for the team to look up the final names of game elements. Oftentimes during production, game features and elements have temporary internal names and will change for the final in-game version.
- **Lore Documents:** Lore documents establish the relevant narrative background for the game required to build the player-facing narrative and make creative decisions regarding gameplay and artistic direction. This lore can include a backstory of events before the game, or descriptions of locations, social structures, culture, nature, natural laws, history, and more.
- **Character Profiles:** Character profiles are a series of documents establishing important characters of a game, like playable characters, enemies, and relevant NPCs. The more screen time a character gets, the more in-depth their character profiles should be. These documents delve into the key attributes of a character, their personality, biography, role in the story – and their game function as well.
- **Plot Outline:** An outline of the key plot points, structured on a dramatic curve and, eventually, in relation to connected gameplay moments. This can be anything from text, a timeline, or a flowchart.
- **Narrative Roadmap:** A document that, specific to live games, describes any plans for future additions after the release of the game. This includes planned expansions, season packages, time-limited and live events, as well as pacing and intended release schedule..

PLAYER-FACING NARRATIVE

The following list lays out the narrative tools that shape the story inside of the final game, which the players will get to see and experience.

- **Context:** The general visual and narrative context given to game loops and player actions offers a small arc of conflict and resolution that repeats itself in varying forms throughout the game. The context given to an action will influence the narrative meaning and experience of it and can be textual or purely artistic.

- **Plot:** The dramatic story arc that the player progresses through while playing the game, driven by player actions toward completing the game.
- **Cutscenes:** Noninteractive cinematic scenes that are meant to drive the plot forward, signal progress, and serve as rewards.
- **Dialogue:** Conversations between characters, which are used to drive the plot forward, give insights into the character's personalities, but also serve an informative function. Dialogue can serve as mission briefings, feedback during missions, and reward after completion of a mission.
- **Quest Design:** The context given to game objectives, offering a small arc of conflict and resolution, usually including a reward or progression of sorts.
- **Barks:** Brief audio cues that are meant to serve as contextual narrative, feedback or helpful instructions during gameplay. They ideally manage to capture the personality and language quirks of the speaker, may that be the avatar, an ally, or an enemy. Examples: "Shit, a grenade!", "I'm too pretty to die!", and "Sire, could I bother you for a moment?"
- **Names:** Names for characters, locations, weapons, items, and other game elements can say a lot about what they're referring to.
- **Descriptions:** Descriptions for characters, locations, weapons, items, and other game elements. They are often part of a general codex or inside feature-specific menus. They are part of the worldbuilding emerging in the game.
- **Documents:** Unlockable texts of any format, with common examples being letters, audio logs, stories, and descriptions. Often a collectible that can be unlocked or found during gameplay.
- **Interface Texts:** Any text that is part of the UI. Even though many of them will be primarily functional, they can express lore and tone through specific phrasing.
- **Tutorials:** Anything that is meant to help players understand how to play the game. Ideally, this is naturally embedded in the story itself and taught in context, with the help of character dialogue, tool tips, and action, rather than like an instruction manual.
- **Player Guidance and Feedback:** Any feedback for the player's actions, designed to improve a sense of agency, teach the game's rules, and give hints on how to progress and make the world seem more alive.
- **Narrative Systems:** The rules of the dynamics between player actions and narrative triggers, determining how the story is revealed, progressed and presented in-game.

CROSS-FUNCTIONAL NARRATIVE

There are additional ways to reveal the game's narrative to the player, and that is through the collaboration with other crafts. These cross-functional tools are unique, insofar as that the narrative designer isn't the only designer of these game aspects, but the one who seeks to infuse them with narrative meaning in collaboration with the craft specialists.

- **Game Design:** Core gameplay, game mechanics, game dynamics, game systems, character skills, etc.
- **Level Design:** Environmental design, level architecture, level mood, player guidance, map design, etc.
- **Art and Animation:** Creative direction, lighting design, concept art, environment art, character design, character animation, object design, UI design, etc.
- **Sound Design:** Voice acting, environmental sounds, sound effects, music, etc.
- **Marketing:** Advertisements, announcements, trailers, banners, articles, etc.
- **Transmedia:** Short films, music videos, movies, comics, novels, social media accounts, etc.

SUMMARY

- Narrative designers can use a **variety of internal documents** to build a game's narrative (story vision, narrative pillars, narrative guidelines, tone documents, localization guidelines, narrative system design, glossary, lore documents, character profiles, plot outlines, and narrative roadmaps for live games).
- Narrative designers can express narrative through a **variety of player-facing narrative tools** (context, plot, cutscenes, dialogue, mission design, barks, names, descriptions, documents, interface texts, tutorials, player guidance and feedback, and narrative systems).
- Narrative can be expressed with **cross-functional tools** as well (game design, level design, art and animation, sound design, marketing, and transmedia).

3 Why Does Narrative Design Matter?

If you've picked up this book, it's safe to assume that you already have a passion for narrative in videogames. You don't need to be convinced why story shouldn't be treated as an afterthought, but a key component that deeply influences all aspects of a game, and the player's experience of it. But, working in the industry, you might need sound arguments to sell the importance of narrative design to a doubtful team searching for a feature to cut. Educating your team (or superiors) about the negative consequences of bad narrative design might give you that edge when suggesting a new game element. Besides, the awareness of your craft's purpose can make creative decision-making just a little easier – since you know what it's meant to achieve. You want to tell an engaging story, of course, but narrative design in videogames is striving to do even more than that. Its goal is to oil the metaphorical gears of the game and improve the player's experience on many levels.

These are the key aspects we'll look into:

- **Narrative Bias:** Players will see a story, whether it's intentional or not!
- **Motivation and Feedback:** Why are players supposed to do something? And what is the effect of their actions?
- **Contextualization:** How should players feel about their actions? What do they mean?
- **Flow and Immersion:** How can players lose themselves in the game?
- **Attachment and Caring:** Why should players care about these characters?
- **Understanding and Learning:** How can players make sense of the provided information?
- **Pleasing Coherency:** How to make the game feel like a consistent experience?

NARRATIVE BIAS

Narrative Design answers: What do the patterns mean?

Some videogames don't appear to have a traditional story at first glance, that much is true: They can be design-driven, rather than story-driven. The original Tetris or Pong wouldn't really fall into the "narrative game" category. There is no plot to recount to your friends, no clever dialogue, no cutscenes, or dialogue. But that doesn't mean that there is no narrative experience.

There is a psychology phenomenon called *narrative bias,* often used in the context of scientific experiments,[1] user experience[2] and videogames.[3] In a negative context,

DOI: 10.1201/9781003297628-5

such as misinterpreting unconnected information as being causally connected, it's called narrative fallacy [4] – based on the concept of illusory correlation (as defined by Chapman and Chapman, 1967 [5]). But it's not negative in itself. It describes the human tendency to interpret information as part of a bigger story or pattern, irregardless of the objective reality (or intention of the creator). Humans make sense of the world and structure their observations by trying to connect information by causality-and-effect, even if events happened at random. This phenomenon is often talked about when it comes to scientific studies and logic fallacies, when random data is wrongly connected to one another or misinterpreted as meaningfully evolving, just because it "makes sense" from a dramatic perspective. It's hard for the human mind to accept things as random and meaningless, and it makes memorizing things much harder too, so the bias is an essential part of us. The original purpose for this behavior is to help humans interpret rules and better anticipate the future. So, in theory, this narrative bias is there to help us speculate upon an outcome of a situation and be smarter for the next time. There is an evolutionary reason to it.

As an example: A person eats red berries. A few hours later, this person dies. Narrative bias would lead us to believe the berries were toxic, even if the person was actually just very old and died of old age or had a fatal accident we weren't informed of.

There's lots of uncertainty and randomness in our lives, and way too much information, so narrative bias helps us to make sense of things and plan what to do. Humans think in stories, communicate in stories, understand the world in stories. We *really* love stories.

In short: The narrative bias refers to people's tendency to interpret information as being part of a larger story or pattern, regardless of whether the facts actually support the full narrative.

To make use of a well-known game example, let's take a look at chess. The original chess has no authored plot, in any shape or form. Just a board, 32 pieces in two differently colored sets and two players moving them in turns, according to individual mechanics of the piece, which means that we have a scenario with two opposing factions facing each other. They are each composed of a king and a queen, many pawns and army members with various skills. When the king falls, the faction loses. Doesn't that sound like the story of two kingdoms at war? Well, there's our story after all! Alas, the exact way this conflict will play out, and who wins, is all based on player decisions. Two players play the same premise over and over again, but in a different way every time. The game offers a pre-defined story space, made of pieces, names and rules – and the players make the story happen. All without cutscenes or dialogues. The story is told purely though player action.

Let's look at another famous example that doesn't seem to have a story at first glance. In Tetris, players take the role of an engineer building a rocket to fly to the moon and win the space race for Russia. This isn't a joke. The start screen and the music suggests a Russian setting, and when players win the game (yes, there is a way to win Tetris), the screen will show an animation of a little rocket taking off into space. These context clues might go over many a player's head, but that doesn't mean they don't feel the narrative experience through what they're doing. As a Tetris player, you're trying to build something using only what you have, which demands improvisation and fast decision-making. It's a rush toward completing the construction of something, but there are endless setbacks, which makes the task almost feel insurmountable. You know though that it's not about completion, but trying to stay in the race for as long as possible.

Applied to videogames, a narrative bias means that players will try to see story in the information they get, even if there is no authored plot, so they can make a better plan of action. Every game element is part of the information players will try to connect in a narrative way (consciously or not). The game's systems are the story. The audiovisual experience is the story. What players do is the story. Players will perceive story in everything, whether we consciously author it or not, so we might as well design it with purpose. This way, all other creative decisions can be inspired by the narrative core and reinforce it, creating a coherent experience. This train of thought can also help us be more aware of our game's implications – what kind of statements are we expressing through our game's systems and elements? Does that fit the story we want to convey?

In short: Humans have a narrative bias and will interpret game systems, dynamics and audiovisual elements as a story either way, so we might as well design everything with purpose and make sure it fits our intentions.

MOTIVATION AND FEEDBACK

One of the most important goals of a game is to get players to play it and keep playing it. But without proper motivation, they will eventually stop and put down the game. This rings especially true for live games, which are intended to go on indefinitely (or at least for as long as they remain profitable) and therefore have a lot of mileage to cover. Narrative design plays a key part in doing just that.

Feedback is the other key tool for keeping players playing. If they don't know if what they're doing is correct or incorrect, it can have a devastating effect on their motivation. Motivation and feedback are intimately linked, and both rely on narrative design.

MOTIVATION

Narrative Design answers: Why am I doing something? Why should I care about it?
There are two ways to boost motivation in an interactive system such as a videogame. On the one hand, there are extrinsic rewards (such as currency, items, new characters, etc.) and on the other hand, there are intrinsic rewards (such as enjoyment of play, self-image, self-improvement, satisfaction of curiosity, etc.).[6] Extrinsic rewards are the things given to players when they've done something right, which they can then use or collect, while intrinsic rewards play into motivations that come from within the player. The latter promises no compensation for their actions, but an emotional value, such as the joy of destruction, social connection, or being proud of a victory. Narrative design can reinforce both of these reward types, but especially intrinsic motivation relies heavily on narrative design. On that note, intrinsic rewards are more likely to form long-term motivation – although videogames usually use both of these reward types.

Imagine your team has designed a fetch quest in the adventure game you're working on. It could be very straightforward, a pop-up telling players exactly what to do: "Get item at point A, bring it to point B." Maybe they'd do it once, but chances are, it wouldn't keep them motivated for very long. Sure, you could promise them currency for it, but that only makes use of the extrinsic rewarding method.

Now, imagine the item, location and context were a little more specific: "Find a seed in the forest and bring it to the farm." Here we're getting some context – this seed is probably for the farmer who wants to plant it.

Next, imagine players receiving the quest from a quest giver NPC: "A draught killed all my crops, my family will die in a few months if we can't plant new seeds. Please fetch me some and I will reward you." As you can see, what started as a simple chore has turned into a self-contained short story. It is, admittedly, not a Shakespearean play, but it drastically improved the likelihood of players being motivated to actually do it. They know why they're doing it and can anticipate the effect of their actions on the world. This makes the task much more meaningful.

What if the player had known the NPC beforehand? They're a friend, albeit fictional, and they enjoy seeing them happy. This means that things just got personal. We're making use of the player's curiosity regarding how the story arc will end, their desire to be helpful toward characters they like, and their desire to witness how their own actions have an impact on the world. Seeing your own actions within a story world and feedbacked by its characters is more emotionally meaningful than abstract rewards.

Quest givers and dialogue aren't the only way to create a narrative context for a player's actions, either. A meaningful item name and design, making use of symbols and semiotics on the interface, as well as a meaningful choice of objectives and settings can also go a long way.

This narrative contextualization, tying an objective to a world and its people, improves short-term motivation due to the increased emotional involvement and curiosity. For long-term motivation, we just have to look at the bigger narrative picture, the sum of the player's actions in the game. By establishing the player's role within the world, and their overarching goal, they know what the short-term goals can be anticipated to amount to. Are they saving the world, looking for treasure, trying to become the best?

This importance of context can be applied to all types of motivation. The given example plays into the motivation of immersion and emotional attachment, but this isn't the only motivational type commonly found in players.

According to player research company Quantic Foundry,[7] gamer motivations can be separated into the following categories:

- **Action** (Destruction and Excitement)
- **Social** (Competition and Community)
- **Mastery** (Challenge and Strategy)
- **Achievement** (Completion and Power)
- **Immersion** (Fantasy and Story)
- **Creativity** (Design and Discovery)

Narrative design can enhance these types of motivations the following way:

- **Action:** Narrative design can show the impact and meaning of a player's actions, making everything more epic.
- **Social:** Narrative design can give meaning to the fictional world, its situations of collaboration and competition, as well as a player's role, status, and relation to others.
- **Mastery:** Narrative design can show the increasing impact and meaning of a player's actions, making gradual growth more satisfying.
- **Achievement:** Narrative design can underscore the gravity and meaning of player's achievements, making everything more worthy of pride.
- **Immersion:** Narrative design can immerse players in the game's story and world through engaging storytelling and characters.
- **Creativity:** Narrative design can give meaning and purpose to the player's tools, options and choices, which they can use for creative expressin and problemsolving.

Additionally, narrative on its own can also serve as an **extrinsic reward**. If players are rewarded cutscenes or new unlockable narrative content, this can be considered an extrinsic reward that motivates them to continue. This narrative reward will always have an element of intrinsic value too though, since it caters to curiosity and can be emotionally rewarding due to the way the story progresses.

FEEDBACK

Narrative Design answers: Am I on the right track?

The second pillar of player motivation is regular feedback. When trying a solution for their objective, proper feedback helps to keep players motivated – both negative and positive feedback. This makes them see that their suggested solution was registered (and that the game didn't experience glitches), giving them a sense of agency, while helping them learn whether it was a feasible solution or not.

Positive feedback to a correct solution is a rewarding experience. Players feel praised, proud of their actions and see their work properly acknowledged. This feedback can be anything, from visual feedback, a ticked box or a change in the world, to characters verbally acknowledging it.

But even negative feedback in the case of failure is helpful because it helps players eliminate how *not* to do things and therefore encourages them to try again, with more information, better equipped for success. Negative feedback is better than *no* feedback.

Additionally, feedback can serve as a reminder of their current missions because they're in the right location, or enough time has passed, or they just accidentally drove progression forward. If they know that they've something to help their mission along, they get a little boost of serotonin.

This type of feedback and signposting (=guiding a player with reminders and visual cues) can be purely abstract as well – a sound, a visual impact, a tick on a list.

But it can also be framed within the narrative: A metal detector that beeps when you get close to the metal item you're searching, a companion remarks that you're walking the wrong way, your avatar mumbles that they can't leave yet, etc. This helps embedding the player's actions within the game world and increases their sense of agency (which is also central to motivation and enjoyment of the game). Additionally, having a fictional audience to your actions can create all sorts of interesting emotions – from feeling supported by friends to feeling opposed by antagonists. Either way, it makes players feel that their actions matter in the grand scheme of things and motivate them to press on.

In short: Creating a dramatic structure around game loops helps to keep short-term motivation, while overarching stories help long-term motivation. To further reinforce player motivation, purposeful feedback in the form of dialogue or other signals is essential – responding to error, confusion, logical wrong solutions and correct solutions with contextual triggers.

CONTEXTUALIZATION

Narrative Design answers: How do I feel about my actions? What do my actions mean?

Gameplay doesn't exist in a vacuum, but always comes with a *context* implied through visuals, audio, text and other creative aspects of the game. This narrative context influences how players perceive their gameplay experience[8] – not only their moment-to-moment gameplay but also the general meaning and purpose of their actions. Changing the context of the very same gameplay has drastic consequences to the final game experience, shifting the gamefeel, story genre, or even target audience.

To clarify the point, let's compare two rail shooters: House of the Dead and Gal*Gun. Their core gameplay is similar: They are first-person-shooters where the player automatically advances on a pre-determined path (also called rail shooters). You aim a reticle at targets popping up left and right and need to hit them several times until they're down.

House of the Dead is a gritty horror shooter where you shoot an invasion of the undead to survive the day.

Gal*Gun is a cute anime shooter where you're a cupid in training and shoot girls with pheromone arrows until they faint happily.

Playing these games offers a drastically different experience. This has nothing to do with the game design but everything to do with the narrative context, the visuals and the meaning given to the player's actions. One is a tense horror game full of violence, while the other is a tongue-in-cheek romance game full of fan service. One could argue that violence isn't even part of Gal*Gun, despite being a first-person-shooter. As a player, you do pretty much the same things in the core gameplay loop of these games, but the experience couldn't be more different. (It is of note that they emphasize their contexts with differently designed meta layers. While House of the Dead is an arcade-style experience with campy horror cutscenes, Gal*Gun offers another meta layer with a dating sim, where interactive dialogues influence the relationships of the protagonist to different girls and eventually the ending.)

However, context isn't only found in the overarching theme of a game but also **moment-to-moment contextualization** for each of the player's actions. This aspect of contextualization directly feeds into emotional attachment, motivation and proper feedback. Anything previously mentioned during those sections of this chapter is most often set up through the context given to a situation. This moment-to-moment-contextualization should give the player an idea of the setting, the current conflict, their role in it, the emotional meaning of their actions, their current objectives, and their eventual goals.

So, next time somebody on your team says *"We can just add the narrative later, it doesn't matter that much!"*, consider that the narrative context plays a key part in how the core gameplay is perceived and is essential for boosting player motivation and emotional attachment.

In short: The game's setting and narrative context change the meaning of a game's gameplay and should be considered core to the creative vision, rather than a separate decision. Furthermore, moment-to-moment context is crucial to building player motivation and emotional attachment.

FLOW AND IMMERSION

Narrative Design answers: How can I lose myself in the game?

As developers, we want players to fully immerse themselves in the action of the game – because sometimes having fun doesn't mean laugh-out-loud entertainment, but an enjoyable state of focus and immersion (no matter if the experience is uplifting or stressful). This psychological concept, called *flow*, was described by the psychologist Mihaly Csíkszentmihályi as a mental state of hyperfocus, in which a person is fully immersed in the execution of an activity. Flow is characterized by the complete absorption in what you're doing, and the resulting transformation in one's sense of time.[9]

In games, this is achieved with a well-designed challenge progression – an ever-rising wave of challenge, improvement, success and relief (*see Chapter 13*). But achieving a state of flow isn't only about difficulty design. Narrative design also plays a central role in players getting into a state of flow and staying in it.

The key to entering a state of flow lies in quick recognition and understanding of what you're trying to achieve and what your current options are. This way, there is no need to stop and think, you can just act. Sometimes it doesn't take much to drag players out of the moment, where metaphorical bumps in the road ruin the smooth ride. If things don't make sense at first sight and instructions are unclear (or already forgotten), it makes things harder. For many games, reaction times matter. And that extra second of wondering what you're supposed to do right now might be too slow, and failure ruins your flow. The keyword is *intuitive design* – something that allows players to interact with the game world naturally, helping designers to create challenges beyond "How does this even work?" Of course, frustration, trial and error aren't something that needs to be avoided at all cost, but it's always better to either create moments of confusion with purposeful intent (related to narrative or pacing), rather than making things counterintuitive by accident. This will hinder getting into the flow and staying in it.

Flow is about intuitive understanding and always knowing your next goal and your possible options, even if you don't know the solution yet. Flow means that you can understand your situation at first glance, so that you don't have to waste mental resources on doing a double-take, guessing randomly, or worse, being lost. Narrative design can help to clarify what the player needs to do and how they can approach the problem, reducing mental friction. The secret to intuitive narrative design is creating self-explanatory contexts, straightforward instructions, and semiotics[10] – making use of established symbols and metaphors to benefit from a mental shortcut to an established meaning. These symbols can stem from other videogames or even real life. And if we use them (in a way that fits the narrative circumstances and the game genre), we can free up some mental space that players can then use for other cooler things.

For example: A key is a symbol for the ability to unlock something. We know that in real life keys open doors or boxes. So when we find one in a videogame, we expect it to serve as a door or box opener. It sounds obvious, but that's the idea, it's meant to be intuitive. Another example: A players encounter a boss fight. The giant creature seems unbeatable – when a giant red orb becomes visible inside their palms. Many players who have played action games will have encountered this visual shorthand for weaknesses. So they're likely to try attack this spot next, intuitively understanding the rules of the boss fight.

These examples might make it seem like these shortcuts are always meant to refer to something established in real life or other videogames, but there's a third option: Using symbols that are intuitive inside of your game's *own* lore. Those need to be established narratively, but can help to make game elements unique to your project, even if only in name and design. For example: The Fallout games are a post-apocalyptic RPG series, where improvisation and do-it-yourself solutions are everywhere. Fittingly, the main currency is not dollars or gold, but *bottle caps*. This symbol makes immediate sense in a post-apocalyptic setting where trash is turned into treasure – besides, bottle caps are hard to counterfeit and exist in limited numbers.

As you probably noticed, semiotics require previous knowledge from players. If your game is for hardcore gamers of a specific genre, you can safely draw from special knowledge of that target audience. But if you're working on a game that is intended for a broader audience, perhaps to introduce a casual audience to a niche game genre, these symbols might not be intuitive for everyone (and need more explanation – if you choose to include them anyway). Often, symbols referring to real life are rooted in a specific cultural environment as well, so especially when it comes to worldwide releases, it's important to check your own assumptions. To make sure your semiotics are understood by your target audience, cultural advisors and playtesting will be your best friends.

But what we can take from this section is not only that we shall use established semiotics to reduce the player's mental workload. It's equally important for things to make intuitive sense within your game. If they don't fit your world and seem out of place, they can also create friction, even if they're understandable from a functional point-of-view, or refer to something from real life. Using cyber credits as currency in a science-fiction world? Makes sense. Using cyber credits in a historical medieval setting? Not so much. This disturbs the narrative coherency and intuitive understandability of your game.

If all semiotic choices naturally emerge from the game's narrative base, it helps players quickly understand their meaning and creates a sense of coherency. Your semiotics are part of your worldbuilding and general narrative design, after all. And the more things make sense, the less mental friction players will experience, and the more easily they will get into a state of flow. The same applies to immersion. Often used synonymously with flow, immersion can also refer to being immersed in a fictional world, its people and stakes. It doesn't only refer to moment-to-moment focus, but an overarching investment. Using symbols and semiotics that intuitively fit your game world will improve both, flow and immersion.

In short: To help players quickly understand the game, their goals and options, the lore-appropriate semiotics and symbolism can serve as mental shortcuts. This will decrease needless mental friction and make it easier for players to get into a state of enjoyable flow and immersion.

ATTACHMENT AND CARING

Narrative Design answers: Why should I care about these characters?

If a game is narrated well, players get attached to its fictional characters and care about what happens to them. Great characters can drive a game – even if they're nothing more than a colorful bar, like in Thomas is Alone. When their personality, dreams and fears are expressed through the game's story and narrative design, players are more likely to get emotionally involved and keep on playing. They're more likely to feel with them, making every moment of defeat and victory all the stronger. This emotional attachment ties directly into immersion, motivation and contextualization. But it's also important for all the things that happen outside of the game, like fandom participation and brand loyalty. If people get attached to the characters, they want to see more of them – by sharing cosplays, fanarts, fanfictions, hopes, and theories – or by eagerly awaiting the new official content or merchandise release. For a live game that is supposed to keep players around for a long time, getting them to care about your characters is essential, arguably even more important than investment in the plot. If we look at Fortnite (a seasonal battle royale game) and Overwatch (a multiplayer team-based hero shooter), two long-running multiplayer games, it's undeniable that the marketing of a charismatic core cast and pop-cultural crossover characters has played a key role in their success. Despite little plot progressions inside of these games, they've created emotional attachment by leveraging engaging characters (which show their personality in how they look, talk, act and function) and transmedia content (like websites, comics and short films). What we can learn from this is that lovable characters don't necessarily require plot-driven in-game features to charm players. With narrative design tools alone, such as visual design, function, skills, animations and barks, players can get a feel of a character's personality as if they're a person, and not just a game element. Anything beyond that, like in-game or transmedia stories, make them even more effective.

To expand upon this train of thought, it's important to remember that the game character they get attached to can also be *themselves and their avatar.* Even a blank slate avatar, who comes with little or no backstory or personality, can become a source of deep attachment due to the narrative *surrounding* the avatar, or the narrative that the player projects onto them. This can happen through player choices, actions, personalization, or roleplay. Players can therefore also get attached to their role inside the world, and the way it expresses their own choices and personality. In such a case, narrative design still remains a key to attachment, because why would I care about my role in the world if I don't care about the world?

In short: Narrative design can enable emotional attachment to the game's characters, which improves immersion, motivation and contextualization.

UNDERSTANDING AND LEARNING

NARRATIVE DESIGN ANSWERS: HOW DO I PLAY THIS GAME?

Videogames face the challenge of having to teach their rules to the player when they play it for the first time – no matter how much it adheres to established conventions. Some games need minimal onboarding, while others need more explanation, but there are no games without any new information to learn. Nowadays, game boxes don't even come with instruction manuals anymore, so the responsibility lies in the hands of the game itself – both in the form of tutorials and any design choice that is meant to teach a function and strategy to the player. Narrative design helps to understand and retain information, due to the effects of narrative contextualization of gameplay and game elements. You will recognize some of these following points, as semiotics, context and emotional engagement all play a role in supporting learning and understanding. Let's take a look at narrative design aspects that help players to better understand and learn how to play the game.

SYMBOLS AND SEMIOTICS – WHAT DOES IT MEAN?

As mentioned in flow and immersion, **symbols and semiotics** can be used as a shortcut to refer to existing knowledge in the player's mind and to explain complex concepts more quickly. Instead of having to explain the use and meaning of a new game aspect, established semiotics can imply its meaning by the use of visual, auditory, tactile, or otherwise manifested signifiers. They can be derived from other videogames, videogames of the same genre, real life or the game world itself. This makes it easier for players to understand a game element's meaning at a first glance, and eventually helps them remember it due to the narrative context of the attached symbol.

GROUPING – HOW DO I CATEGORIZE THIS?

Grouping (also called *chunking*[11,12]) is a memorization method where units of information are separated into coherent groups in order to facilitate learning. Recalling information within a group will come easier by association with an umbrella category and the other units within that group, in contrast to a big pool of individual unrelated units. This is also applied visually, in Gestalt psychology and UX Design, where we have the Gestalt laws of grouping,[13] which describe various ways how to group information visually. Users tend to group elements together based on visual characteristics because it makes it easier to understand and remember their meaning at first sight.

Videogames[14] do this in many ways, like grouping game mechanics as features or grouping interface elements in menus. But grouping can also be done in a *narrative manner*. To group aspects of a game together under a narrative umbrella enables the player to remember many more game aspects much more easily. A feature representative can be the personified grouping mechanism for all information related to a specific feature – for instance, a weapon's specialist, a strategic specialist or a shopkeeper. It doesn't have to be a character though: It can be a specific menu, a specific location, a specific narrative framework. If players read a tutorial about every aspect of the game all at once, without a change of scenery or mentor, it will be close to impossible to memorize. Group them into narrative contexts and categories, and things immediately become easier to digest.

CONTEXT – WHAT'S A PRACTICAL APPLICATION?

Whenever players receive new information, narrative design can create a specific **situational context** and practical application for it. This way, players don't have to learn dry facts, but engage in learning-by-doing. Information becomes easier to remember if there's a context associated with,[15] such as: Who told us, where did they tell us and what was our first application of this new information?

This connects to Prince and Felder's **inductive learning**,[16] a teaching approach where you are using specific examples to infer general knowledge, rather than only explaining theories. Using scenarios with practical use is said to help retain the information much better than theoretical explanations. This means that the player will remember the game's workings much easier if they're given a situational application. Additionally, these examples can be played, turning players into active participants, rather than just listeners – which brings us to Constructivism.

Kolb and Fry's **Constructivistic learning method**[17] advocates for sensory and activity-based learning. They claim that a concrete experience, which learners can observe and reflect on, helps to build abstract concepts and learnings. In short, a virtual environment with a specific scenario and observable outcomes is a Constructivist learning environment, which is reinforced by narrative contextualization.

PURPOSE – WHAT AM I LEARNING THIS FOR?

Narrative context turns gameplay into a **purposeful interaction**[18] with the game world, therefore giving a deeper meaning to the player's actions. Instead of instructing players with objectives, narrative framing explains them *why* they're meant to do it – their goal, purpose, and effect on the virtual world. Having a purposeful application for knowledge makes it easier to keep it memorized because your subconscious understands why it's important to remember it – just like you're more likely to remember common phrases of a foreign language if you're planning to go on vacation there, instead of learning random vocabulary without practical application. This relates to…

Emotional Engagement – Why Should I Care to Learn This?

By providing a situational context, narrative design also creates **emotional engagement**[19] and the urgency to retain certain information. Players are presented with a specific situation with characters they feel sympathy for, or might even feel emotionally attached to. Even if the characters are fictional, if they are written in a way that strikes a chord, players will start to care about them. If the players are emotionally attached to the stakes at hand, they are more likely to retain information, just as if this was a real-life emergency. If people are emotionally involved in the information they're trying to retain, they are more likely to do so – because said information is given more psychological weight.

It's important to note that there are different types of learners. Narrative, however, can enhance all learning strategies, may they be visual, auditory, kinesthetic or readable information. The key to an effective tutorial lies within well-contextualized game challenges as tutorials, which make use of several different learning channels, and give a narrative framing for the information at hand.

In short: Narrative design can improve learning and understanding with the use of semiotics, grouping, context, purpose and emotional engagement.

PLEASING COHERENCY

Narrative Design answers: How does it all fit together?

A videogame is made up of many creative decisions from many different people, putting it at risk for dissonance caused by pieces that don't perfectly fit together. This is detrimental to the game flow (as already mentioned in *flow and immersion)* and overall enjoyment of the game experience. But this is where narrative design comes in, the craft whose main purpose is to ensure the coherency of all the game parts – by the unifying factor of the player's (narrative) experience. If all creative decisions stem from the same narrative basis, no matter if they apply to story, gameplay, visuals or sound, we get a coherent experience that conveys a purposeful vision. The creative direction of each game element should be an expression of the narrative foundation, reinforcing the game's lore, intended themes, and philosophies. It's a way to make sure that everything makes sense together and doesn't feel like an assortment of random creative decisions. A player's perception of quality, and overall enjoyment, will depend on whether everything is seen as coherent. This general impression of things "making sense" will make it easier for players to get into the flow of the game, understand its features, and perceive it as a well-crafted product. Naturally, enjoyable experiences increase retention (because players want to continue playing) and brand loyalty (because players understand and like the game's creative vision).

In short: Narrative coherency makes a game feel like a coherent whole, which enhances flow, learning, brand loyalty, and player retention.

CONCLUSION

All the above-mentioned aspects are reasons why you should care about narrative design in your game, even if your project isn't meant to be story-driven.

If you make sure to **implement good narrative design**, you can reap the following **benefits**:

- **Create Engagement:** I want to play this!
- **Decrease Friction:** It feels intuitive to play this!
- **Enable Immersion:** I am invested in this!
- **Give Meaning and a Sense of Agency:** My actions mean something!
- **Improve Learning:** I understand this!
- **Improve Experience:** I enjoy playing this!
- **Boost Retention and Brand Loyalty:** I care about this!

And to turn things the other way around, if you **disregard narrative design**, you risk the following **disadvantages**:

- Decreasing engagement
- Interrupting flow
- Impairing understanding and learning
- Slowing players down
- Decreasing enjoyment
- Failing to create emotional attachment
- Failing to create motivation to keep on playing
- Decreasing the sense of quality of the game

SUMMARY

- Narrative Design is important, because of...
    - **Narrative Bias:** Humans will interpret gameplay and creative direction as a story either way, so we might as well design it intentionally.
    - **Motivation and Feedback:** Narrative design helps players be motivated and know what they're doing.
    - **Contextualization:** Context of actions changes the player experience.
    - **Flow and Immersion:** Narrative design is essential for getting players into a state of flow, making it more likely they like the game and keep on playing.
    - **Attachment and Caring:** Narrative design makes us care about what we do.
    - **Understanding and Learning:** Narrative design facilitates understanding the game and how to play it.
    - **Pleasing Coherency:** Narrative design helps to create a pleasing game experience.

REFERENCES

1 Shahram Heshmat, "What is narrative bias?: The illusion of causality," *Psychology Today*, December 12, 2016, https://www.psychologytoday.com/gb/blog/science-choice/201612/what-is-narrative-bias

2 Don Norman, "The Psychology of Everyday Actions: People as Storytellers," in *The Design of Everyday Things: Revised and Expanded Edition*, Basic Books, November 5, 2013, 56–59.

3 Raph Koster, "Chapter Two: How the Brain Works," in *A Theory of Fun for Game Design*, Paraglyph Press, November 13, 2004, 12–19.

4 Nassim Nicholas Taleb, *The Black Swan: The Impact of the Highly Improbable*, Random House, April 17, 2007.

5 Loren J. Chapman, "Illusory correlation in observational report," *Journal of Verbal Learning and Verbal Behavior*, May 25, 1965.

6 Carol Sansone and Judith M. Harackiewicz, Intrinsic and Extrinsic Motivation: The Search for Optimal Motivation and Performance, Academic Press, July 24, 2000.

7 "Gamer Motivation Model," Quantic Foundry, accessed April 20, 2023, https://quantic-foundry.com/wp-content/uploads/2019/04/Gamer-Motivation-Model-Reference.pdf.

8 Zack Hiwiller, "Milieu," in *Players Making Decisions: Game Design Essentials and the Art of Understanding Your Players*, 2nd edition, New Riders, December 7, 2015, 151–162.

9 Mihaly Csikszentmihalyi, *Flow: The Psychology of Optimal Experience*, Harper Perennial Modern Classsics, July 1, 2008.

10 Katie Salen and Eric Zimmermann, "Design," in *Rules of Play: Game Design Fundamentals*, MIT Press, September 25, 2003, 42–46.

11 George A. Miller, "The magical number seven, plus or minus two: some limits on our capacity for processing information," *Psychological Review*, 1956.

12 Mirko Thalmann, Alessandra S. Souza, and Klaus Oberauer, "How does chunking help working memory?," *Journal of Experimental Psychology: Learning, Memory, and Cognition*, 2019.

13 Don Norman, *The Design of Everyday Things: Revised and Expanded Edition*, Basic Books, November 5, 2013.

14 Raph Koster, "Chapter Two: How the Brain Works," in *A Theory of Fun for Game Design*, Paraglyph Press, November 13, 2004, 20–26.

15 Maija Kozlova, "How do video games provide effective learning," Cambridge English Blog, May 19, 2021, https://www.cambridgeenglish.org/blog/how-do-video-games-provide-effective-learning/.

16 Michael Prince and Richard Felder, "The many faces of inductive teaching and learning," *Journal of College Science Teaching*, March/April 2007, https://www.pfw.edu/offices/celt/pdfs/Inductive(JCST).pdf.

17 Christopher W. Totten, "Teaching in Levels Through Visual Communication," in *An Architectural Approach to Level Design*, CRC Press, August 20, 2014, 161–169.

18 Maija Kozlova, "How do video games provide effective learning," Cambridge English Blog, May 19, 2021, https://www.cambridgeenglish.org/blog/how-do-video-games-provide-effective-learning/.

19 Maija Kozlova, "How do video games provide effective learning," Cambridge English Blog, May 19, 2021, https://www.cambridgeenglish.org/blog/how-do-video-games-provide-effective-learning/.

Part II

Interactive Storytelling

4 Introduction to Interactive Storytelling

Games are an interactive storytelling medium, defined by the players' ability to act upon the game's world, no matter if they can influence the progression of a plot or not. Through their actions, they at least decide the exact order of actions and the pacing of the game. Most games give players a level of freedom in how they approach a situation, so that there isn't only one possible playthrough, and some games tip the scales a little more in favor of player freedom. They give players the power to become co-authors of their own experience, deciding how a story progresses and plays out. There are many different approaches for designing games like that.

A central topic of interactive storytelling in games is striking a balance between **authored intent and player agency**.[1] Narrative designers author a narrative, but they also design the player's freedom and limitations in how far they can influence their own story experience. Depending on the game, a narrative experience can fall on different ends on this scale from **author-driven narrative to player-driven narrative**. The author-driven narrative is the predetermined story, as it will be experienced in the game. It is created with the writer's full control, and players only follow each plot beat as the writer intended. The player-driven narrative, however, is when players obtain the freedom to define their unique story experience through their actions in a more significant way. They may explore branching story paths, non-linear narrative, optional moments or emergent narrative (narratively meaningful moments that naturally emerge from their interaction with the game's systems), and more.

Although live games are ambitious in and of themselves, they can have different approaches to designing their level of player freedom and might even choose to offer player choices and nonlinear storytelling. Some live games are entirely designed as interactive fiction, consisting of branching storylines that players can shape with their decisions – such as the mobile games Choices, Episode, or Love Island. Additionally, there are live games with vast open worlds, MMOs such as World of Warcraft, Red Dead Online, and Sea of Thieves, which allow for vast player freedom with modular narrative, parallel story progressions, and emergent storytelling.

The following chapters seek to take a closer look at the interactive aspect of storytelling in videogames, starting with general musings such as balancing player agency and authored content, as well as making choices meaningful. This will be followed by an overview of interactive storytelling structures, for when player choices are meant to influence your live story in some way.

SYSTEMS OF INTERACTIVITY

An interactive narrative is defined by the player's ability to execute an action that causes a reaction from the game. This can be as small as reaching triggers that drive

DOI: 10.1201/9781003297628-7

story along or as big as choices that deeply influence how the story continues. Narrative interactivity can work with a variety of systems, all of which can be boiled down to variables that need to be saved and loaded – choices influence variables, and variables influence the story. Some are big, some smaller, but in the end, the interactive narrative is all about variables and systems connecting these variables, which decide which narrative is triggered in which way and at which point in time. Here are a few **systems of interactivity**, beyond branching stories that usually come to mind when speaking of interactive storytelling.

- **Triggers**, which are programmed consequences to certain actions. Each player's action receives a reaction from the game (consequence). This applies to all games, no matter if there are story choices or not: The player has to take specific actions to cause a string of effects that drive the game along.
- **Story Branches**, where player choices unlock entirely new scenes and/or endings, which can be additional, parallel or alternative story content.
- **Story Variables**, where choices influence the details in the story, such as the presence of a character, the actions of characters, details of moments or whole plot development. This means they cause alterations in scenes without the creation of entirely different story branches.
- **Relationship Systems**, where choices influence relationships between a playable character and an NPC (or between NPCs). This shift in a relationship can be reflected inside the story, with newly unlocked or alternate scenes, as well as gameplay.
- **Character Stats**, where choices influence the personal attributes of a character, which in turn have an effect on story, story choices, or the success of story choices. This system is an RPG-like gameplay element. Examples would be charm, fitness, magical power, etc.
- **Morality and Affinity Systems**, where choices influence the position on a scale from one extreme to the other. Most often used for a morality or honor system, this scale can be about any kind of attribute. The player's location on this scale usually influences how characters act, which options are available to them, or what kind of ending they're steering towards.
- **World States**, where choices influence the state of locations and actors in the world. This can be for the whole world or individual locations. This state can act as a variable inside story moments, influencing how characters act, which things happen, if the story progresses, etc.

PLAYER AGENCY VS AUTHORED INTENT

One of videogames' greatest strengths also poses their greatest narrative challenge: Player agency and freedom.[2] Player agency describes the feeling of your own impact of the world, like your actions matter and have an effect. Player freedom, on the other hand, is the option to choose what to do and where things are heading. While the writer seeks to provide a narrative experience with specific plot points, pacing and a dramatic arc, players want to play the game as it suits *them*. You could assume they are in natural opposition, fighting over control of the game's direction. Because the more freedom a player receives, in what they do, how they solve things, and how

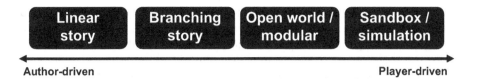

FIGURE 4.1   Spectrum of narrative agency, from author-driven to player-driven.

the story continues – the more control the writer has to abandon. And depending on the type of freedom given in the game, they must invent new ways to deliver a story because the traditional ways of story progression doesn't apply in the same way anymore.

But it's a flawed assumption to think that this means that the narrative experience is ripped out of the game writer's grasp. There is no need to feel threatened by sandboxes or some procedurally generated content – narrative teams are still the ones designing the experience – the game and the player just become more influential actors within the story space. Narrative designers are still the ones developing the story intent, vision, building blocks, the spaces of opportunity, the triggers, and outputs. The more player freedom a game provides, the more central the role of narrative designer becomes – the expert on storytelling through systems and all aspects of the game, rather than just traditional writing (Figure 4.1).

On the left side of the spectrum from *authored story to player-driven story*, we have **linear experiences**,[1] where every step, solution and plot point is decided before the player even begins playing. It is a journey laid out for the player to follow, without any power to change the course of things. There is only a limited right way of progressing in the game, and players can't end up anywhere where the writer hasn't intended them to go. Games like this aren't inherently more frustrating due to the limited range of influence, they're actually quite popular (such as action adventures, first-person shooters, jump'n'runs, etc.), since they don't make their limitations visible.

The feeling of player agency, in these cases, comes from being the one executing the solutions and seeing their effect on the world. A linear pre-scripted experience doesn't prevent a sense of agency at all – it's all about giving feedback on the impact on a player's actions through audiovisual design, systems, and story. Even if they are pre-determined to solve things a certain way in order to continue: They are the ones who found the solution. Even if it is a scripted experience, they must discover that scripted path and walk it themselves, roleplaying as the protagonist of the journey with a given script that they discover along the way. The general assumption that you need to give the player choices that influence the game's story in order for them to feel a sense of agency is incorrect. As long as they feel like their actions matter, and they have the power to exert influence over the game's world, by controlling an avatar and interacting with systems, a sense of agency can be created. It's more about clarifying options and consequences, helping the players to know what to do and feel its impact.

If you add choices to these linear experiences that result in alternate story scenes, they become **branching experiences**.[1] These give the player more freedom in determining the progression and possible outcome of the narrative. There is a vast variety of possible branching structures (*see Chapter 5*), that are composed of story scenes connected by branches determined by choices, making use of alternative routes, variations, and variables. In a branching experience, the player chooses from a variety of authored paths, while the narrative designer still defines all possible paths and available choices (like the narrative games developed by Quantic Dream or Telltale Games).

Further down the spectrum, we have **open narratives**,[1] in open world (or otherwise modular) games, that give an even broader freedom regarding how to progress through the game. Here, the narrative designer offers a whole selection of activities, some obligatory (and usually tied to a main story) and some optional (usually tied to side stories). They provide tasks sorted into various progressions, regions, or categories, with bigger milestones connecting more free-form activities along the way. Players interacting with the world, for emergent storytelling, usually completes the narrative experience of an open world game. On top of that, open world games might choose to make use of branching story paths as well. Managing to keep the story coherent becomes more challenging, due to the increased player freedom.

At the other end of the spectrum, we have **sandbox games and simulations**. This is where game writers stop being the author of a pre-determined experience, and the game itself becomes a sort of story generator – in interaction with the players themselves – based on the narrative designer's vision, rules, and systems. The focus lies on stories that emerge from the player's interaction with game and narrative systems, and might even use procedurally generated content. Players interact with game systems that react to their input, thus creating meaningful situations that create emergent narrative. Since this narrative, although not pre-written, is still based on rules and limitations that are meant to result in something in line with the creative vision and intention of the game's narrative. The narrative designer still decides on the intent and vision of the experience and what stories can be experienced in the game – therefore creating the space of possibility, and the structure in which it will be presented. The role of an "experience author" remains in the hands of the developer, the tools just change.

Even though games can provide drastically different levels of player freedom, that doesn't make one or the other more enjoyable to players. It doesn't matter on which end of the spectrum your project falls, players can still feel a satisfying sense of agency when interacting with the game. If anything, if you give players a lot of freedom, it becomes more challenging to create a consistent story experience, and it might fall apart. The next section will explore how we can achieve this feat.

CREATING STORIES WITH PLAYER FREEDOM

The great challenge for games with a lot of player freedom is to consistently deliver its vision and themes and to ensure good dramatic pacing within its vast systems, despite each player playing the game their own way. After all, we cannot control what they're doing at any given time, and the more options they have to *stray from the ideal path*, the harder it is to make sure the intent of the story remains visible and well-paced. There are, however, a few general tips how to make this possible. Not *all* of them need to be part of your specific project, though.

- **Worldbuilding** is still needed to serve as the narrative foundation of all the game's mechanics, dynamics, and stories. Even in the most open game, there is a setting and an underlying story that has informed all the creative decisions that went into its creation. So no matter if you choose to add information about the world in text, like documents or dialogue, or if you don't, it's still there. In the architecture of buildings, flora and fauna of the world, and the way things work. That worldbuilding is always a part of narrative in games, even if the pre-authored plot is missing completely.

- Use **restricted player actions** for a guided experience. No game gives players the option to just do everything (since each action needs to be programmed and implemented), so the choice of which actions to allow is a big part of the story experience. No matter in which order players then do actions in, they only have access to the actions you designed. You may also choose to restrict actions by chronological progression, location, or playable character – context matters here too. As an example: If you implement features for peaceful collaboration, this expresses your game's themes. If you implement features for competition and power fantasies, it will make for a very different game.

- **Let the options tell the story**. As a subset of restricted player actions, the available choices are also part of the game's story identity. If every option is situated within the context of honorable or dishonorable, this becomes a central theme of the game, no matter which actions players choose. For example: Will you react to a violent and lawless world with criminal ruthlessness or will you try to protect others and fight for the law? This is the core theme of Red Dead Online's honor system, which separates player choices into honorable and dishonorable. But such options could also adhere to something other than a morality-like scale, such as being rational vs emotional, various approaches that fit the mindset of the playable character or general philosophies that would earn the favor of certain characters or factions. The kind of options you offer, and what kind of structure they adhere to, says something about the story and the character's (and player's) role within it.

- **Author a well-paced main progression and regularly guide players back on track.** A game doesn't always have to allow the same level of absolute player freedom and may combine more linear experiences with freedom of action. Create pockets of player freedom in between your structured plot, where players can go wild until they're ready to continue the main progression (or several main progressions). Create narrative systems that can trigger plot points at specific moments of play – like when players arrive in a new location, when they've completed a set amount of missions, rooms or levels, or after they've leveled up enough. Create narrative systems that allow you to pace a story in a satisfying way, working around the amount of player freedom you're planning to give in between. The freedom in between this main progression can be filled with a variety of content that can be completed in any order, or other open activities. This type of structure is often found in Open World games.

- Work with **nested story arcs**, where bigger story arcs consist of smaller story arcs, allowing players to experience a satisfying sense of pacing in smaller and bigger loops of conflict and resolution throughout the game. The big story arc can be one or several main progressions, possibly out the game's obligatory content, traditionally structured with a dramatic arc – while the small story arcs should relate to smaller actions the player can take, such as singular missions, side stories, or even just game loops. These smaller story arcs are often candidates for more player freedom, with optional and procedurally generated content, in addition to all the free roaming they can do (in e.g., Open World games). The reason is that it's much easier to hold the audience's attention if bigger plot points are bridged with smaller satisfying story arcs. It's the same way that all fiction is structured. A movie has acts, and acts have scenes. A novel has chapters, and chapters have scenes. And in such, videogames have acts, levels, and missions: Increasingly smaller dramatic arcs that make up bigger arcs.

- Create **systems** that allow **emergent storytelling** that aligns with your vision, something that fits your world, themes, tone, and worldbuilding. In these systems, limits and rules convey the narrative intention. Player stories emerge from actions they take in the game, and by deciding which actions they are allowed to take, you define their space of possibilities. These possibilities are narratively charged, so you can use them as a storytelling medium. To use Red Dead Online as an example: If you give players the option to hunt down other players to collect their bounty at the sheriff's office – this is not a scripted story. But this game mechanic enables emergent player stories around this theme of being an outlaw or bounty hunter and chasing somebody or being chased for their financial gain. The game provides a variety of options for player interaction, from different weapons to emotes or using a lasso to hogtie somebody. And these options define the space of possibility for emergent stories between players.

- Separate the narrative experience into **several themed progressions**, like one or more main progressions and side progressions. This way, players get more freedom to complete tasks in any order they want, while still experiencing a sense of progression in an order you designed. These progressions can be structured by location, type of task, class or role, questgiver, playable character, or following a main story versus following side stories. In Red Dead Online, for example, you receive two different series of quests for being an outlaw or a gunslinger (determined by your position on the honor scale, a morality system defined by player actions and decisions), which tell a story with cutscenes and missions when played in sequence. Players can play these missions whenever they want, though. With this kind of structure, game writers can simply write several smaller and bigger progressions, which allow players to go through them as they want. This is kind of a theme park approach: There are several attractions you can go to, but they all have a pre-defined progression. The player's freedom lies in choosing what to do, when to do it, and whether to stray from it to do something else. But clear thematic coherency (e.g., by binding these progressions to specific icons, names, or quest givers) helps being able to follow the narrative arc. This is the challenge: Creating satisfying story arcs that allow player freedom but still land, despite their interactivity. Pacing needs to accommodate the player's whim.

- To make sure players are never lost in their freedom, offer a **structured list of possible tasks** and clarify what they mean – or another way to access options of what to do next, or track what you've already started. To be able to guide a player's path along a nonlinear experience, it's crucial to remind them of their options and discoveries, so they never feel lost, stuck, or confused. These lists of tasks can be made up of tasks that players have already discovered, icons on a map, or a clear location where to get new tasks of a specific kind if needed. In Sea of Thieves, for example, players can receive quests from different trading companies with specific philosophies and quest types. When they want a specific type of gameplay, they simply speak to the representative and purchase a voyage/quest to then put it on their map table and start it. The Order of Souls, for example, provides players with Bounty Maps and Ghost Ship Maps, therefore sending them on more eerie and supernaturally charged missions than other trading companies.
- **Reminders** become more important, the more time can pass between two story beats. These reminders can be of the possible progressions players can pursue at any given moment (future), or of the story that has happened so far (past). When it comes to progression reminders: Narrative momentum can get lost if players forget their options or if their actions don't get structured in smaller narrative arcs. By reminding them of their options how to pursue smaller arcs or the bigger main arc, they can be gently swayed back on track. Those reminders can be as simple as lists of tasks (as mentioned in the previous point), but can also come in the shape of characters contacting them via phone calls, or markers on the map when they're nearby a possible mission. When it comes to story reminders: Make sure that characters might have to remind players of key information if a lot of time can pass in between these points, or otherwise, think of offering glossaries, story summaries, or cutscene libraries.

MEANINGFUL CHOICES

Choices in games can be as big or small as you want to design them, from impactful choices that alter the entire game, to small decisions that don't change the big picture. Videogames are, after all, a series of decisions that come together as a bigger experience. Do I walk straight ahead or do I check out the side of the path, hoping for a collectible? Do I rush in guns blazing or should I try to be sneaky and take my enemies out one by one? Do I jump now, or 1 millisecond later? Even if a game is linear and pre-scripted, small decisions are everywhere.

When it comes to interactive stories that allow players to change the course of the narrative, we are faced with the question if these offered choices are *meaningful* and satisfying to players. As soon as a game is advertised as an interactive experience that allows choices and a personalized narrative experience, expectations are high.

Imagine this situation: The player has to pick whether they want to sacrifice person A or person B, but no matter which one they choose, person A will always be the one to die. They just influence whether they're sacrificed now or killed by an accident later. Sure, it influences the player's role in the death of the character, and their emotional reaction, but a lot of players would still feel cheated by this choice and become frustrated with it. The problem was that their choice didn't feel meaningful, since the end result is the same. By being able to check the result (with the help of the internet), they are likely to lose their sense of agency. The illusion is broken. They're just a helpless audience member who can't change anything. In interactive stories, this question of *agency* becomes central.

If you were to ask a player what they consider a *meaningful* choice, they'd probably say that it should influence the story progression, in an endlessly branching story tree. However, this isn't feasible for most games, especially longer ones, since it results in a lot of content players might never see. This doesn't mean that choices can't be made meaningful in various types of interactive narrative structures. So, how do we make a choice meaningful, emotionally involving and satisfying? We need to support the player's **sense of agency**. Let's take a look at several techniques, which can be used for a multitude of interactive narrative structures.

LIMITATIONS AND FEEDBACK

- **Limiting the number of choices**. If players have too many choices available at once, they may get overwhelmed, and can't properly weigh each option against one another, which then results in them feeling powerless. The so-called **choice paradox**[3] applies: More choices are only good to a certain extent, after that, the selection makes people miserable. There are too many factors to properly weigh all possible actions against each other, causing anxiety and uncertainty. Also, if somebody chooses from a larger selection, they will be less satisfied with their choices than if they had chosen from a smaller selection. After all, if there are so many different options, there is a chance for a perfect option for *them*, they just don't know which one it is (and will usually assume it's not the one they ended up picking). In addition, they might care less about all individual options, assuming them to have a low impact – after all, they all had to be produced by the game developer, just how impactful can they be if there are ten or more of them? This might simply be a psychological coping mechanism to lower the frustration of choice paralysis, however. Lastly, people can only handle around 7 (±2) elements in their working memory at once, according to psychologist G. A. Miller,[4] while some scientists even suggest as little as 4.[5] So giving players between 2 and 4 options for one choice is usually a good range.
- Announcing the **importance of an upcoming choice**,[6] so players can make a conscious decision, knowing it will have some form of influence on the game. This means that, if a game has both minor choices and big plot-changing choices, those big choices should be marked as important *before* players make them. For example, a romantic choice could be marked with a heart (as in Assassin's Creed Odyssey), so players know when they can romantically pursue a character with a dialogue option. Cyberpunk 2077

has a whole range of markers that imply the meaning of choices: Yellow dialogue options progress the plot, white options are optional information and a 'seat' icon implies that you would stand up and end the conversation. Additionally, there are informative icons next to choices that require certain character stats, or which are based on your chosen character's backstory. In general, you can add any visual markers for important questions, a glowing dialogue box, another font color, shaking letters, a big exclamation mark popping up on the screen, anything. Additionally, characters can also clarify the importance of a question inside of the dialogue itself, or ask if a player is really sure that this is they want. You can get creative with it – but stay consistent with your own creative choices. This way, players know when they have the room to be playful, and when they should be really careful about making a choice. This isn't obligatory for every type of game, of course, especially when you want to focus on immersive roleplay, where you need to weigh every choice carefully.

- **Clarify the consequences of a past choice**, both, **short-term and long-term.**[7] The game should show unique reactions to either choice and make the player understand the impact that the choice had. Remember, we're talking about meaningful choices, which doesn't mean that every single choice has to adhere to this (although a small influence should be shown – otherwise why add this choice at all). This can be as little as an immediate feedback in the dialogue, visual feedback, or a visualized stats change (like The Sims' relationship improvement stat, visualized with a *green* ++ over the Sim's head). Naturally, more meaningful choices should have a longer effect than just a short immediate feedback. If the consequences of an action can still be felt later on in the story, players have an increased sense of agency and impact on the story (by changing the plot or otherwise harkening back to it). Proper feedback is key and doesn't *only* have to be within the dialogue of the story, or whole new story branches or endings. It can also be reflected in the presence or absence of characters, the state of the world, abilities or disabilities of the avatar, and more. There's even the option to use visual UI feedback, such as floating hearts (as in Mystic Messenger, when a character liked the player's dialogue choice) or a text overlay that remarks that "*[Name] will remember that!*" (famously employed by the developer Telltale Games).

CHOICES WITH IMPACT

- Additionally, your most important **choices should actually be impactful**, instead of only being feedbacked as such. Not all choices need to be big, but important choices should have their appropriate impact. Something that actually **influences the plot** in one way or another. This can take shape in variations in scenes, alternative scenes, story routes, or endings. We can draw from a few **topics relating to basic human needs**, which tend to be especially impactful for alternative story developments. If we take a look at Maslow's Hierarchy of Needs,[8] we can see that the most important ones start at the bottom third, with basic needs (physiological, safety). In the middle, we find psychological needs (belonging, love, and esteem). At the top, there is self-fulfillment (self-actualization). In his system, he describes that the lower the need on a pyramid is located, the more central it is for a person's comfort. It's more important to fulfill the lower needs before you tackle the higher ones.

However, for videogames, it is likely a little different, based on the fact that we as a player cannot feel the physiological needs of an avatar as much as we would in real life, no matter how good the game design is. We'll never truly feel hunger, cold, or fear of death due to a game. We can just understand that our avatar does. Inspired by Maslow's Hierarchy of Needs, I'm suggesting a **list of impactful choice consequences** (not sorted by any hierarchy). They can be related to **death, suffering, love, self-fulfillment, success, and belonging**.

– **Death and Suffering:** Choices don't always have to be a matter of life or death, but there's a reason this proverb exists. A character's death can be a powerful moment. May that be about the life and death of the player's avatar, a party member, or other emotionally relevant characters (such as NPCs or villains). Being able to **cause or avoid suffering** in general has a similar effect, may that be physical or emotional pain. Players may want to cause suffering for reasons of punishment, catharsis, or simply morbid curiosity – or because they want to roleplay as a character who lives their life that way. There's a reason why this other proverb exists as well, "*a fate worse than death.*" Sometimes extended existential suffering (or being able to narrowly avoid it), is even stronger than the death scene of a character.

– **Love:** Romantic developments are also a powerful story tool, may that be in the choice between romantic options, or changing a relationship by picking the right (or wrong) choices. Love doesn't only have to be about romantic or sexual love. It can also refer to love for family, friends, or a community – or simply a player's love for a character. If your choice can visibly influence relationships or allows the player to bring happiness to beloved characters, it makes a choice immediately meaningful.

– **Belonging:** Humans are social creatures, so being able to gain a sense of belonging can be very captivating. This can be about the avatar belonging to a social group or a purpose, earning a place or a rank, or being accepted by a social group in-game. Giving players the ability to influence whether other characters are part of an in-group or not can be a powerful tool. This also applies to the opposite end: The ability to exile others from a group through player choices, even if that character is your own avatar. Players might choose to play as a character in exile on purpose because they find that story more interesting (following other motivations) – but that doesn't mean it's any less meaningful to be able to choose.

• **Self-fulfillment and Success:** Another impactful story consequence can be related to topics of self-fulfillment and success of the player, the player avatar, or other characters the player cares about. Players want to see characters they like succeed (or fail, if they dislike them). This can be about allowing a character (avatar or other) to fulfill their dreams, reach a goal, or fail at it. These themes can often be found in alternate endings, which either give a happy resolution to a game's conflict or frustrate it (as a bad ending).

MORAL DILEMMAS

Another way to make a decision impactful is to make it a **moral dilemma,** rather than a question with a clear right or wrong answer or a matter of taste. To create a moral dilemma, the choice must be between two (or more) available options, but where either choice can only result in a moral failing or a negative emotional reaction (such as regret, conflictedness, uncertainty, guilt, etc.). They will either cause an undesirable outcome or the absence of a desirable outcome – the character will be forced to do something wrong or fail to do something right. These dilemmas can come out of self-imposed situations (the character got themselves into this mess) or world-imposed situations (they were thrown into this mess). Let me propose this set of ludic **moral and dilemmas,**[9] adjusted and restructured to be best applicable to videogames.

- **Desirable vs Desirable:** Both options A and B have drastically different but equally desirable effects. These can be story-based consequences, gameplay advantages, and more. That means that the player waives a desirable effect automatically, as soon as they pick the other choice. They must decide which positive opportunity they can bear to lose, or taken the other way round, which of these options would be *better.* Depending on what they have to choose between, this can be quite a tough choice to make. Even though this choice guarantees them something good, the psychological effect of *loss aversion* makes it harder (if players perceive it as such). Players don't want to lose something good, which they could hypothetically have. For example: Between two equally charming characters, which one do you choose to romance? This is at the core of many dating sims, such as Mystic Messenger, where your actions during the first 4 days of gameplay define the romantic route you're unlocking.
- **Undesirable vs Undesirable:** Both A and B have drastically different but equally undesirable side effects if chosen or not chosen. This can be tied to personal choices, where a character is in a situation where they see no other choices but those that would have undesirable effects. This can either be a choice between two negative effects, or negative *side* effects. The player must pick the lesser of two evils and then deal with the negative consequences that they caused themselves. This potentially forces the player to take a deeper look at their own core values, questioning their moral codex and which evil they can commit more easily.
- **Multiple Moralities:** Both options are based on morality codexes that the character or player adhere to, but in this situation, they contradict each other. There could be a conflict between a personal loyalty to a party member, and the duty of a heroic role, for example. What if a close party member turns out to work against the group's intention, but they have their own good reasons to do so? Would the player stay loyal to them, or would they

stay loyal to the cause? This could also be about asking the player to choose between two factions who both have good arguments, or intentions, or at least enough charm. An example would be in Far Cry 4, when Ajay (the player) gets the choice between killing Pagan Min, a tyrant and the lover of his late mother, or letting him live. The conflict is between the fact that Pagan Min considers Ajay his family and has only been kind to him, wishing to patch things up, and the fact that he's a deadly tyrant who Ajay was sent to assassinate.

- **Ethical/Obligation Dilemma:** These moral dilemmas are about conflicts where personal desires stand in conflict with social responsibility. One is a personally advantageous, emotion-driven option and the other a lawful, ethical option (based on whatever ethical dogma is referenced in this situation). The emotional option might be related to a character the player grew to like, whereas the ethical option might be more lawful and perhaps advantageous to more people. An example would be in Life is Strange, where the player must choose between saving Max's (the protagonist's) best friend and love interest Chloe, or saving the entire city. The ethical choice, based on utilitarianism, is clear. But the emotional attachment to Chloe, both from the player's and the protagonist's point of view, makes it hard to decide. This specific example would fall into the **trolley problem** of moral dilemmas: The choice to sacrifice one person (you care about) for the greater good of many (who you aren't as close to). This obligation dilemma can also play with morality scales that align player characters with a certain category. Making these decisions could influence the scales in a way that the player initially didn't intend to do. For example: They want to play as an evil outlaw, but are suddenly faced with the decision to sacrifice their best friend to support that moral alignment or to choose something else, and mess up their initially intended morality.
- **Prohibition Dilemma:** In a prohibition dilemma, all available options are illegal or morally reprehensible. Therefore, even when there is a solution to the conflict at hand, the player and/or character would have to bear the guilt and cognitive dissonance of having done it. This isn't about the undesirability of the outcomes, as in "*undesirable vs undesirable*," but the way that the action would change the characters perception of themselves, as well as society's perception of them. As videogames are a playful realm that are experienced differently from reality, pulling off this dilemma requires a very strong narrative setup. After all, if the game makes the player choose between two horrible options (especially if required to progress), it takes some of the moral responsibility away from them. They don't *really* have a choice (unless they want to stop playing). But if the narrative sufficiently sets up the moral self-perception of the player and/or their character, or this choice is optional, it can still work.
- **Uncertainty Dilemma:** Here, the outcome of either choices isn't completely predictable and both might end in tragedy. The inability to gain all required information, paired with the sense that there is more we don't know, creates insurmountable pressure on the player. The element of randomness makes

taking *'the right decision'* much harder. In videogames, where everything can be checked in online walkthroughs nowadays, these dilemmas are a little harder to pull off and usually require an equal level of desirability and undesirability on both options. Giving a dominant strategy here would remove the aspect of dilemma. This type of dilemma also removes some of the player's sense of agency. That doesn't mean that this type of dilemma can't be very powerful. Looking at the example of Papers, Please!, we find that the game contains tons of dilemmas that partially fall into this category as well. The player might spare a family father who tries to illegally sneak into the country (= obligation dilemma), based on their personal ethics. But they later find out that he was actually a secret agent, losing the player a lot of money in punishment fees that they needed for their own family. In this case, the constant looming threat of uncertainty becomes part of the moral dilemma.

SUMMARY

- Interactive fiction must find a **balance between authored intent and player agency** – which differs from project to project.
- There are several **ways to add interactivity**:
  - Triggers
  - Story branches
  - Story variables
  - Relationship systems
  - Character stats
  - Morality/Affinity systems
  - World states
- **Interactive Narratives can be:**
  - Linear experiences
  - Branching experiences
  - Nonlinear open world experiences
  - Procedurally generated experiences
  - Sandbox experiences
- There are several ways to **enable player freedom** while still **creating a meaningful story:**
  - Worldbuilding as your narrative focus
  - Restrict player actions for a guided experience
  - Author a well–paced main progression that players can return to when ready
  - Create nested dramatic arcs, to provide short–term and long–term narrative pay–offs
  - Let the options tell the story
  - Define purposeful systems for emergent storytelling, where limits and rules convey the narrative intention

- Separate narrative experiences into several progressions
- A structured list of tasks, so players don't lose track
- Reminders, so players don't forget things while they're roaming
- There are several ways to **make choices** in interactive narratives **meaningful**:
  - Limiting the number of choices
  - Announcing the importance of an upcoming choice
  - Feedbacking the consequences of a past choice (short–term + long–term)
  - Creating **impactful consequences** to player choices (topics relating to basic human needs, like death, suffering, love, self–fulfillment, success, and belonging
  - Making the choice a **moral dilemma**, such as:
    - Two desirable outcomes
    - Two undesirable outcomes
    - Multiple clashing moralities
    - Ethical/obligation dilemma
    - Prohibition dilemma
    - Uncertainty dilemma

REFERENCES

1 Tobias Heussner, Toiya Kristen Finley, Jennifer Brandes Hepler, Ann Lemay, "Story," in *The Game Narrative Toolbox*, Focal Press, 2015, 105–124.
2 Janet H. Murray, "Agency" in *Hamlet on the Holodeck: The Future of Narrative in Cyberspace*, The MIT Press, April 7, 2017, 126–153.
3 Barry Schwarz, *The Paradox of Choice – Why More Is Less*, Harper Perennial, January 18, 2005.
4 George A. Miller, The magical number seven, plus or minus two: some limits on our capacity for processing information, *Psychological Review*, 1956.
5 Amanda L. Gilchrist, Nelson Cowan, Moshe and Naveh-Benjamin, Working memory capacity for spoken sentences decreases with adult aging: recall of fewer, but not smaller chunks in older adults, *Memory*, September 2008.
6 Sid Meier, "Interesting Choices," Game Developers Conference, March 5–9, 2012, https://www.gdcvault.com/play/1015756/Interesting.
7 Sid Meier, "Interesting Choices," Game Developers Conference, March 5–9, 2012, https://www.gdcvault.com/play/1015756/Interesting.
8 Saul Mcleod, Maslow's hierarchy of needs, *Simply Psychology*, March 21, 2023, https://www.simplypsychology.org/maslow.html.
9 "Moral Dilemmas," Stanford Encyclopedia of Philosophy, July 25, 2022, https://plato.stanford.edu/entries/moral-dilemmas/.

5 Interactive Storytelling Structures

Many games promise an experience of absolute player freedom full of exciting story choices, turning them into the true protagonist of the narrative. But the released product can often end up being perceived as disingenuously advertised, where the real influence on the story doesn't live up to the promise. On the other end of the extreme, some games offer so many narrative choices that the average player only ever gets to see a small fraction of the full content, ballooning the project's scope for a limited playtime. Additionally, with so many possible playthroughs, there is the risk that not every single one is equally enjoyable. The sweet spot usually lies somewhere in between, or more accurately, each individual project determines that ideal balance. Not every game needs to have a lot of branching choices to create a sense of agency. But games can be extremely ambitious in their goal to tell an interactive story, allowing players to truly decide how the story will progress. One thing isn't better than the other, but you need to be aware of the kind of game you want to create, and how ambitious you can be, based on team size, budget, development time, etc. It's always best to be smart and simplify things as much as possible, but if your project needs a vast branching story, then that's what you're going to do. By taking a look at the role of variables and different narrative structures, we'll try to find plenty of inspiration for possible solutions for your project.

CHOOSING VARIABLES

Before we go into different interactive storytelling structures, it's important to realize that branching storylines aren't only determined by offering a choice between two or more paths. They're not always a UI element that directly asks the player: *"Do you choose A or B?"* They can be driven by a compound of previous small choices, which are recorded as variables. These variables, determined by player actions during gameplay, dialogue choices, and more, can have several kinds of **effects on story and game elements**.

Such **variable effects** can be:

- **Story branches** (resulting in alternate scenes and plot developments)
- **Ending variations** (resulting in alternate endings of the game, and when those endings trigger)
- **Story variations** within a moment (e.g., references to past player actions and events, how a character acts, which exact lines are triggered, which character is present or missing, etc.)
- **Available choice options** (e.g., only aggressive options based on previous aggressive gameplay, choices that only unlock with specific knowledge,

DOI: 10.1201/9781003297628-8

choices that only unlock playing as specific classes, choices that only unlock
at specific charisma levels, etc.)
- **Available gameplay options** (e.g., an avatar played as evil cannot purchase
from an honorable shop dealer anymore, choosing an alliance with a coven
gives you magic powers, etc.)

The content of these variables can be set based on a variety of **choice types**. What
type of choice sets a variable is an essential part of the narrative as well, being the
action leading to later consequences. How players can influence variables defines the
type of world you're describing, and which choices matter most in it. If you sort your
variables into *good* and *evil* behavior, then this contrast of morality is going to be a
core element of your narrative. If your variables define the relationships with NPCs,
then this relationship tracking is going to be a core element of your narrative. If your
variables track the information your character has revealed, then information and
investigation is going to be a core element of your narrative.

Some common examples for **choice types** are:

- **Character Choices** (What has the character done?)
- **Personality and Skill Stats** (What are the inherent personality and skills
of a character?)
- **Moral or Faction Alignment** (Which philosophy does a character adhere
to? Who are they loyal to?)
- **World States** (What is the state of the world? What has happened and what
hasn't happened?)
- **NPC States** (What is the state of the NPCs? How do they feel, what do they
know, what are they doing?)

LINEAR INTERACTIVE STORY

Just because a game has no story choices that create branches or alternate endings,
doesn't mean that it isn't an interactive story. Games are interactive by nature, as the
player acts upon the game to cause a reaction from the game. A linear story[1,2] in a
game still doesn't happen without the purposeful action and gameplay decisions of
the player. In a linear interactive story, the interactive engagement comes from the
player's discovery of the pre-determined path, with the freedom to choose how they
want to do it. A linear game story is still likely to contain endless amounts of gameplay choices, both big and small, from moment to moment. Which weapon do I use?
Which route do I take? Do I sneak around the enemies, or do I run in guns blazing?
Which room will I explore first? All of these gameplay choices influence the player
experience of a story, the acted-out narrative while being devoid of "classical story
choices" or branching storylines. This puts the biggest emphasis on a pre-authored
plot and dramatic sequence of events and emergent storytelling during gameplay.
Players have an influence over their personal pacing and how the action parts of the
game play out (see Figure 5.1).
Examples: Uncharted and Gone Home.

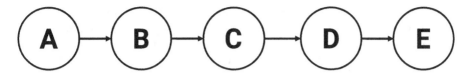

FIGURE 5.1 Flowchart of a linear interactive story.

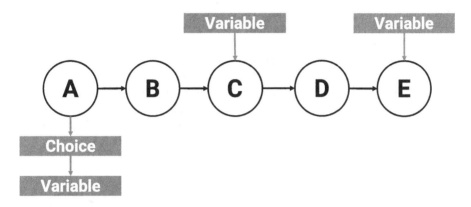

FIGURE 5.2 Flowchart of an interactive story with variables.

LINEAR INTERACTIVE STORY WITH VARIABLES

If you want to add player choices and story alterations that aren't as complicated as branching narratives and entire alternate scenes, it is possible to combine a linear interactive story with variables.[3] That means that the dramatic plot points remain the same, but vary slightly, depending on player choices (during gameplay, dialogue, or other choices). These variations are so contained that every playthrough follows the same plot development, with personalized variations here and there. This can even include whole alternate or optional scenes, but never fully branching story structures. This could be, for example, that a cutscene plays out differently, depending on which character has been chosen in the beginning or the game, altering a few sentences to refer to their unique background. Or players have chosen to attack an NPC instead of sparing them, which results in receiving feedback to that action in a later scene. Or due to a failed mission, they skip a cutscene, and later see another one, reflecting the impact of that failure. Or the personality stats of the playable character are influenced by player behavior and reflected in the way NPCs are speaking to them (see Figure 5.2).

BRANCHING NARRATIVE

In branching narratives,[4,5] each choice creates a new branch of the story, leading to one of several possible subsequent scenes. This means that players choose one path through a branching net, with each choice multiplying the amount of possible scenes at any given step of the story. This type of storytelling, a pure branching narrative that only branches out more with every significant choice, is extremely ambitious and gets out of hand quickly. Even if you only give two choices at a time, this means that after your first choice, you have two alternate branches. After the second choice, you have four alternate branches. After that one, it's eight. Considering your amount of parallel scenes doubles with every choice, you can already see how quickly this would escalate – if used in its pure form. This structure will result in a lot of unseen content for a single playthrough, but comes with high replay value. This is why a purely branching narrative is rarely used for longer games, and usually reserved for short games, or games with very limited assets (such as interactive fiction, visual novels, or short adventures). This structure can be combined with decision variables that just change single elements in a scene without creating a branch, to limit the amount of actual branches but keep a high sense of player agency. Some paths can also end up in a premature end, to additionally help with limiting the scope. In any case, this structure is rarely seen unaltered and usually tamed by combining it with some of the other structures. For these hybrid options, look at *parallel narratives* and *convergent narratives* (see Figure 5.3).

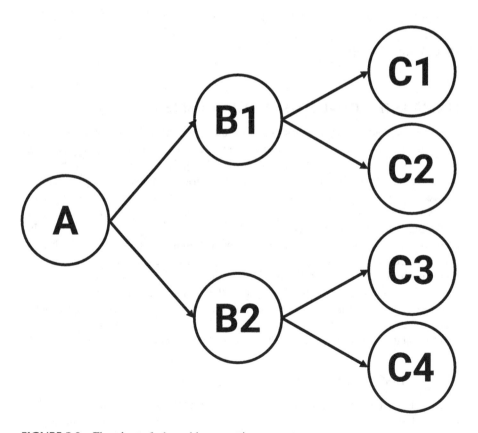

FIGURE 5.3   Flowchart of a branching narrative.

PARALLEL NARRATIVE

To make branching narratives more feasible to produce, they can be limited in their branching scope. In parallel narratives, players can play through two or more parallel paths.[6] They either enter one route at a specific point in the game and then keep on going on it or possibly switch between the routes based on their choices. Here, choices don't split into new story branches, but each choice feeds into a scale that determines which path the player is on. Most often, this concept is tied to morality systems which influence the scenes players see. This can also result in a different ending, to bring a conclusion to the player's allocation on that choice scale. Sometimes games offer the choice to switch over into the other paths during the game, while others branch out at a specific time and then don't converge anymore. (see Figure 5.4).

Examples: Red Dead Online and Mystic Messenger.

CONVERGENT NARRATIVE

Another way to limit your branching narrative for a more achievable production effort, you can add a foldback structure.[7,8] In this approach, player choices create story branches that lead to different parallel scenes, but they eventually merge again. This keeps the experience more under control (retaining key plot points that the player is always supposed to see) while allowing unique player experiences and alternate scenes and even endings. You can still carry over player decisions and refer to them by combining this structure with variables, which can be queried to then trigger one line or another in a shared scene. This approach often creates a montage effect, more specifically the Kuleshov effect, where players will interpret the exact same subsequent events in a different way based on their individually experienced context and information. The convergent key moments should, if done well, not be perceived as a cancellation of the previous choices, but a natural progression (even though players got there differently). This is a good way to feedback a lot of player choices without having to write several different plots. For your project, you can create as many branching paths and converge them how you want, to mix and match obligatory and alternate moments. (see Figure 5.5).

Examples: Detroit Become Human and Until Dawn.

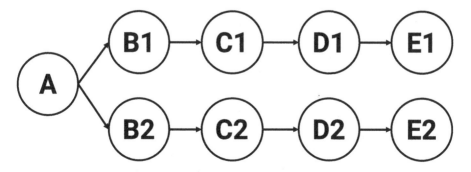

FIGURE 5.4 Flowchart of a parallel narrative.

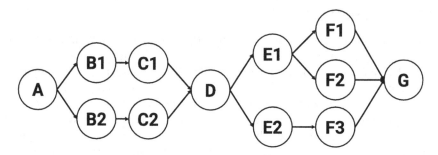

FIGURE 5.5   Flowchart of a convergent narrative.

WORLD STATE NARRATIVE

This type of interactive narrative removes itself from the linearity of logic flows and branches and focuses more on actors within the story world and the variables that determine possible story moments.[9] Imagine an open world game where moments unravel depending on your actions and the state of the world and its inhabitants, which are tracked through variables. The game world is narratively structured by possible story events, which have dependencies on several actors, such as NPCs, enemies, locations, or other. For example: If a guard stands in front of the town gate, running into them triggers a story moment – if they don't, it doesn't. So, when the player runs into one of those actors, a series of possible story moments can happen, depending on the player's previous choices and interactions with other actors. Driven by dependencies and variables, this type of storytelling structure can create very unique player experiences, but usually needs to be sorted into coherent story pockets, akin to an event-based storytelling. It's closely related to emergent storytelling, but usually has pre-scripted variations of scenes that depend on a whole set of variables and actor states. To better explain the structure, let's picture a fictional event in an open world game.

Picture an Old West setting. There's a dangerous criminal gang in town and the player may get involved. The actors in this scenario are the player, the criminal gang and the town sheriff. The criminals can be encountered in a variety of ways, each situation playing out differently depending on previous player actions.

The **key variables** in this event are:

A. Have the criminals been encountered?
B. Have the criminals been locked up in prison?
C. Have the criminals been killed?
D. Has the player heard about the criminals from the sheriff?
E. Has the sheriff been killed?

Meeting the criminals can have two different scenarios, depending on whether the sheriff has been encountered beforehand or not.

- **Scenario 1:** The player didn't know about the criminals and encounters them for the first time. They are immediately spotted and can now choose to kill them in defense or run away.

- **Scenario 2:** The player has already heard about the criminals from an interaction with the sheriff. The player character can now spot them from afar and has the option to approach them with stealth. They can now choose to kill them, capture them or run away.

  Meeting the sheriff also has different varieties, based on the previous actions and world states. This element is independent from the part relating to the criminals and can be combined in multiple ways.

- **Scenario 1:** The player hasn't met the criminals yet and now hears about the situation from the sheriff. He asks the player to help out, maybe adding some pressure by talking about the suffering this has caused the town.
- **Scenario 2:** The player has already met the criminals and escaped them. The sheriff doesn't need to explain all of it, but asks the player for help.
- **Scenario 3:** The player has already met the criminals and killed them. The sheriff is relieved and explains why the player did the town a great favor, handing out a small reward for the effort.
- **Scenario 4:** The player has talked to the sheriff before, gone to the criminals, and captured them. The sheriff is relieved and hands out a bigger reward for the effort.
- **Scenario 5:** The player had already encountered the criminals, but decided to run away from them. The sheriff is now dead, and his wife can be found crying over it.

As you can see, this story encounter can begin in multiple different places. There is no traditional order of having to seek out a quest giver to start something. Maybe they first hear about the situation from yet another NPC, who complains about the criminals, too. You could also choose to add even more actors and variables, like the weather and time of day influencing where the criminals hang out, or when players wait too long after first hearing about them, they find more and more NPCs that have been robbed and killed.

Using world states as a way to track and trigger narrative can be interesting for story environments that seek to give the player a lot of freedom, and create a sense of a living world (see Figure 5.6).

Examples: Elden Ring.

STORY MAP

Story Maps are composed of narrative nodes connected by decisions, not in the shape of a branching tree, but in any shape the narrative designer chooses. Each story node can consist of something as small as a piece of dialogue, or as big as a whole story arc. The player navigates that storyscape like geographical locations made of moments. Not every moment can be triggered from every location in the map.

Story Maps can be found in more experimental interactive narrative games and story simulations, where the narrative is the core feature of the game, such as the experimental simulation Façade, or The Sims.

When used in open world games, the connections between nodes are often not only story decisions, but geographical decisions. To travel through the story map, players may physically travel through the game world, as well. This creates a net

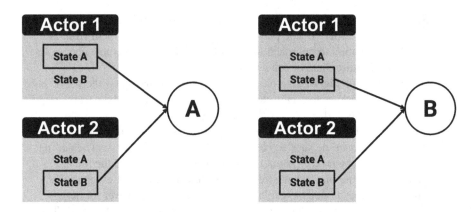

FIGURE 5.6   Logic flow of a world state narrative.

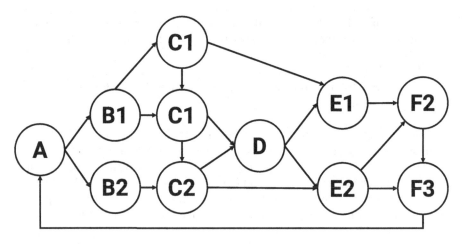

FIGURE 5.7   Logic flow of a story map.

structure that often consists of a variety of modular self-contained stories, which are part of a larger experience. These self-contained stories can be completed in any order (or with some dependencies between one another) and often take the shape of quests or missions.

Open World games often combine story maps with a linear interactive narrative or a converging narrative on top of the map – combining a main progression that ties into an open story map, with both structures mutually influencing one another. Often, players get the freedom to explore a variety of moments in any order they want, until the next part is unlocked (like a main mission). Sometimes the unlocking process of main progressions is connected to gaining enough experience points with the open world missions, such as in Far Cry 5. Here, players have a separate progression for three different regions, driven by missions. They can experience these short story missions in any order, with some dependencies, and the order of completion of the three regions is also free to choose. After three are completed, the fourth final region unlocks (see Figure 5.7).

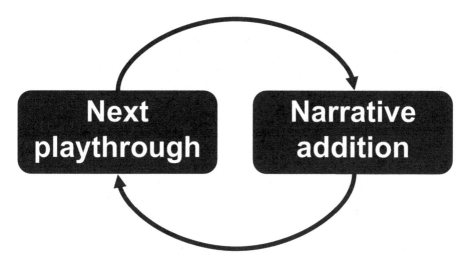

FIGURE 5.8   Logic flow of a loop and grow structure.

LOOP AND GROW

In this structure, the player is expected to play the game several times to experience the whole narrative.[10] This can be combined with any of the other structures, but adds the element of repeatedly restarting the same story with new knowledge, choices, options and story developments. A loop can, for example, be necessary for trial and error to find out paths to new endings – whereas information gained in one run can be used in the next to get to a new narrative location. This can include that you gain a piece of knowledge too late in one run to use it, but after starting a new run, you can use that knowledge right away. Or the story changes on its own, the more often you play it. The goal of these loop and grow narratives is often the exploration of a single story's depth and variations, with several possible end points such as true endings. This can also be intertwined with a rogue-lite game structure, where each death triggers a new story development – and players don't replay the same story with new changes and developments, but continue a story on a meta layer, combined with a repeating game loop (See Figure 5.8).

Examples: Hades, 12 Minutes, Doki Doki Literature Club.

DESIGNING AN EFFICIENT BRANCHING NARRATIVE

The challenge of branching narratives is striking a balance between how much is produced and how much is seen in any given walkthrough. A key aspect of that consideration is how we want the player to interact with the game, and remember that the medium is the message. The way a story is experienced is part of its message and themes. Do we want them to play the game once, maybe twice, but make a playthrough unique to each player? Or do we want a highly replayable experience that offers new content in an interesting and motivating way for a long while? Or do we want them to play the game multiple times to reveal its true meaning and ending?

Balancing how much each player sees versus how much content actually exists is a battle between production investment and experience pay-off. If a game is extremely complex but most players never see most of it, they might come out of it feeling the story was lacking. Or even if they don't, the project might come out far more expensive than it needed to be to get the same point across and make players happy.

This is about picking your battles and developing smartly. This is about clarifying a narrative strategy for yourself (and your team) and then make meaningful choices that support this strategy. Put resources into aspects that lots of players will see and which are central to the game's narrative experience and put less resources into sidetracks and Easter eggs.

If everything is equally excessive, it's easy for players to lose sight of the central idea. Don't create so many branches that players get lost in the woods. Design in a way that enables most players to play the game in a way that aligns with your intended experience.

To reduce your production effort in an elegant and clever way, to allow your team to create the game with the biggest bang for your buck, you need to plan ahead. You should think about these aspects:

- **Define your intended player interaction** with the story and plan accordingly. Do you want them to play it once, multiple times, or give them an almost infinitely replayable experience?
- **Define the narrative freedom** you plan to give players and then stick to it. Not every project should give the players as much freedom as possible, even if it can be tempting to let players do *everything* you can think of. Limit yourself, but do it in a smart way, so that players don't even feel restricted but pleasantly focused. Try to be as efficient elegant and purposeful as possible. Sometimes less is more, as too many choices can be overwhelming. This applies to both development teams and gamers. And when too many features drown out the interesting core, maybe even taking development time away from it, that's no good.
- **Create interactivity using elements that don't depend on big branching stories**, such as variables, gameplay, and game systems. Using this, rather than creating new branches for every decision, limits the amount of content that will remain unseen to a majority of players. Not every moment needs multiple possible scenes, sometimes it's enough if small things change within it to get the same effect and sense of agency in players.
- Think about ways to **contain your branches**. Use convergent narrative structures, leading players back to one (or more) main story progression(s), with variables from past decisions influencing details. Whenever you decide to add branches, also consider limiting branching storylines within a certain perimeter, such as locations, chapters, missions, or DLCs.
- Consciously differentiate **big decisions and small decisions**. Don't carry all decisions with you throughout the entire game and don't give them the same weight. Limit how many big story-changing decisions you offer. Not everything needs to show a long-term effect and can either be irrelevant in the long run or just show very small changes. A big decision could, for example, create a story branch with an entirely new scene, while a small

decision just influences a variable that changes a line in one dialogue, or only shows immediate feedback and is then never referred to again. Limit how many choices have a big impact, and even consider cutting those that don't really improve the experience at all.

- Use **context as a tool to shift the meaning** of an identical scene. In cinematic montage, there is something called the Kuleshov effect.[11] Here, the exact same scene gains another meaning through the context of what happens before or after. The same face can indicate sexual desire or a hunger for food, depending on which other image is combined with it (a seductive person or a nice meal). In videogames, this effect can be used as well: An identical scene can entirely shift in meaning depending on how the player got there, how much they know, and what happens afterwards. Playing with different levels of information is one of the more interesting potentials for interactive narratives because they can change with every playthrough.

INTERACTIVE NARRATIVES IN LIVE GAMES

When you're working on a live game, keeping your choices under control becomes even more important. Just imagine a branching narrative that is continued for seasons to come! You're going to keep this game going for as long as you can, adding more content over time. And the more long-term you want player choices to be, the more complicated (or impossible) it will get. What works for one season might give you a headache in the next. Don't get lost in ambitious short-term plans.

Let's take a look at some ideas **how to insert interactive narrative** and player choices **into live games**, without losing control of your project. Be aware that you don't need to implement all of these in the same game (not all games have the same vision), but you can often make use of several of them.

- **Limit story choices, branches, and alternate scenes** as much as you need in order to have a realistic production roadmap. Track how long the production of a narrative package would take when you choose to include as many choices and story alterations as you intend to have, so you know how quickly you'll be able to produce content when you intend to have live. During this experimental phase (ideally pre-production or production), you may find out that it's just not feasible and that you should adjust your plans. And don't forget that if you keep on branching out existing branches, it means that your production effort would rise exponentially! Use variables, use converging or parallel narrative structures, or find other ways to contain the expansion of your content.
- **Limit the long-term effects of choices**, by (for example) containing them within seasons, storylines, events, DLCs or missions, and not having them carry over to later points. And if you still choose to, out of important narrative reasons, keep it simple. Carrying branching storylines across many seasons, and having them branch out indefinitely, is downright impossible to track and manage. At some point, players don't gain anything from it anymore, either. So it's usually a better idea to limit choices to a certain part or phase of the game and then let the story converge again. If you want to include player choices with long-term impact, you could also provide a limited number of

parallel stories that depend on player choices, but don't branch out indefinitely either. For example, by letting players experience the story from the perspective of different factions. You need to make sure players can start from the same starting point in each season. If there is a difference, it should be fairly limited and offer a default entry point or the option to make a past choice, for the players that weren't around to play the last season.

- **Attach individual choices to personality, morality, or alignment scales**, instead of creating a new variable for each individual choice. This allows players to shape their narrative standpoint no matter when they enter the game, even if they missed previous (time-limited) seasons and choices that happened then. The story can refer to the value from this variable regularly, creating a different experience for players depending where they are on that scale – without the need of having played through past time-limited experience. This also avoids having an increasing amount of variables and branching scenes.

- Another possibility is to use **player choices as a voting system** for upcoming narrative content. This means that players can make choices, but not all possible consequences need to be produced. They need to be planned for, but in the end, only the chosen option needs to be added to the game. It's important to mitigate player frustration if their choice isn't the one that influenced the story in the end – this can be circumvented by giving it a narrative framing that explains the reason for it. For example: There is a battle between teams, and players choose a side. The side that gains more points wins – and their victory comes with an attached a narrative choice. Splatoon's Splatfest events have implemented voting systems, albeit without a narrative consequence, where teams pick a side in questions such as "What's better, Pizza or Burgers?" Team Pizza and Team Burger collect points, and in the end, the winning team determines the answer.

- If you have a live game with time-limited seasons and sequential narrative content, **make plans for players who enter the game later on**. If you give players choices in each season, new players won't have taken these decisions and need a way to make up for them. There are several options how to handle this. For example, they can be assigned a default set of variables, either persistent or at random (which takes the experience out of the players' hands but could be made invisible and rectifiable later on). Alternatively, these required choices might be part of the onboarding, which allows them to catch up on those past choices needed for the live season – these choices could even be added to the moments where they become relevant, instead of general onboarding. Lastly, of course, you can contain your choices to each individual season (or story arc, such as missions or DLCs), which means that players don't actually need to make choices that had happened in the past – they have become irrelevant in the new season.

- Another solution to this issue is to **limit all your choices to onboarding content**, and therefore putting none into your live seasons. This part of the game would be permanently accessible for all new players, no matter when they start. This could either remain self-contained or result in an alignment that influences the game afterwards – no matter which live content is currently active. For example: Red Dead Online's Honor Missions during onboarding align players on a scale from Gunslinger (honorable) to Outlaw (dishonorable). They feature moral choices which later determine available missions (and story). While they play the game, however, players can freely influence that honor scale through their in-game actions, making it possible to be an Outlaw in one moment, and a Gunslinger in the next.

- If you do want to make a choice-driven game, however, these solutions might not scratch that itch yet. Alternatively, you can make the interactive narrative central to the core gameplay and **create a design with low production costs**, such as interactive novels or dialogues with modular graphics (like Chapters or D4DJ Groovy Mix). Limiting the production complexity of each new narrative chapter makes it more feasible to produce a lot of them over a long period of time, while still keeping up with a schedule. Here, the same previously mentioned rules apply: Think about using variables, converging and parallel narratives, instead of only using branching narratives.

Your choice design will depend on your type of project, of course. Single-player live games don't have the problem of onboarding players that join later into the game, since there *is* no time-limited live season that forces players to jump into the middle of a story. They can all start in the beginning. But multiplayer live games, with seasonal structures that tell an ever-progressing story, need to consider how to handle a belated entry into the seasonal story progression. And self-contained arcs or limited choices are one way to do it. Additional factors are the production complexity of your narrative chapters, the game's vision, and general gameplay. In general, it's important to make the creative choices that fit the vision of your individual project, while trying to make it worth with your production setup, budget, and time constraints.

SUMMARY

- **Variables** can enable players to have an **effect on story**:
  - Story branches, alternate scenes & story developments
  - Different endings
  - Variations of the same moment
  - Available choice options for dialogue or actions
- Variables can be determined by various **types of choices**:
  - Character Choices
  - Personality and Skill Stats
  - Moral Alignment
  - World States
  - NPC States
- **Linear Interactive Stories** are pre-authored narratives where player choices don't influence the story, except for pacing, action and gameplay choices.

- **Linear Interactive Stories with Variables** are pre–authored narrative experiences where player choices influence variables that slightly influence the story, but without extensive branching.
- **Branching Narratives** branch out with each choice the player takes.
- **Parallel Narratives** offer several story progressions that take place in parallel, and the player chooses which route they want to follow – often connected to moral or group alignments.
- **Convergent Narratives** are an adjusted version of the branching narrative, where a foldback structure allows branches to merge back together occasionally, limiting scope.
- **World State Narratives** focus on several actors within a story space, their connections, and their different possible states.
- **Story Maps** are composed of narrative scenes that are connected by decisions, but not in the shape of a branching tree – it can create a storyscape with or without a set ending.
- **Loop & Grow** is a structure where players play (part of) the game several times to experience the whole narrative.
- In order to design an **efficient branching narrative**, it's helpful to:
  - **Define intended player interactions** with the story and build the game around that.
  - **Define the narrative freedom** given to players (and be realistic about it).
  - **Create interactivity** with elements that **do not depend on branching stories**, such as variables or gameplay.
  - Consciously **differentiate big and small decisions**, limit how many have a big impact, and cut small decisions that don't add anything to the experience.
  - Use **context as a tool** to shift the meaning of a scene without having to actually write a different scene.
- When designing **interactive narratives for live games**:
  - **Make choices self–contained** within a season, storyline, DLC, event, or mission.
  - Have **individual choices influence a** morality or affinity alignment, instead of having one variable for each choice.
  - Use **player choices as a voting system** that then applies to all players.
  - **Make plans** for **people who enter the game later** and haven't made choices in the past.
  - **Attach choices to onboarding** content that is permanently accessible.
  - **Create a design with low production cost** and combine this with strategies to limit branching storylines.

REFERENCES

1 Josiah Lebowitz and Chris Klug, "Defining Interactive and Player-Driven Storytelling," in *Interactive Storytelling for Video Games: A Player-Centered Approach for Creating Memorable Characters and Stories*, Focal Press, April 5, 2011, 117–147.

2 Lee Sheldon, "Modular Storytelling," in *Character Development and Storytelling for Games*, Course Technology, 2nd edition, April 3, 2013, 312–316.

3 Steve Ince, "Writing and the Development Process," in *Writing for Videogames*, Methuen Drama, September 29, 2006, 47–54.

4 Josiah Lebowitz and Chris Klug, "Defining Interactive and Player-Driven Storytelling," in *Interactive Storytelling for Video Games: A Player-Centered Approach for Creating Memorable Characters and Stories,* Focal Press, April 5, 2011, 181–204.

5 Lee Sheldon, "Modular Storytelling," in *Character Development and Storytelling for Games*, Course Technology, 2nd edition, April 3, 2013, 316–324.

6 Steve Ince, "Writing and the Development Process," in *Writing for Videogames*, Methuen Drama, September 29, 2006, 47–54.

7 Emily Short, "Storylets: You Want Them," Emily Short's Interactive Storytelling, accessed April 24, 2023, https://emshort.blog/2019/11/29/storylets-you-want-them/.

8 Lee Sheldon, "Modular Storytelling," in *Character Development and Storytelling for Games*, Course Technology, 2nd edition, April 3, 2013, 316–324.

9 Jon Ingold, "Narrative Sorcery: Coherent Storytelling in an Open World," Game Developers Conference, March 1-3, 2017, accessed at https://youtu.be/HZft_U4Fc-U.

10 Emily Short, "Storylets: You Want Them," Emily Short's Interactive Storytelling, accessed April 24, 2023, https://emshort.blog/2019/11/29/storylets-you-want-them/.

11 "Kuleshov Effect: Everything You Need to Know," Nashville Film Institute, accessed April 22, 2023, https://www.nfi.edu/kuleshov-effect/.

6 Open-Ended Storytelling Structures

When we're talking about narrative design for live games, we're talking about stories that are meant to go on for a long time. As long as a game stays profitable, its (hypothetical) intention is to last forever. This fact points us toward a need for open-ended storytelling, where we plan for a space for endless continuation. As the title of this book suggests, one of these options is to simply continue the story. Add more over time. Treat it like a TV series, with many exciting seasons to come. This, however, isn't the only approach we can take to make a game story a little more open-ended. And since games are often composed of several features, these approaches can even be combined.

To understand what we mean by open-ended design, let's clarify what separates it from limited design. A limited design would be a story that you can clearly complete within a limited number of playthroughs. On the other hand, an open-ended design provides a significant amount of content with no set end, allowing players to play with the game until they get bored, without running out of significant new experiences. While open-ended narratives might not hold a player's attention for the rest of their life, the goal is to offer countless hours of playtime. They're story sandboxes, playgrounds, and toys – interactive experiences that allow players to explore.

Open-ended systems therefore offer another way of adding content to live games besides the persistent continuation of one sequential story. The open-ended structures can serve as a basis for players to spend a lot of time in, potentially being expanded with the addition of new modules over time, whereas you can still add seasonal content.

There are a handful of different approaches in how to create open-ended narratives.

NONSTORY NARRATIVE

A game doesn't need cutscenes, dialogue, or even dramatic plot beats to be a narrative experience. Like a game of chess, these games without a scripted plot still express a core theme and conflict that are explored through player actions. This means that we can create an open-ended narrative experience by giving players repeatable gameplay that tells a story through its actions – each experience is unique due to the fact that players also behave uniquely in each run. Depending on how complex the game systems are, this can also contain *systemic narrative* and *emergent narrative* (which I will define further in later sections).

EMERGENT NARRATIVE

SYSTEMIC NARRATIVE

Systemic Narratives replace a traditional pre-authored plot with a story experience driven by dynamics between actors (game units that can listen to input, give output,

DOI: 10.1201/9781003297628-9

and have behavior) – though a mixed approach is possible. This systemic narrative is made up of actors and a set of rules that connect them with each other. These actors can be NPCs, enemies, or animals, but also sub-systems for missions, weather, physics, weapons, etc. Actors in a narrative system are defined by the following aspects:

- **State of being** (e.g., Being idle or active, living or dead, aggressive or peaceful, wet or dry, etc.).
- **Unique goals** that motivate their behavior (e.g., An enemy having the goal to kill every player, starting with the weakest ones, an NPC patrolling the same path unless something disrupts them, etc.).
- **Dependencies with other actors**, with rules that define how they're influenced by each other (e.g., An NPC cowers in fear when a hostile enemy is near, an animal flees into a burrow when it's raining, an enemy yells *"Grenade!"* when a grenade lands near them, etc.).
- They **listen to inputs,** certain triggers that would warrant a reaction from them (e.g., Fire, encountering enemies, being attacked, etc.)
- And they **emit outputs** in reaction (e.g., being visible, audible, etc.)
- So when the inputs and outputs of two actors meet in a meaningful way (whereas the player can also be involved in this) an **action is triggered** (e.g., Conflict between two enemy types, fire going out when it's raining, an NPC being in a good mood because we liberated their city, etc.).
- And lastly, units have **consistent rules** to allow players to make plans and perceive the game as a logical game world that operates by intuitive and believable rules.

In this structure, the player is an agent who acts upon the narrative system to cause interactions and reactions and, in turn, reacts back at them. This is a purposefully constructed space for emergent narrative – player stories that weren't pre-scripted to happen at this exact point of play, but which are envisioned and enabled by the system designed by the game developers. They can contain dialogue or barks as well, and don't only need to contain game dynamics and *"pure gameplay."*

Narrative systems can take different shapes, depending on how we define our actors and rules, and where we place our **focus of the player experience:**

- **World Systems:** Focusing on the whole game world, and the dynamics of nature, locations and peoples.
- **Character Systems:** Focusing on individual characters and their relation to the world, like the behavior of NPC companions or love interests.
- **Dialogue Systems:** Focusing on believable interactive dialogue dynamics between the player and another actor.
- **Story Systems:** Focusing on the structure of the story itself, and how each action and triggered moment influences the development of the story.

These narrative systems can have varying experience intentions, too, namely a focus on emergent player stories during gameplay, a dynamic story, or the procedural generation of content.

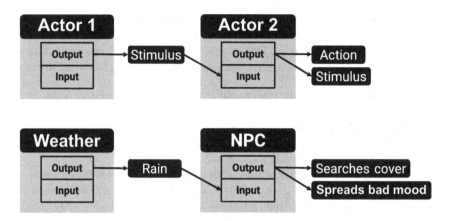

FIGURE 6.1   Logic flow of a systemic narrative.

- **Simulation-Centric Approach:** Creating a game world to dynamically interact with, which feels alive, reactive, and allows for emergent situational storytelling and player stories. *(Examples:* The Sims, GTA Online*)*
- **Narration-Centric Approach:** Creating a story space which the player can navigate, creating a dynamic story with player choices, high replay value and a lot of unique possible playthroughs. *(Examples:* The Novelist, Façade*)*
- **Procedurally Generated Content:** This can be simulation- or narration-centric, but it includes randomly generated content to create the content of the system – usually conceived to be limitlessly scalable. This allows the creation of (otherwise impossibly) large story libraries for players to experience, and the opportunity for randomized playthroughs that are completely unique to players. *(Examples:* No Man's Sky, Watch Dogs: Legion*)* (see Figure 6.1).

ROLEPLAY SYSTEMS

In multiplayer games, some game features and systems can also be an opportunity for roleplaying with other players. Closely related to systemic narrative and often intertwined, the central actors here are not one player and their surrounding actors, but rather, a group of players who all serve as actors within the game world. This player interaction allows for emergent narrative – you write stories by interacting with other people. While people interacting with one another isn't something we, as narrative designers, design, we still give them the game world to do it in, and the tools with which they can express themselves. We give them tools of interaction, and these tools determine the possible narrative of their actions. Beyond in-game chat, the way players *can* act with each will deeply define *how* they will act with each other. If we only give them guns to shoot at each other, this will be their dominant narrative – showdowns with strangers who want to kill them. If we give an opportunity to rob players, or tie them up, that allows emergent stories about robberies and abductions. But we can also offer non-lethal interactions, such as emotes, collaboration, going bounty hunting together and sharing the reward, horseriding alongside each other, or even getting drunk together and falling into each other's arms – or starting a harmless and non-lethal fist-fight. All examples listed here are taken from Red Dead Online. Some of these things don't even give players any experience points or rewards, except for the opportunity to roleplay with others. We can, however, also encourage specific interactions by adding rewards to them. Anyway, when creating games with intricate systems around player-to-player interaction, it's extremely valuable to think about your roleplay value for the opportunity for emergent narrative. And what kind of stories do you encourage with the behavior you offer them as tools of expression.

MODULAR NARRATIVE

A modular narrative provides a world full of *story modules* that are thematically connected but can (mostly) be played in any given order, although usually with some logical constraints. A module can be a dialogue, a mission, an event, or whatever you want to separate your narrative experience into. Some of them may be grouped together in a sequence, where completing one is a prerequisite for unlocking the other, while others may be independent and stand on their own. There can be other dependencies which determine whether a module is available or not, too, such as geographical location, player level, current moral alignments, or other variables. These modules function as short stories or self-contained scenes along the path of a greater story arc. These modules can be added upon indefinitely, meaning, the player explores a pool of different story modules that grows with every update. An example for this could be an open world game (such as MMORPGs) filled with self-contained missions in different locations, which are tied together by the general themes and the player journey. Expansions of modular narratives can simply add new modules or even a whole new type of module (such as a mission type or a new area with local missions). An example can be found in World of Warcraft, where new expansions add new zones to explore, which come with a story, game features, gameplay, and items.

These modular narratives can be combined with procedural narrative systems – where your narrative modules are composed of sub-modules that get randomized and recombined based on your defined rules (see Figure 6.2).

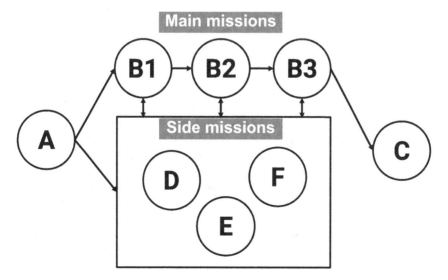

FIGURE 6.2 Logic flow of a modular narrative.

Player-facing   **Internal**

```
You enter the dungeon.          Listen for...
It's too dark to see.
                                Actions:
What do you do?                 "Look", "Search", "Go to"...

                                Objects:
                                "Doors", "Walls", "Floor"...

                                If A1 + B1, then...
                                If A1 + B2, then...
                                ...
> [Type reply]
```

FIGURE 6.3   Example visualization of a story simulation.

DYNAMIC NARRATIVE/STORY SIMULATION

A dynamic narrative is a net of complexly interconnected possible story moments without a pre-determined progression or golden path. Players can move between them and play these story moments in any given order. It is different from a modular story in the way that it consists of story moments that are deeply influenced by player actions, rather than just a selection of short stories that can be played in any order, and closer to a *story simulation*. Depending on its structure, it can look almost identical to a story map, as mentioned in the previous chapter, but is defined by its more simulation-centric approach. A dynamic narrative puts player choices first, and might even allow direct input, such as a chat system or text input (like in text adventures). Some examples would be Façade, The Stanley Parable or Event [0] (see Figure 6.3).

PROCEDURAL NARRATIVE

Procedural narrative adds the element of randomization and computer generation to a game's narrative design. It's the method of programming algorithms to procedurally generate entire stories, parts of stories, or individual elements of stories (such as missions or character biographies). The output of these algorithms is defined by a pre-determined set of rules, restrictions, and contents – A narrative designer defines the intended shape of the final output (such as a story in ten scenes, a mission in two sentences, a biography with five keywords, etc.), all possible content and how said content will be shuffled and connected, rather than writing the final player-facing version. The authorship thereby lies in the definition of the tools, limitations, and manner of output. Procedurally generated content can be helpful to create an almost endless amount of unique content, by adding the element of randomness and recombination with the help of a tech tool. The challenge lies in defining rules in a way that the output comes across as logical, meaningful, and unique to the player. It should not read as computer-generated, unless you want that to be part of your narrative vision (when you're interacting with a fictional AI, for instance).

An example for procedurally generated narrative would be in Watch Dogs: Legion, which prided itself on having *endless* amounts of unique NPCs that can be recruited into the player's team. Each NPC has a list of attributes that are assigned randomly, with some dependencies to give off the impression of coherent personalities. Each NPC gets a unique design, as well as a name, job, fun fact, age, occupation, salary, important associates, and some random facts called "metadata," which read a little like an excerpt from a biography without dates. Each of these aspects gets a pool of possible answers – only numbers between a certain range for their age, in accordance to the 3D model given to them, for example. Through a set of rules, the tool for procedural character generation can create countless technically unique NPCs, unique to the player's game.

Procedural narrative can be used on a global game scale (as No Man's Sky's procedural generation of entire planets and universes) and on a small scale (like individual character biographies or item descriptions). Another example for procedurally generated characters would be Darkest Dungeon, where every unique (and mortal) character is created from a randomized list of roles, aspects, and psychological weaknesses. In the case of this game, these elements influence their behavior in gameplay as well.

Whether a procedurally generated aspect is the right choice strongly depends on the project – because there is always the risk that the result doesn't feel as meaningful as a pre-scripted narrative might have. And if the pool of options is too small, the curtain lifts and reveals the technical workings of the game – possibly taking away from the emotional gravitas of the content. But, on the other hand, it can help create growing amounts of content more easily – by expanding the pool of options over time or adding new procedurally driven features.

PLAYER-GENERATED CONTENT

Another way to create an endlessly increasing amount of content is to turn your players into co-creators. By providing tools for content creation, such as levels, missions, or stories, players can create and share new content with each other. For player-generated content, the challenge lies in providing accessible and flexible tools, with limitations in accordance with your game's vision. Players don't need to be able to create everything and anything under the sun – a purposeful focus on tools and options can guide your players' creations to fit the game's general philosophy and gamefeel. Implementing curation and community management becomes central in approaches like these as well, with the help of rating and reporting systems. This might not fit every kind of game, but has been used in a huge variety of genres, such as VRChat (room and experience creation), Roblox (game creation), Super Mario Maker (Mario level creation), Choices (visual novel story creation), Far Cry 5 (FPS level creation), or Riders Republic (racing track creation).

SEASONAL NARRATIVE

Lastly, there is the most straightforward option to keep a story going: Simply write more of it. Much like TV shows, comic books, and serials in magazines, live games can go seasonal and keep adding a continuation of what came before. This can either be temporary – like a live broadcast on TV – or a permanent addition – more like a TV streaming service. For something that continues over a long time, a simple continuation is likely to lose audiences because it leads nowhere. Therefore, the dramatic structure must be a sequence of arcs (seasonal or otherwise), just like TV shows do. Keeping the audience's tension over a long period of time is a masterclass exercise in building and releasing tension, opening conflicts and closing them, without risking them wanting to stop at any given point. How to write a game season, and what we can learn from television shows, will be described in more detail in *Chapter 13*.

SUMMARY

- **Nonstory narrative** games convey a narrative meaning through their general narrative design, gameplay and game systems.
- **Emergent narratives** can be created through game systems in which several actors that influence one another, where player input and world dynamics create situations with narrative implications.
  - **Systemic narratives** are stories built from world, character, dialogue, or story systems, and can have a focus on simulation, narration, or procedural generation.
  - In **Roleplay systems**, game features enable players to roleplay and create their own stories.
- **Modular narratives** provide a story world full of interconnected story modules that can be played in different orders (which can be expanded with new modules).
- **Dynamic narratives** are nets of story units that are connected by rules and dependencies, functioning as story or chat simulations. They don't have a pre-defined progression and react dynamically to player input.
- **Procedural narratives** are partially randomized and computer-generated, based on rules and pools of content defined by the narrative designer.
- **Player-generated content** builds a growing library of narrative content by offering tools for players to make and share own creations.
- **Seasonal narratives** are the creation of seasonal story content, possibly similar to a TV show, where players are provided with new narrative additions in regular intervals.

BIBLIOGRAPHY

Josiah Lebowitz and Chris Klug, "Defining Interactive and Player-Driven Storytelling," in *Interactive Storytelling for Video Games: A Player-Centered Approach for Creating Memorable Characters and Stories*, Focal Press, April 5, 2011, 117–245.

Tanya X. Short and Tarn Adams (Editors), *Procedural Storytelling in Game Design*, 2nd edition, Routledge, March 21, 2019.

Part III

Live Game Storytelling

7 Introduction to Mobile Game Storytelling

WHY MOBILE GAMES ARE RELEVANT WHEN DESIGNING LIVE GAMES

You might be wondering about our little excursion into the world of mobile games, when this book is supposed to be about live games. We've already caught glimpses of the reason for this in the introduction chapter of this book, but since you might have chosen to jump right into this chapter – or it's been a while since you've started reading this book – let's summarize those reasons.

1. Many live games are **released on mobile** devices, either exclusively or in addition to console or PC releases. Not all live games are on mobile, but most popular mobile games are live games.
2. Live games for PC and console frequently take inspiration from methods of **monetization**, UI and UX design in mobile games nowadays, due to the mobile industry's vast financial success, which blurs the lines between these platforms.
3. There are now several popular **hybrid consoles** on the market which can be played in handheld mode, in very similar ways to mobile devices (such as the Switch or Steam Deck). Designing for consoles like this can benefit from understanding how a mobile device (phone or not) is perceived as a gaming device.

In that regard, there's a high value in understanding the unique challenges and best practices of mobile game development, no matter if your live game project happens to be on mobile, or is developed for PC or consoles. These learnings might vary in usefulness, depending on the structure of your project, but there is a high chance that *some* of it will become relevant to you.

CHALLENGES OF MOBILE GAMES

Mobile gaming is meant to be fun. But since smartphones are always at your fingertips, it's also a tool to zone out and kill time wherever you are. Casual mobile gaming can pass the time during breaks while commuting or to wind down in the evenings. In fact, it's not uncommon for casual players to watch a movie on a bigger screen while they have their smaller screen in hand.

Smartphone users have developed a **specific way in which they interact with their phone**, which emerged from the design of its touchscreen interface and individual apps. They consume micro content from multiple sources, most of which is

DOI: 10.1201/9781003297628-11

served as **bite-sized entertainment** and information. Social media and news apps are an endless scrolling dash of short content, no matter if you're reading opinions on Twitter, looking at photos on Instagram, or watching videos on TikTok. And if one dash is starting to bore the user, they can switch to another app. This creates expectations for every interaction with the device and influences the general average attention span. This means that the **average attention span** for a mobile game is **shorter** than for a console game. Couch gaming sets the expectation of sitting down for an extended period of time, focused on the TV screen and in the relaxed comfort of the living room. A mobile game can be played in a crowded subway or during your lunch break at the office.

This means that the **biggest competition** for player attention isn't only other games, but also **other apps**, such as social media, messaging, video streaming, music, and shopping.[1] They have easy entry points, extremely short content, and, some of them, an (figuratively or literally) addictive *"just one more piece of content"* structure. On top of that, mobile games also have to compete for attention with other activities, like watching TV, listening to music, or eating food. Combined with the smaller screen (which takes up less space in the player's total vision), mobile game players are more likely to be less attentive. Therefore, our narrative design needs to accommodate for low attentiveness.

It's important to keep in mind that there are different mobile **player types with different motivations**, though. When it comes to players of midcore or AAA-like games, they might choose to play mobile games in similar circumstances as a console player would. They might choose to lie down on their couch and fully focus on the game for an extended play session. Especially during the pandemic, these types of play sessions seem to have increased – seen in the rising number of (AAA) Midcore games (such as Call of Duty Mobile, Diablo Immortal, and Genshin Impact) and their high download numbers.[2] Yet the general rule of thumb is still that mobile games are more accessible for a wider audience with the possibility of short play sessions to accommodate for the general decreased attention span and time availability – the longer the play sessions, the less often people might find the time and the less accessible these games will be to general audiences. Our narrative design needs to accommodate for short play sessions.

Besides user behavior, the **technical specifications** of smartphones are the other challenge of mobile games. In recent years, mobile specs have skyrocketed, allowing for more ambitious game concepts. These capabilities are still lower than most PCs and current-gen consoles, of course, which means that mobile games need to be designed for these technical limitations – especially when it comes to ambitious multiplayer games. This includes the size of the phone or the tablet, too. When games are meant to work on a smaller screen, they need to be designed for this format. This has implications for the interface design, with fonts that are big and clean enough to be readable, combined with short enough texts. Additionally, we need general visual clarity that allows players to know what they're actually seeing. At any given time, players need to understand the events on screen and their options of interaction – this will influence your choice of art style, proportions, object sizes, or camera placement. Some of your visuals are likely to be covered by the player's fingers *(or the front camera)* too, since your virtual controls need to be placed on the screen somewhere. You need to plan for those blind spots.

A smartphone also has two different possible orientations: portrait and landscape. For each game, developers need to make a decision which phone orientation they want to use.

When users use their smartphone, they usually do it in **portrait** mode, which means that portrait mode has very low friction for all mobile games, especially casual games for all audiences. It has low friction, can be played with one hand, and demands less attention. It can also be discreet in public. So it's no surprise that casual and hypercasual games like Candy Crush and Knife Hit are played in portrait mode.

When it comes to tablets, the default orientation is more akin to a laptop or computer screen, which is **landscape** mode. This implies that games that are meant to be played on a larger scale can go with landscape mode easily. This doesn't mean that landscape mode games aren't played on mobile phones; it just implies that it's more intuitive for non-casual players and tablet users. This orientation is usually more associated with midcore or AAA-like games. It requires two hands to control and demands more attention, which also implies the potential for longer play sessions. This orientation is often used for games that require a deeper focus, more thinking and live interaction with other players. Examples for this format would be Call of Duty Mobile and Genshin Impact.

And lastly, many mobile games are **designed to be live games**, receiving regular updates and extensions over a long period of time. This creates issues of onboarding for new players, release schedules, keeping a story interesting over a long period of time, and handling the issue of player memory. If a story is getting too long, players might forget the beginning, after all. To create something that potentially works as an endless experience is perhaps the biggest challenge of all, which is why it's the main topic of this book. How to handle these unique challenges of live games will be further explored in *Chapters 8–15*.

To summarize, the unique challenges of mobile games are an expectation of shorter play sessions and a decreased level of attention due to the platform and context of play. The game's narrative needs to be understandable even if played inattentively, making use of visuals optimized for a smaller screen format (which includes visuals, large-enough font, and short-enough text blocks). It needs to align with short play sessions too, providing a sense of progression and small narrative arcs, mixed with reminders and other methods to keep things together. Midcore and AAA-like titles might have longer play sessions, but they're usually still shorter than PC and console games. Besides this, as live games, mobile games aspire to continue and grow endlessly – creating challenges for onboarding and long-term storytelling.

BEST PRACTICES

The following best practices aren't exclusive to mobile games, instead, they can be inspiring for any kind of videogame. But considering the challenges of shorter attention spans, smaller spaces, and long-term live operations, these will be all the more essential when working on a mobile game. You'll find that a lot of it comes down to putting extra care into everything that isn't cinematic storytelling – all the other tools that narrative design gives us. That, and paying attention to the following general tips.

Mind Your Conventions

Your project comes with a set of expectations from the get-go. The fact that it is played on a mobile device, your game genre, your brand (if there is one attached), and your target audience – they all come with a set of conventions. The more you adhere to these conventions, the less you have to explain and the more mass market appeal the product is going to have – but that comes with the caveat of not sticking out from the competition. Finding a unique selling point is just as central in establishing your place in the market, so it's important to consider when you might want to break expectations without disappointing your audiences. The other kind of conventions to be aware of come from inside of your own game. With your initial marketing and first-time-user-experience, you set player expectations as well. Some of these conventions will be based on internal decisions that you make during pre-production, such as your long-term plans for the live operations of your game. What kind of release conventions are you planning to adhere to? Seasons, episodic releases, big DLCs, something else? It's perfectly fine to adjust your trajectory and grow your game based on player reaction, of course, but you should record and adhere to your game's laws and conventions, and if anything changes, make sure it gets updated and everyone knows about it. And lastly, conventions also refer to the narrative architecture and narrative guidelines. Stick to the limitations and purposes of your narrative units, remember to keep a consistent tone and way of addressing the player. Accessible, up-to-date documentation and collaboration with other crafts is key when it comes to sticking to your own conventions.

Keep Consistency

All your creative choices need to be complementary to each other, without accidental narrative contradictions. This doesn't only apply to the plot or dialogue, these narrative dissonances can appear in all elements of the game. If an inconsistent narrative element doesn't stem from the narrative basis, it may contradict another element, or at least feel out of place.

On a larger scale, this applies to **consistency of style**, with the game's general style, tone, and naming conventions. This is reflected in the game's genre, intended emotional experience, and idiosyncratic phrasings. It's important to keep in mind that this style isn't only found in texts but also in the entire creative direction. For this to work out, creating and sharing style documents and glossaries is key.

On the other hand, there is also **consistency of lore and story**. Every game element (and I mean *every* game element) is an expression of your game's underlying narrative – your worldbuilding, plot, past events, characters, or even the level of information any individual character is meant to have. No matter if you write a dialogue, design a mission or just outfits for an NPC, they need to be consistent with the narrative basis of the game. The key is to involve your lore and narrative guidelines in all creative decisions (or at least check things for consistency after the fact). Keeping lore documents and sharing their information with everyone concerned is crucial for this to work out.

Another aspect of consistency is the **consistency of information levels**, in relation to the current knowledge of the player. In each moment of the game, players have a specific level of information. Some things are established and some events have happened, while others haven't. Especially with games that go for a long time, or that have a lot of non-linear storytelling, it's important to check that NPCs only refer to things that have already happened, and if they refer to something the player doesn't know yet, they should sufficiently introduce the aspect as if the avatar is also hearing this for the first time (or needs reminders). Try to hunt down possible inconsistencies with logic flowcharts (defining all possibilities of when a moment can appear), spreadsheets, and tracking of all your variables.

Lastly, there is the **consistency of possible contexts**. Each narrative unit might show up in a variety of situations, depending on your game structure. So you need to make sure it will stay in tune with the logical and emotional state of the story, the speaker and the player, in all moments where it might show up. They shouldn't feel disjointed, but as if they're always meant to show up at this exact point, with a smooth transition from the previous and into the next moment. This applies to both, the logic of plot and the emotional state of the player and involved characters. If something is meant to appear during victory screens, make it celebratory. If something is meant to appear during a variety of dialogues, make sure it would fit into all situations – and if it doesn't, perhaps you need more variations of it to accommodate these variables.

Don't forget that these contexts might also be influenced by **player choices**. No matter what the player has done before, either during story choices or during gameplay, your narrative units should be able to fit into their experience at all possible moments they can appear, without seeming out of place. If a player has just burned down a village, it would be strange if a villager NPC would speak normally to them, just to name one extreme example.

When it comes to consistency of contexts and player choices, logic flowcharts and spreadsheets can also help you track these consistencies – even before you stumble upon all your little inconsistencies during playtesting and QA.

In summary, narrative elements should be...

- Consistent with style guidelines
- Consistent with lore and story
- Consistent with the player's level of information
- Consistent in all possible contexts, fitting the logical and emotional state of the story and speaker
- Consistent with the player's choices

ESTABLISH YOUR CONTEXT

In mobile games, we often want to throw the player right into action to experience the core gameplay. There's nothing wrong with that, of course, since it quickly gives the player an idea of what to expect from the game, and we lower the risk of losing players during onboarding. But if the actions of the core gameplay are just a list of objectives, players are less likely to stick around for long. As we've mentioned in previous chapters (*Chapter 3*), the key to setting up player motivation lies in properly setting up the context of their situation. Context deeply influences the way players perceive their actions, therefore shaping their game experience. It increases emotional attachment and motivation, and improves learning. Even when they're playing simple casual games, players need to understand why they are here, what are they meant to do, and what results they can expect – it simply makes for a better experience.

Situational context is composed of the following aspects:

- **Setting:** Where am I? What's going on? How does this world work? Which events have led to this current moment and are important for me to understand?
- **Conflict:** What's happening right now? Which conflict requires my actions? Who is involved?
- **Role:** What's my (or my avatar's) role in this? How do I relate to the world, its inhabitants, and the conflict?
- **Emotional Context:** What's the emotional and moral meaning to my actions? Who does it affect, and how?
- **Objectives:** What am I supposed to do right now?
- **Goals:** What am I doing this for? What rewards or effects am I hoping to achieve? How does that relate to my long-term goals?

These aspects, however, don't always have to be established with a questgiver or a textbox filled to the brim with information. Not every game has the same structure, and as a general rule, less is more. You can also use your visuals (depictions, symbols, semiotics, etc.), and short texts (such as names or titles) to do the heavy lifting for you. For example, think of a match-3 game level. In example A, a text instructs you to *"Clean the Yard!"*, and then you see that your game pieces are garden utensils, and breakable blockers look like dead leaves. Your gameplay is automatically implied to rake the leaves to clean the yard – and you barely needed any words for it. In example B, you have the same gameplay, but instead, a character asks *"Can I get some mint candy?"* In the background of your match-3 level, you see a candy shop, and now, all the game pieces are candies, some of which look like swirly white-red mint candies. When you match through them, they fly into a bag on the side of the screen and a counter in the corner goes up, maxing out at 20. You now understand that you're a candy shop owner filling mint candies into a bag for a customer.

There are always ways to give context, even if you don't get a lot of space to work with. What is appropriate always depends on your kind of game – but make use of everything you have at your disposal!

For more information about how to properly creating narrative context of a game loop, see "Contextualization" in *Chapter 13.*

MIND PLAYER AWARENESS

Not every gameplay moment is the same when it comes to player attention. If they're in the middle of a player-vs-player fight, they don't have time to read long textboxes popping up on the side of their screen. If they can't pause the game and need their full focus on the core gameplay, how are they supposed to? But when they've completed a core gameloop and return to the meta layer, with nothing urgent to react to at that moment, they can lean back and give all the attention you need for cutscenes, debriefing or even reading documents. The lesson here is to match the format of your narrative units with the situation they will appear in, keeping in mind if players would have the mental capacities to spare, of if they would feel bothered by it. High-octane moments require narrative design that is quick to grasp or okay to miss, like action, instructions, feedback, and barks, while slower moments or game interruptions allow for longer sequences, like cutscenes and dialogue – like when a mission has been completed or players return to the meta layer. Put yourself into the players' minds to figure out their mental head-space, and plan your complexity accordingly.

BALANCE PERSONALITY AND CLARITY

Texts in videogames often have to convey information necessary to play – explaining how the game works and what the player is supposed to do. Especially in mobile games, these texts usually need to be short and to the point, since players (a) don't have the time to read a lot of text, (b) don't have the patience to read a lot of text, and (c) don't have a lot of space on screen. But games aren't instruction manuals, they are narrative experiences, and thus, this information is rarely described in a purely instructional way, but rather in a fun, creative, narratively meaningful fashion. These texts aren't just instructions, they're part of the narrative experience – they have personality.

However, you might run the risk of adding "*too much personality*" and therefore muddle the meaning. To balance a text's clarity and personality is one of the main challenges of microcopy in videogames. If a text is long-winded, prosaic, and mostly focuses on personality and flavor, key information might become unclear and drown in a sea of words. Players may be entertained then, but don't understand what they're supposed to do.

On the other hand, if you only write neutral informative texts without any personality, it will make the game less enjoyable, less emotionally engaging and information harder to remember. Each text is an opportunity to expand your game's narrative, by giving each and every part of the game some narrative weight – even if it's a tutorial text, a small item description or the way a mission objective is phrased. That is not to say there aren't locations where you should absolutely make your texts as neutral and to-the-point as possible (for instance, in your in-app store), but if you choose this approach for everything, including your missions, the game simply loses a lot of personality.

Finding the balance between the two is essential, allowing players to always recognize the central takeaway of a text after they've read it (or even just skimmed it). To achieve this clarity, there are several things a narrative designer can watch out for.

- **Balance** your **narrative and informative aspects**
- Keep your **texts elegant** – as short and succinct as possible, but as complex as needed to get the desired experience
- Be a **word perfectionist**, and use terms that are narratively expressive and stem from your game's lore, while still being straightforward and easy to understand

- Apply the same **sentence structures** to the same type of information (such as mission objectives, weapon descriptions, or skill effects), so that players know where in the sentence to expect the action verb, object, location, numbers, etc.
- Highlight key information with **visual aids**, such as color-coding, bolded words, other fonts or symbols inside of the text, so players can understand your texts at first glance, even when they don't read the whole text
- Use **UX and UI design** to support information (such as arrows, highlights, counters or markers)

It is crucial to make things make sense *at first sight*, without sacrificing style and lore-appropriate wording. Even if players decide to skip texts and just barely caught a glimpse of what was on screen (a valid concern in mobile games, and all games for that matter) the key information needs to be clear. Striking a balance between information clarity and narrative personality is the key to achieve this.

Minimize Mental Workload

No matter the game situation, it's always important to minimize the players' mental workload as much as possible. If the screen is cluttered with objects and information, texts are overwhelming and hard to process, and players need to memorize a lot of information to be able to make decision, they will feel slowed down, confused, and have a harder time getting into a state of flow.

If your game is on a mobile device, that means that your players will likely have even less capacities to pay attention and memorize things, which is why this becomes even more important. Some PC games, especially for *strategy* audiences, have a high mental workload, due to all the things players need to track at the same time (either in menus or on a cluttered interface) – for mobile games, this type of gameplay might not find a big audience, and would need to be simplified into a more casual approach.

When it comes to narrative design, there are several ways to **reduce the mental workload** of a player. On the one hand, you can refer to everything mentioned in the previous section (*Balance Personality and Clarity*) – Balancing narrative and information in your texts, keeping your texts short and elegant, using standardized sentence structures for repeated information, using visual aids to emphasize key information and using UX and UI design to further support given information. *Additionally*, the following aspects help reduce the mental workload, *too*:

- Try to **simplify your game narrative** as much as possible without compromising the experience, both in general and on a moment-to-moment basis
- Make sure your **creative decisions stem from the game's lore,** which means that they make sense narratively and are therefore quicker to understand and easier to memorize
- Use **feature representatives** to structure your game features narratively by assigning them a character or location
- Deliver the **right information at the right time** – instead of infodumping everything in one place, cut it into little pieces that appear right when they become relevant

- Allow for **reminders when needed** (so players don't need to memorize everything), either by keeping something on screen, or letting it return to the screen when needed

HOLISTIC NARRATIVE DESIGN

Lastly, it's good practice to use all the narrative tools in your belt and not only get stuck on plot, dialogue, and documents. Especially when a game has no progressive plot, which is often the case for more casual mobile games, it becomes all the more important to reveal narrative in all other aspects of the game. Even if you only have names, visual designs, animations, and some sounds to work with, you can make the best of that to create a narrative context for your game. Your narrative should be reflected in the big picture (setting, plot, dialogue, etc.) and the small details (names, visuals, game loops, missions, etc.) all the same.

SUMMARY

- **Understanding mobile games** is **relevant for live game developers**, either because their live game is on mobile or because it draws monetization and design practices from it.
- Mobile games have **unique challenges** that are important to understand when developing them.
- These challenges are…
  - Users are accustomed to **bite-sized entertainment** from many **different sources**.
  - **Players play inattentively**, during commutes or while doing other things.
  - Mobile devices have **technical limitations** (but they're constantly improving).
  - **Many mobile games are live game**s and constantly need new content.
- **Best practices** for mobile games are…
  - Mind your conventions
  - Keep consistency
  - Mind your context
  - Mind player awareness
  - Balance personality & clarity
  - Minimize mental workload
  - Holistic narrative design

REFERENCES

1 Marilyn Latham, *The Most Popular Apps on the App Store and Google Play*, Clevertap, accessed April 21, 2023, https://clevertap.com/blog/most-popular-apps/.
2 "The Rise of Midcore Mobile Games: Snapshot Report," GameRefinery, July 2022.

8 Introduction to Live Game Storytelling

The idea of providing games as a continuous service, rather than a completed and unchangeable product, is an ambitious concept. It's not the first time that a medium has attempted such a thing, keeping a story going with continuous new releases. An obvious example would be TV shows with continuous seasons, adding to a story for as long as the ratings remain high enough. But the tradition is much older than television, what with fiction serials being released chapter by chapter in magazines, or even the oral tradition of myth, fairytales, and legends, continuing the stories of popular characters at the hands of several storytellers.

The attempt of *videogames* doing something like this – not as sequels but a *living* piece of media – began to emerge with the advent of MMOs (massively multiplayer online games), such as World of Warcraft (launched in 2004). It wasn't the first MMO, as that honor would go to Neverwinter Nights from 1991 (as the first *graphical* MMO) and Island of Kesmai from 1985 (as the first *commercial* MMO), but World of Warcraft was essential in popularizing the medium and monetization model. The reason for live games to exist has always been driven by monetization. In MMOs such as WoW, a subscription model was introduced in order to finance the creation of new content over a long period of time.

With the introduction of game patches for console games (Unreal Championship on the Xbox having been the first in 2002), videogames were starting to become less of a fixed product in general and were able to deliver bug fixes and even content expansion after release, via an internet connection of the console. Computer games contained this feature for longer, but it often meant that you'd have to manually download a new version or patches, and it wasn't an automatic process. Before this, you'd buy a cartridge or CD-ROM, and it would contain the final build of a game that would never change in any way – especially when it came to consoles. Nowadays, every game is launched via a client that regularly checks for updates, sometimes even with notorious "day 1 patches" for new games that can be larger than the data on the disc you've purchased.

The impact of social gaming, first on the internet (with social online worlds like Club Penguin and Facebook games like Farmville) and then later on mobile phones (multiplayer games such as Free Fire, Among Us, and Pokémon Go), further expanded on this concept of having a malleable product that would change over its course of existence, adding more content for more monetization opportunities. These social games and worlds provided platforms for social interactions, providing a selling point beyond bug fixes and updates through natural emergent player stories and game expansions. Valve's game Team Fortress 2 had also had an impact on this idea, as Valve tried to combat a shrinking player base of their multiplayer team-based shooter by releasing several free updates in 2008, with

  DOI: 10.1201/9781003297628-12

additional in-game purchase options for opening loot boxes. As they transitioned to focusing their revenue on in-app purchases, the game became free-to-play, laying the groundwork for many games-as-a-service (GaaS) (that weren't MMORPGs) that would follow after.

The element of social gameplay has always been deeply intertwined with live games, although it's not required. In their early days, mobile games had a tendency toward social games and casual free-to-play titles, instead of MMOs and subscription services – an effect of the more limited possibilities of the technology and the shift in target audience. But that too has changed by now, and you can find mobile live games that are not that far off from computer games and MMOs of old (such as Genshin Impact). Based on the way mobile games have been published on smartphones, with the store being flooded with games of drastically varying quality, competition has been fierce. By now, it can be tough to sell a game with an upfront price, just based on the expectations of players to be able to download something for free when they play it on their smartphone – something certainly born from the distrust caused by a lack of quality control in mobile games in the past. Therefore, free-to-play has become the norm in mobile games, and premium paid games feel like an exception. But games don't develop themselves for free. So the concept of in-app purchases and continuous monetizable content releases have been established over time to deal with this. Now, with the mobile games industry making so much money with free-to-play live games, a lot of premium games have opened up their structure to offer live game support, taking pointers from the techniques and monetization strategies of mobile games.

And here we are now.

This live release structure demands new ways to write, design, and monetize games, and the following chapters will provide a deep dive into narrative design and storytelling for such live games and their unique structure. A live game needs to tell a story over an extended, often unpredictable amount of time. You may need to tell a story over the course of a year or 15 years. This doesn't mean that it has to be one single story you need to stretch out into a painfully slow experience, of course (and you really shouldn't). You need to rethink the very structure and content of your narrative and design it as a long-form narrative from the ground up. Writing for live games is completely different from writing for a single-purchase packaged game, considering its unique set of update structures, challenges, and opportunities.

LIVE GAMES

Live games, also called Games-as-a-Service or GaaS, is a term for a release model in which new additional videogame content is provided for a long time after the initial release. This is a means to monetize a game after the first buy-in (premium games with a live game model), or a structure to monetize free-to-play games. These new contents would either be accessible through a subscription service, in-game purchases, or both. The ongoing release of new content is meant to encourage players to play a game continuously, rather than complete it once and put it aside. These games are meant to become a hobby, often with a social aspect, rather than a completable one-time experience.

Usually, a live game falls into one of the following **monetization structures**:

- A **premium game**, requiring players to buy initial access, which releases **new live content** over an extended period of time, often as new chapters, DLCs or expansions to multiplayer modes. Some of these may require additional purchases or a season pass to access (the latter being defined as an access ticket to future or already existing expansions). *Examples:* GTA Online, Far Cry 6, The Division 2, and Fallout 76.
- A **free-to-play game** with no initial buy-in, which provides continuous new content that is, in some way, monetized through in-game purchases such as items, expansions or battle passes (a time-limited progression with unlockable items, also called season passes). *Examples:* Fortnite, Genshin Impact, Apex Legends, and Pokémon Unite.
- A **subscription game** that needs to be paid for on a monthly/yearly basis, which provides continuous new content, either for free or at additional costs. Nowadays, some subscription-based games offer a free-to-play entry point for new players for a limited time or until their characters reach a certain level. *Examples:* World of Warcraft, Final Fantasy XIV, and Star Wars: The Old Republic.

COMMON LIVE GAME STRUCTURES

Live Games can provide drastically different experiences to players, depending on how they choose to structure their game content. During pre-production, you're likely to decide on the general content structure of the live game you're building, since it deeply influences how the gameplay experience will be structured, and the game's narrative too. Experienced players have expectations for each of those content structures, so you will have to either fulfill those expectations or consciously move away from some of them to differentiate yourself from the competition.

As we look at the following **popular content structures**, keep in mind that some games fall into more than one category. As games are composed of many features, it is possible to have several of these in the same game. Usually, a game has a bigger focus of one of these, though.

- **Linear Progression:** Live games with a linear progression are focused on delivering a linear experience with a clear progression that is constantly being expanded as part of its live services. The live aspect comes in the form of adding new content over time – new endgame content, new side progressions, new spin-off levels, and new live events. These games are often level-based and can sometimes be story-driven (in the shape of unlockable narrative). Their genre is often action adventures, puzzles, time management, and narrative games, but they can be just about anything.
  Examples: Candy Crush Saga, Homescapes and Episodes.

- **Match-Based:** Match-based live games put a focus on repeating matches of core gameplay (usually between 5 and 45 minutes), without a traditional level progression. Think of matches in FPS games, beat-em-ups, or playing a song in a rhythm game. They're often player-vs-player, but can also have a collaborative or even single-player environment. Players repeat the same kind of gameplay in a limited time in one or various modes, to win and gain a permanent progression on a meta layer, such as character levels, trophy roads, or other progressions. Permanent progression usually *only* takes place on the game's meta layer, and any kind of progression during a match will be *reset* by the end of it. This means that a progressive narrative is likely to take place on the meta layer, or at least be tied to meta progressions, besides narrative tied to real time. Popular game genres in this category are MOBAs, shooters, battle royale games, rhythm games, and other multiplayer games.
  Examples: Clash of Clans, Brawlstars and Call of Duty Mobile.
- **Open World:** Similar to theme parks, these games offer an open world with many different options for activities. They provide a semi-guided experience with loads of options, meaning that players aren't forced to play them in one specific order, but gain freedom of choice. These games are often composed of a selection of quests and progressions, separated into a variety of areas that can be played in parallel. Like different areas of a theme park, activities are likely grouped by gamefeel and experience. They're driven by pre-scripted content and pre-made experiences and suitable to be played in single-player, but often with the option of social interaction, collaboration, and competition. MMOs and open world games often fall into this category.
  Examples: Genshin Impact, The Secret World: Legends, and World of Warcraft.
- **Sandbox:** Sandbox games offer a system-driven world with lots of player freedom and opportunity for emergent gameplay, roleplaying, creative expression, and social interaction. Instead of mostly pre-scripted content, they provide complex game systems, generated content, and/or creative tools that allow players to create their own content to share with others. They can contain quests, raids, and some form of progression, but usually put more emphasis on social player interaction or creative play, at least after players have completed the onboarding process. MMOs and creative platforms often fall into this category.
  Examples: Roblox, GTA Online, and EVE Online.

GAME SEASONS

The term *game season* describes a time period of additional videogame content releases after the initial game launch, combining several pieces of content as one season or several consecutive seasons. A season usually groups its content thematically, often by a name, theme, and/or story arc that gives each season a unique vision and can be used for marketing. The structure of a game season also serves as a way to set expectations for players, regarding when and what kind of new content they can expect to see in the future, which is why many game seasons see regular release schedules. The exact content of a game season can vary drastically from game to game.

However, while this definition applies to all game seasons, the term has been used in different ways, usually depending on which game genre they're referring to: Non-live games, episodic narrative games, live games, and games with live support. They slightly differ in structure, content, and intent.

- Various **Non-Live Games** have defined a *game season* as the access ticket to DLCs and bonuses that will be released sometime after the initial launch of the game. When players buy this type of season pass, they will receive a series of upcoming DLCs and bonuses as soon as they're available, such as additional levels, items or modes. If they buy the season pass after everything has been released, they immediately get access to everything. This type of season pass doesn't refer to any time-limited or live content and doesn't have the ambition to continue – it's simply a purchasable batch of extra content.

- **Episodic Narrative Games** define a *game season* as a grouped set of episodes that tell one coherent story arc, much like a TV show season. This means you're purchasing the entirety of the game (all episodes) before all episodes have been made available. Therefore you'll receive new content packages over a period of time, in usually regular release intervals, until the season has been completed. Not all episodic narrative games are designed to be endless (and actual live games) though, but rather released over a longer period of time (such as Tales from the Borderlands or other Telltale games) – therefore, a season might not be followed by another. If players buy the season pass after all the season's episodes have already been released, they normally immediately receive access to all episodes. Games may also choose to continue with more seasons afterward, meaning, they continue the story beyond one season and possibly choose to monetize each season separately. This definition was used *before* "game seasons" became a widespread term in the monetization of content in free-to-play games-as-a-service. Some live games still use this way to define a season (a package of narrative episode that combine to one arc) most prominently narrative games (such as Episode or Lovestruck).

- **Live Games and Games with Live Support** define a *game season* as a period of time during which you can play the game in its current state, with a seasonal set of new content and (possibly) time-limited events tied to it. This new seasonal content is a set that may be composed of new game features, modes, progressions, items, cosmetics, or other elements, which all go on top of the already existing base game from the previous season. Each of these individual parts can be a permanent addition, and thus remain after the season ends, or only be made available for a limited time (either for the whole season or an even shorter time frame) – which means that if you don't play them now, you'll miss them forever. One season will usually focus on a new exciting theme, main conflict, and a handful of (new) game features – possible offering new unlockable items and progressions that tie into it. The entirety of content of one season isn't necessarily released at the beginning of it, but rather spread out over the whole duration of the season – possibly including time-limited events.

A popular monetization method of (live) games, which plan to release new content after their initial launch, is *season passes*. Just like the term season itself, a season pass can have different definitions, some of which conflict with one another. In general, a season pass is an in-app purchase that grants the player access to the additional contents of a season.

There are different **definitions of a season pass**:

- **DLC Season Pass (Permanent Content)**: This usually comes into play when a game is a premium game (with an initial buy-in) or a narrative episodic game. This season pass grants access to all additional content that will be released over time, such as new DLCs and expansions. This content will then be accessible permanently. This type of season pass can be purchased on release, to be able to download new content as soon as it's available, or long after the last piece of DLC has been dropped, to be able to access all included contents at once. This monetization method is often found in premium games with live support that have a predetermined roadmap for new DLCs, but don't strive to be a game-as-a-service, but can also appear in games that add a lot of permanent additions to their game (such as new regions, classes, and progressions). Some games might only have one season pass after release (such as Far Cry 6), while others may have several season passes for several packages of content (such as Borderlands 3).
- **Live Season Pass (Temporary Content):** This type of season pass grants access to all content tied to the active season, or additional content on top of the free season pass that is available to everyone. This usually means that the content is only temporarily available (for the duration of the season). Parts of it may be permanent and remain in a player's account even after the season ends, such as special items that players receive or unlock within the given time period. This content can either be made available at the beginning of the season or be released over the course of said season, sometimes only for a limited time.
- **Battle Pass:** As a sub-category of the live season pass (and often used synonymously), this type of season pass grants access to a game progression that allows you to unlock time-limited items and contents. It's usually (but not always) driven by XP gained in the game or a specific mode, and acts as a combination of progression and unlockable rewards that can only be played for as long as the season is active. Any earned rewards, however, remain in the player's possession even after the season ends. Battle passes reset and change with each season, making each individual season's battle

pass a unique release that pays off the most when players buy it early on in the season. Many games offer a free (accessible for everyone) and a premium (purchase required) version on parallel tracks, so that players can purchase the opportunity to unlock more things per time investment. Showing both at the same time usually serves as an incentive to purchase the premium battle pass, since players get to see how much they could have already unlocked if they had the additional reward boost. Battle passes are often also called season passes, or even use a unique name tied to the game's lore, usually ending in "pass."

In addition to these season passes, there's also **another type of subscription** that some games choose to offer.

- **VIP Subscription:** This type of subscription is a time-limited pass that grants additional content, much like a live season pass, but isn't tied to a specific season. They're renewed in intervals (often weekly or monthly) or need to be purchased regularly for the player to keep benefiting from their offered advantages. These bonus contents are usually gameplay boosts (such as increased resource earning) or "free" items and are intended to give players additional goodies and a quicker way to progress. This type of subscription is often offered in single-player casual games, but has been used for multiplayer games too (such as the Fortnite Crew subscription that offers players exclusive items, in-game currency and the battle pass).

CHALLENGES OF LIVE GAMES

Live games come with a unique set of challenges, most of which arise from their ambition to release continuous content over a long period of time. This means that the game has an ever-growing amount of content and the demand for meaningful open-ended continuous narrative. This never-ending narrative can either be set in an ongoing continuity, like a series of events taking place in real time, or an ever-growing expansion of an existing story that permanently remains available. Some games do a bit of both. Not every player will be there on day one and instead joins later on, some will leave and return after some time has passed, and some others will be there continuously – but designing a narrative for a live game means that *all* these players have to be catered to. On top of that, there's the demand to release new game content on a regular schedule, proving a challenge to production and designers, with lurking dangers of feature creep, a term used for excessive expansion of a game until it's not user friendly, coherent or enjoyable anymore. From a narrative standpoint, the core challenges of live games are the following:

Telling a Story That Goes on Indefinitely: Whatever type of story you're trying to tell, as a live game, it needs to continue for as long as the game stays live. Even if the initial production focus will be on the release build of the game, you need to plan for the ambition of an endlessly expandable game. You can't simply *add more* after the fact, since this risks production complications and narrative issues. There is a need to plan ahead to make sure the narrative foundation you're building can actually carry season after season to come. On the one hand, this means setting, main conflicts, and characters, and on the other hand, the structure and conflicts you intend to explore over time and whether it'll give you enough variety to work with.

If you want players to care about the narrative aspect of the game (which always influences how much they care about the content in general), you also need a plan for keeping up suspense and telling a story with a sense of coherency and meaning. Of course, some games will heavily lean toward gameplay and social interactions to keep their game interesting, but even with a limited scripted narrative focus, things such as themes, characterization, setting, and gameplay contextualization remain relevant as a means to draw players in and keep them motivated. Player retention depends on motivation, and the pacing and format of releases are deeply related to this topic (which will be planned by the live production team, most likely, but which is also a question for narrative design).

Long-Term Development, Changing Teams & Story Coherency: Keeping a long-running story consistent is a challenging task, even if you were a single author working on your personal vision. The longer a story continues, the higher the risk of creating inconsistencies. With a collaborative team effort like videogames, these chances rise even more. Plus, when a project is meant to keep on going for a long time, we can expect teams to change eventually, with old members leaving and new ones joining. Maybe you're going to switch to another project or company yourself, or you're the one joining a live game after it's been going on for a while. This brings its own set of problems when it comes to story continuity and content development, making proper documentation and employee onboarding crucial to keeping things on track.

Players Join at Different Times: Since players don't join the game at the same time, their first-time-user-experience will be different depending on when they do. Especially in a game that is always changing and shifting, players will have different entry points. If the game's story is being told on a season-by-season basis, this either means that late players have an ungodly amount of content to catch up on before they can participate in the currently active *live story* of the game, or they are thrown into the middle of an active story that they don't fully understand. A live game needs a solution for this onboarding problem, and design an onboarding that helps late-comers to be up to speed as quickly as possible, and hook them too.

Live Content Access: Since your players will join at different points of the game's life cycle, there is also the issue of how you make your new content accessible. If your game is telling a permanent story that adds new chapters at the end, and that part is only available for end-of-content players, you're ignoring players that aren't that far into the progression yet. Deciding on the accessibility of new content, and how to cater to different player types, will be an issue that you need to plan solutions for. The key usually lies in a balance between content available to end-of-content players and earlier players. You can offer several entry points into the story, either by seasonal arcs which allow a new entry point in the beginning of each season, or by adding new parallel progressions, rather than just more to one long progression.

Player Memory: When a player is able to complete your game's content within 10–20 hours, they can possibly get through it in a couple of days or weeks (depending on whether they're a hardcore gamer who sinks a lot of time into games or a more casual gamer who takes their time). They are fairly likely to remember what happened in the beginning if it hasn't been that long ago and a narrative designer can refer to the knowledge gained within that playtime. But when a game is intended to run indefinitely, for months and even years, some information will get lost and forgotten over time. Often literally (not accessible in-game anymore) and also psychologically (in the player's memory). Players might not remember a certain piece of information that you want to refer to, or a character that emerges from the depths of the story to become relevant again. Or even a whole plot point of a past story arc, if we're being honest. A narrative designer for live games needs to design with that memory issue in mind: Just because something was mentioned before, doesn't mean it will be remembered now. In fact, some players will not have seen that specific piece of information in the first place, because they never got that far in the season, or they joined the game at a later date. This is why contextual reminders, or perhaps archives, can be crucial to keep the player's level of information exactly where you need it to be.

Managing and Curating an Ever-Growing Library of Content: When you consistently release new content, the game keeps on growing. This can become a problem, especially when it's released on storage-limited mobile devices. To manage this, your team might plan to release some content for a time-limited only, and other content as a permanent addition. But even the content that stays in game will need to be structured in a way that makes it accessible to players, and not an overwhelming amount of things – this means that you have to plan for how current content as presented and past content is archived (if you want to do that at all). The most important thing is to make sure that players know what the game offers and where to find it, as well as being able to follow the story even without a specific piece of content they might have missed. Having summaries or records of past time-limited story contents is an option – may that be inside the game or on an external platform (such as websites, wikis, or YouTube). Some games have such a dedicated fanbase that there is always somebody uploading videos of a time-limited piece of content, so that even players who missed it can see a recording after the fact. You shouldn't count on external fan activity though, but plan your own solutions ahead of time.

WHY MAKE A LIVE GAME?

After we got an overview of the challenges of live games, you're probably thinking: That sounds like a lot of risk, why would I even want to make a *live* game? The answer is probably that you're not the person who decided this in the first place, but people higher up the corporate ladder. You're just the person hired for the job. And considering you acquired this book, maybe you're already convinced of this release format, or an avid player of live games yourself, wanting to make your mark on the market. Either way, when you build something, it's important to understand the appeal of it. So let's take a look at the three main perspectives to get a better grasp of the "*why*" before we dive deeper into the "*what*" and "*how*." There are different perspectives on the argument for creating live games, namely business, creative, and consumer.

Business Perspective

From a **business perspective**, successful live games can have an astonishingly large revenue, and keep on bringing in more money over a long time. This isn't a guarantee, of course, and will depend on the actual success, player base, and effectiveness of monetization. But this is probably one of the number one reasons why companies decide to join the market with a live service game. This promise of great financial success actually comes several from different factors. Live Games can …

- Keep players in your **company ecosystem** longer (i.e., they play games your company developed)
- Improve brand and **company loyalty** (making your brand name more recognizable due to more frequent exposure to the game)
- **Stay relevant** for a longer time than single releases, and don't have release gaps like game series
- Get players to invest **more money** across the lifetime of their experience than they would invest in a single-purchase premium game
- Get a **bigger player base** if offered as free-to-play, due to the low cost of entry
- Offer a **continuous revenue stream** to the developer, instead of just a bulk income when a new game is released
- **Keep players playing** your company's games without having to create new games for it, with potentially lower development costs for the same (or better) retention and money
- Have **faster release schedules** (with DLCs, updates, seasons, events, etc.) than a game series
- Inspire players to **interact with the game regularly**, rather than having them "finish" it.
- Be **released earlier** (with additional features on the roadmap), and adjust their trajectory of development depending on player sentiments, giving them more freedom to experiment and adjust.

Creative Perspective

But business isn't the only argument you can make for creating a live game. Luckily, there are also arguments to make from the perspective of the creative forces involved, which would be you, the developer. From a **creative perspective**, specifically that of narrative designers and writers (as this is the topic of this book), live games offer the unique opportunity to tell an epic story beyond a singular game's usual proportions. You can create a narrative that keeps on going for years, which gives you space for a lot of worldbuilding, character development, and experimental storytelling in width and depth. Also, the nature of the live game is that you can refine things, change things and expand things after release, which gives you more time to improve the story with revisions, updates, or expansions. Since the game will be available to players, they can even be included in the shaping of the story – may that be through feedback, features, or reactions to general community sentiment. So, developing Live Games means you can...

- Tell an **epic long-term story** over the course of months or years, allowing for a storytelling experience more akin to a TV series
- Create an **extensive game world** with many, potentially complex characters
- Refine the story, **expand the story**, and deepen the story over time
- **Keep players invested** in your fictional world and story for a long time, creating a deep emotional bond and perhaps a loyal fanbase
- Use **player sentiment, input, and feedback** to revise or further develop the story in a better direction
- Create **virtual social worlds** with an explicit focus on player-to-player interaction, socialization, and roleplay – an interesting creative challenge with great emotional potential

PLAYER PERSPECTIVE

Lastly, there is also the **perspective of the players** and reasons why they would be interested in playing a live game over another game. As a game developer, reminding yourself of the player's perspective is always a good way to inform your design decisions. After all, you want to create a game that is fun and which players want to play, right? So, why would players want to play a live game specifically? Depending on your genre, the usual player motivations apply, of course. Enjoyment, mastery, exploration, relaxation, competition, socializing, and so on.[1] But a few of those motivations might get reinforced by the structure of a live game in a way that non-live games can't do – just because they can share this experience with other people, and there is always something new to explore, experience and to master. They're never "*finished*," but can keep challenging (or relaxing) themselves.

For a player, a live game can offer...

- The opportunity to **try out more games** due to the **low entry cost**, and being able to enjoy huge amounts of playtime without the obligation to invest any money in it. This makes a game more accessible for players who don't have a lot of money to spare for games, too. *(Note: only applies to free-to-play live games)*

- **A hobby,** like sports, which is something they can do regularly to wind down, challenge themselves, and can emotionally rely on to give them the experience they come to expect from it (relaxing, challenging, exciting, etc). The regular addition of content makes it more likely that the experience doesn't get boring for a long period of time. A hobby can be meaningful, and give players a sense of play, relaxation, flow, competition, community, mastery, personal growth, and more.
- **A fandom (meta community),** where they can fully immerse themselves in a fictional world over a long period of time, sharing the experience with a community of other fans. Live games regularly deliver new content that fans can then enjoy, discuss with others and use as inspiration for fanworks such as fanfiction, fanarts, and cosplay. Fandoms can be engaging, on an emotional, intellectual, creative, and social level.
- **A(n in-game) community,** with the game serving as a platform to socialize and interact with others, may that be in a competitive, collaborative, or purely social way. These communities can expand beyond the game, but live games have the opportunity to have extensive social features for players to use it for socializing by itself. A community can create a sense of togetherness and personal value, by being part of something bigger that is shared with other people.
- A sense of **accomplishment and identity**, by treating the game as a sport they want to master and test their skills at. Sometimes this accomplishment comes from getting better as a player, sometimes in the form of leveling characters or completing collections, or other achievements, you can reach in the game. Many live games (especially multiplayer) are also played as e-sports. Live games usually have a wide range of possible ways to feel accomplished and have a stronger social element for showing off your success.
- A space for **playful exploration**, where players can create identities and roleplay with others, in group dynamics or competitive spaces, and playfully explore fictional spaces and their own identity (as another gender, a completely alien species, fulfilling a role in a team, etc). This is the digital version of play, in general, and can be very fulfilling and a method of self-reflection and discovery (or simply fun). This is especially true for games with big social and roleplay elements, such as MMORPGs and Social MMOs.

SUMMARY

- Live games come in **various monetization structures: Premium games** with live content, **free-to-play** games and **subscription** games.
- Common structures for live games are **linear progressions, match-based, open world and sandbox**.
- The term **game season** refers to a way to structure content releases as seasons, which has been differently defined for **non-live games, episodic narrative games** and **live games**.
- Popular season **monetization methods** are DLC **season passes, live season passes, battle passes and VIP subscriptions**.
- The **challenges of live games** are…
  - Telling a story that **continues indefinitely**
  - **Long-term development cycles** with changing teams
  - **Players joining at different times** of the game's lifetime
  - New **content might not be accessible to all players,** and only relevant to a limited amount of the audience
  - Extensive game lifetimes may cause players to **forget parts of the story**
  - Managing an **ever-growing library** of content
- From a **business perspective,** live games are attractive because they have the **potential for great player retention, brand loyalty and a persistent revenue stream.**
- From a **creative perspective**, live games offer an opportunity to **tell an epic story** over a long time and **build large (social) worlds,** with the option to use **community sentiment** to steer the future development.
- From a **player's perspective**, live games can be attractive because they have a **low entry cost** (as a F2P), can serve as a **hobby, fandom, or community**, give players a **sense of persistent accomplishment** and offer a **playful space** for personal exploration.

REFERENCE

1 "Gamer Motivation Model," Quantic Foundry, accessed April 20, 2023, https://quantic-foundry.com/wp-content/uploads/2019/04/Gamer-Motivation-Model-Reference.pdf.

BIBLIOGRAPHY

Oscar Clark, *Games as a Service: How Free to Play Design Can Make Better Games*, Routledge, August 10, 2018.

9 Learning from Other Media

Live games aren't the first medium to try their hands at long-form storytelling. It's only logical to take a look at those who came before us, to try and figure out their shared attributes, and which learnings may apply to our medium. Think of long-running **TV shows** and **cinematic universes**, which tell many continuous stories with the same characters in the same universe. **Comics, mangas, and other sequential art**, which carry on a narrative over many issues. There are also **tabletop RPGs and pen & paper roleplay**, such as Dungeons & Dragons – where players play many sessions within the same group to continue their journey, getting together in a magic circle of make-believe that is like a shared improvisational theater based on rulebooks, procedures, and established worldbuilding. And if we move a little bit away from obvious examples: Even **sports** are interesting for us, with their long-running drama of rivalries, victories, failures, and comeback stories, *especially* those with a certain level of showmanship and performance, such as wrestling.

The further we look into the past, the clearer it becomes that long-form storytelling has been around for much longer than we might initially think. In the past, so-called **literary serials** were a popular form of storytelling, where novels would be split up into chapters that were released in newspapers as regular releases. In many cases, those novels weren't completed before release, but written chapter by chapter, with a defined serialized approach written *for* this episodic format. Famous novels have originally been released in this format, such as Arthur Conan Doyle's Sherlock Holmes novels. But this arguably wasn't the origin of endless storytelling, either.

In fact, expanding existing universes and stories over time is a tradition that's arguably as long as storytelling itself. It has been a deeply ingrained part of **mythology, folklore, legends, and religious texts**, where a canon would be expanded over a long period of time, with many different storytellers contributing to the same lore. What is the Bible, if not an example of that? It was created as a narrative that has been expanded over many years, with many different authors (separating their authorship by "books," such as Book Matthew), ever-growing and separated into phases. The same applies to Arthurian legends. Greek Mythology. Folklore and fairytales. The human desire to expand and continue existing stories, to expand upon a canon, has always been there – creating games that strive to do the same is just a modern form of it. Of course, we're creating a commercial product – but that doesn't mean that it can't become *pop* culture.

In short, to get a better idea of how to tell **long-form stories**, these forms of **media** can be used for inspiration:

DOI: 10.1201/9781003297628-13

- **Literary Serials:** Novels, or other longer pieces of fiction, that have been published chapter by chapter in magazines.
- **Fiction Series:** Serialized novels, novellas, or short stories that have published a large amount of sequels about the same characters or set within the same universe.
- **Sequential Art:** Sequential art strips, magazines or books that have published a significant amount of issues (such as comics, mangas, or webcomics).
- **TV Shows:** TV episodes structured and released in several seasons.
- **(Semi-)scripted Sports:** Such as wrestling, with its dramatic rivalries between heroes and heels.
- **Pen & Paper Roleplay:** An improvised roleplay game (such as Dungeons & Dragons) with a game master and a group of players, in which they go on adventures in several sessions, possibly continuing over the course of years as there is no obligatory end to playing.

SHARED ATTRIBUTES OF LONG-FORM MEDIA

So, what do these story formats have in common, besides their ambition to tell a continuous story? Let's take a closer look. Our learnings will prove as a good starting point for building a foundation for our live game narrative. They've already achieved to tell a long-running story, might as well learn from their experience and build up on that.

A Rich Fictional World

A rich world with a strong core cast and interesting conflicts that have the potential to **inspire many different stories and story arcs**. You will have to look at your foundation and consider: Could I feasibly add 10 more episodes in that world with this cast? How about 20? Or 50? Would there be potential to add or rotate characters, and would that extend its potential even longer?

A rich world can be handled in many different ways, and doesn't necessarily imply an expansive fantasy universe you built from the ground up. In fact, many popular long-running TV shows are actually set in grounded, but specific settings. The more specific a setting, the more unique will be the inspiration you can take from it (instead of risking feeling too generic and thus emotionally unengaging). The mockumentary The Office is a workplace comedy predominantly taking place at an obsolete office supplies company, located in Scranton, Pennsylvania – its main characters are the employees. Breaking Bad is set in the city of Albuquerque, New Mexico, contrasting the lives of law-abiding middle-class citizens with the criminal underbelly of the city, through protagonist Walter White's journey into becoming a drug kingpin. Stranger Things takes place in 1980s Hawkins, Indiana, focusing on the lives of a handful of teenagers and introducing horror and science fiction elements of secret government experiments and the alternate dimension known as The Upside Down. All of these TV shows could build drama and intrigue across several seasons, because their settings are specific, with equally specific perspectives of the main characters within that setting.

The biggest question will always be: Does the setting, in combination with this cast of characters, provide us enough fodder for many engaging and interesting stories to come? This can be driven by external forces (such as a monster-of-the-week structure), interpersonal, character-driven dynamics or the exploration of its characters' emotional developments. As another, older example of a long-running story: Arthur Conan Doyle's *Sherlock Holmes* stories have worked for so long because the core conflict is endlessly repeatable in fresh new ways: There is a crime, and Holmes has to solve it. Since there are endless variants of crimes, there is potential for many stories without it getting repetitive. *Star Wars*, on the other hand, works because there are endless planets and many factions that are at odds with each other – with new factions rising and old factions dying throughout the narrative timeline, as well. You'll also notice that the franchise has a big (ever-expanding) world and charismatic recurring characters, which always brings audiences back in to see more of them.

A CONSISTENT IDENTITY

They have a strong and **consistent identity**, shaped by recurring themes, emotions and conflicts. These core themes remain relevant across the whole narrative property. Characters are usually used to explore different aspects and views on these core ideas.

Audiences should know **which type of experience** to expect when they seek out newly added material, and helps them to estimate if those themes and conflicts are interesting for them. Besides, it helps with marketing to have a strong core. You need to ask yourself:. Is it a comedic action romp about friendship? Is it a tense horror drama about facing the unknown? A sci-fi story about technology and identity? A provocative drama about power and betrayal? Even if your focus shifts over time, with new worlds, characters, and conflicts, there is a story *soul* that needs to be retained before you risk losing what the narrative was originally about (and have audiences jump ship). While things shouldn't remain exactly the same, the identity should remain – it can be a tightrope act to figure out how much change is good and how much is too much.

A RELIABLE STORY STRUCTURE

They have a **reliable story structure** that creates expectations for the audiences in terms of structure, drama and scheduling. They know exactly how long a chapter or episode will be, what the suspense curve will be like, and what kind of conflict they will experience, which makes it easier to estimate if they're in the mood for that (and have the time) at any given moment. From one episode to the next, this is going to stay the same, reliable experience. A comic issue could be 21 pages long, for example, and has one self-contained dramatic curve, while also being part of a bigger storyline across several issues. A TV episode could be 30 minutes long and has a self-contained dramatic arc with a monster-of-the-week structure, where you know that the heroes will face a new antagonist every time and defeat them within those 30 minutes – unless it's a season opening, finale, or otherwise special episode. Often, these reliable story structures can even be formulaic, where you can predict dramatic points and twists by the page or the minute. This isn't necessarily a bad thing for something that is intended to work over a long time – formulas are only bad when they *feel* repetitive, result in audiences not being surprised by the story, or cause a decrease in story quality. TV shows are usually formulaic, but that doesn't mean the story development and character decisions can't still be surprising to the audience.

REGULAR SCHEDULED RELEASES

They have regular **scheduled releases**, such as weekly, monthly or daily new updates. This topic is related to established publishing structures and marketing but also has an effect on the memory of the audience when they consume a new chapter, and therefore how they process the story over time. No matter if a release schedule is quick or slow, providing new content with a regular schedule helps set audience expectations and avoid frustration. Also, as a narrative designer, you'll likely be part of the discussion when it comes to planning the release structure – or at least you'll have to roll with the punches of what other people decide and have to take this schedule into account when planning and writing.

NESTED DRAMATIC STRUCTURES

Each release has a **nested dramatic structure**: A **self-contained small arc** (episode/chapter) is **set within a bigger arc** (season/book), which may amount to even bigger **multi-season arcs** that will have their evolution and pay-off across an even longer time period (entire show, full book series, entire brand). This allows the audience to get a satisfying narrative experience within the chapter/episode they get with each release or session, but keeps them motivated to read the next one, to find out the development and eventual conclusion of the bigger arc. This, of course, implies that one must set up conflicts that aren't solved within the same episode, but carry on across multiple episodes. Equally, solutions should rarely wrap things up too neatly, but rather create even more open questions and new plot directions. Always keep the audience curious, but give them satisfaction through smaller arcs. In General, this is a question of short-term vs long-term motivation, which aligns neatly to what we do with gameplay arcs in videogames anyway. Game loops are embedded within game levels, which are embedded within map areas, which are embedded within the entire game, and so on. It runs quite parallel to how TV shows, comic books, and other long-form media work.

STORY ARC SEQUENCES

Although it is related to the last point, it is worth singling out: Never-ending narratives share that they are a **sequence of arcs and/or collection of stories**. Even if the same characters experience a chronological adventure, this adventure is usually made up of *individual* self-contained dramatic arcs with their own goal, which can come to a conclusion and make way for an all-new goal, conflict, and arc. Audiences need the satisfaction of a big conclusion from time to time – if a big goal takes too long to be reached, they might stop caring about it or get too frustrated. This also

SUMMARY

- **Other media** have already created **long-form storytelling** with episodic structures, which can serve as our inspiration.
- These media are, e.g., **literary serials, novel series, sequential art, TV shows, semi-scripted sports, and pen & paper roleplay.**
- They **share the following aspects**:
  - A **rich world** with a **strong cast** and interesting conflicts
  - A **consistent identity**, defined by themes, experiences, and emotions
  - A **reliable story structure**
  - **Regular scheduled releases**
  - **Nested dramatic structures**, with small arcs within bigger arcs within even bigger arcs
  - A **sequence of arcs or collection of stories**, rather than one long story

allows for a separation of intention – a new focus on themes, a new focus on characters, and a brand new start within the same known universe. TV shows usually do this by season, and comic books do this by story arc.

Keeping these basics in mind will be helpful in planning and writing our live game narratives.

10 Building the Narrative Foundation

Planning a seasonal narrative is comparable to being the architect of a building that is supposed to grow over time. You don't actually know how tall it's supposed to be when you start out, but you know you're going to start with a three-floor building that will receive three more floors, and if things go well, it will eventually grow into a skyscraper. Maybe some floors will have to undergo drastic renovation in the process, too.

Now, maybe this already helps to illustrate why that might be quite the challenge, maybe even a bad idea. And, just to be clear, this approach is certainly not recommended for real architecture (and possibly a slightly flawed metaphor). The foundation of a building needs to be designed in a way that carries the whole final structure. It's a question of calculating for the intended form, weight, and stress, using the right materials, structural engineering, and environmental factors. It's quite similar for seasonal games. You need to design the foundation and the individual floors in a way that will enable them to not collapse under themselves.

This is why we're starting off with this topic: How to build the narrative foundation of a game that is meant to go on for a long time. If we want a game's story to be infinitely expandable, it's essential to build a strong foundation that can carry all future expansions. Like an ever-increasing skyscraper, the stronger and more thought-out the narrative foundation, the more floors it will be able to carry in the future.

CREATING YOUR NARRATIVE DESIGN VISION DOCUMENT

A new project always begins with nothing but an idea. Sometimes it starts with a story premise or a fantasy, but the first creative impulse might as well be a core game mechanic, a game genre, a specific target audience, a current trend, a monetization strategy, or the demand to create a new entry in a long-running franchise. There are many ways to discover that initial spark. When you're a creative, you'll likely collect sparks all the time, stumbling upon things that fascinate you simply by going about your daily life and surrounding yourself with things that excite you. Or you discover them after goal-oriented brainstorming sessions. But more realistically, when you work in the games industry, you're going to get dragged into a project that already decided on that initial spark, most of the time.

But a creative spark alone doesn't make for a great game. The actual execution, the progress of countless experiments, insights, and decisions, this is what makes for a great game. And in order to know *how* to make these decisions (and which guidelines to use), it's important to develop a *vision* of your actual goal. You need to know

DOI: 10.1201/9781003297628-14

what kind of game you're trying to make, in order to make better creative decisions as it takes shape. Therefore, during pre-production you need to create a vision of your game and the game's narrative.

Instead of this being something you set in stone in the very beginning of development, it's likely going to be a back and forth for an extended pre-production period between the various members of the team. You're likely going to adjust the story vision after the game design has been refined in more detail, and the rest of the game vision may change because of new story impulses. But at some point during pre-production, you need to *define* your game's identity and story vision in several documents and stick to it – something to guide creative decisions along the way, while retaining that much-needed flexibility of game development. This type of documentation is a valuable tool for everyone in the team, since it provides a reference point for everyone to make better creative decisions that work toward the same vision. The better your team knows the intended player experience, the better they can estimate if they're going in the right direction. Good documentation helps a team have a shared vision and makes a project viable for long-term development and shifting team set-ups, too. They need to be understandable and accessible, meaning, your team should be able to find the information they need even without your help.

A game vision or pitch document usually contains elements of gameplay, story, and creative direction, whereas we're going to focus on the narrative aspect. A Narrative Vision document may contain the following elements, ideally with some visualizations (placeholders, concept art, graphics, charts, or whatever you have at hand):

1. **Story Overview:** What is the story? What is the main conflict? What is the setting? Who are the main characters? How will the characters go about solving the conflict? What does it all lead up to?
2. **Core Fantasy, Themes, and Conflicts:** What's the core fantasy that you're promising the player? What kind of themes and core conflicts are you going to cover over the seasons? And how is that going to tie into the gameplay?
3. **Setting and Worldbuilding:** Where are we, when are we, and what are the important current events framing our story? What do we need to know about the world to understand the general story vision?
4. **Central Characters:** Who are the main characters? Who are the protagonists, deuteragonists, side characters, love interests, or antagonists? What are their personalities, roles, wants, and needs? How do they relate to each other? Which personal journeys play a key part in the story?
5. **Avatar:** Who do players play as? Is it a unique actor or a customizable character? What is their role in this setting? What is their backstory and motivational drive and personal stake in the story?
6. **Narrative Perspective:** Do players embody the avatar's perspective (narrative first person), do they accompany a character from the outside (narrative third person), are they omniscient like a god, or is it something else entirely? (*Note: A narrative perspective is not equal to the in-game camera perspective.*)

7. **Tone, Target Audience, and Age Rating:** What's the age rating, target audience, and general tone? Is it humorous, serious, relaxing, exciting, etc.? Any restrictions regarding topics and language?

8. **Additional Style Documents:** What are the unique terms of your game, and how are they defined internally and when they're player-facing? What are your UI guidelines?

9. **Narrative Pillars:** How are you going to tell the story? What is the general structure going to be like? Which narrative features are going to shape the core experience of the players? This is meant as an overview of the *most important narrative pillars* (not more than three to five), rather than a place to plan out every single narrative feature that the game will eventually have.

10. **Narrative System:** How do we intend to tell the story? What are the main narrative tools we'll use to deliver that story? For example, will we put an emphasis on cutscenes, contextual barks, missions, environment design, documents, and gameplay? Plot-driven or theme-driven? When creating a Vision Document, you likely won't know *all* the pieces yet, so this is the time to think about the *most important aspects* of your narrative system design. This section builds upon the *Narrative Pillars*, and outlines *all* narrative features, rather than just the most important ones.

11. **Live Narrative Intentions:** As an extension of the Narrative System, the vision of a live game should also include plans for the continuation of the story, and what your future releases will look like. Will you add plot-driven seasons with a new villain to defeat, and story missions to progress through? New progressions focusing on individual characters, with no main story continuation? Themed seasons with a bunch of new cosmetics and game modes, each one catering to a different fantasy?

Now, let's take a closer look at these individual segments of a holistic creative vision document. It's important to add that this list is not intended as a strict template that has to be executed in the exact way I describe. In fact, different companies and different narrative designers likely have their own personal approach. However, even if some documents may have other names or slightly different structures, there's likely going to be a large overlap with several of the aspects that I will go on to analyze in greater detail. In any case, think of this chapter as a general suggestion, and a reminder of the many different aspects of a game's narrative vision, rather than a rule. It can be adapted, shortened, or extended to suit your needs.

STORY OVERVIEW (LOGLINE, SYNOPSIS, OUTLINE AND FLOWCHARTS)

Naturally, before you write a story, you need to figure out what the story is going to be about. Depending on the purpose and stage of creative development, the initial story overviews can go from a brief elevator pitch up to a detailed beat by beat outline. They're essential for communicating the story idea effectively, nailing down your own intentions, and preparing the actual writing process. As a general rule, it's always helpful to have various lengths of story overviews for different use cases, such as pitching, pre-production, or production.

Logline

The shortest story overview is the **logline**. Think of it as the pitch that you can tell somebody when they ask you what your game's story is going to be about. It should convey the **core idea** of your narrative in just **one to two concise sentences** while implying the story's genre, core fantasy, themes, and conflict. This sentence should contain the following key points: Your protagonist, the inciting incident, the goal, the antagonist, and the central conflict of the story. Clearly lay out the story – without mentioning the ending – to clarify the idea and why it would be exciting to explore. This type of short overview is borrowed from movies and novels – if there is a story, it can be summarized in a logline.

Here are a few examples:

- A 20-something American tourist has to save his friends from human traffickers on a pirate-infested tropical island near Bangkok and joins forces with a local tribe to become an enlightened warrior to achieve it. (Far Cry 3)
- A young street hustler, a retired bank robber and a drug dealer must pull off dangerous heists to survive in a Los Angeles-inspired city, while under pressure from the U.S. government and the criminal underworld. (Grand Theft Auto V)
- In a cyberpunk future, a mercenary tries to find a way to free themselves of a mysterious cybernetic implant that threatens to overwrite their personality and memories with those of a deceased celebrity, and the two must work together to be separated and survive. Meanwhile, they bump heads with dangerous gangs and corporations looking for the key to immortality (Cyberpunk 2077).

Synopsis

A synopsis is a **brief summary** of your story, usually **up to one page** long. It goes into much more detail than a logline (which only describes the general story idea), and gives an overview of the story's beginning, middle, and end (or rather exposition, rising action, climax, falling action, and resolution), **emphasizing pivotal moments** of plot development and their impact on the main characters. It should reveal the main characters' motivations, conflicts, and actions, and how everyone will change over the course of the story. Think of this as a summary that would be in the beginning of story vision documents, to define something with more clarity than just the general idea, but quick to present and read.

Outline

As opposed to a synopsis, a story outline aims to summarize and break down **all key scenes** of the story and their major plot points. It's the next step between a synopsis and the final written text: A more detailed beat-by-beat definition of what will happen at what point. Each beat should mention the setting, characters, conflict, and the resolution of the scene's conflict. With this document, you can start to build and see the moment-to-moment story that players will experience, and start building the gameplay flow with it.

This document is needed not only for the writing team but also for your team's game designers and level designers, as it gives them the narrative context for the gameplay moments they're creating, and helps discuss and clarify the game flow and progression. As opposed to an outline for a movie or a novel, an outline for a videogame might get expanded to also contain aspects relevant for game development. You can decide to **mention the related gameplay** (player actions, gameplay types, involved weapons, possible rewards, challenge level, etc.) and key narrative that will be conveyed by **action or creative direction** (such as environmental storytelling).

Since we're working with live games, we're likely going to write **several outlines** eventually, covering several different progressions – for example, a main campaign outline, a season 1 outline, a season 2 outline, a new side progression outline, and so on. Your initial outline, written during pre-production, could cover your permanent main progression and the progression of season 1, for example – but this will depend on your story and plot structure throughout the seasons and whether your story will even require an outline at all.

On average, an outline document can be **several pages** or even **up to 30 pages long**. It can also be formatted differently from a movie's outline, like taking the form of a spreadsheet, with one cell for each story beat, arranged in chronological order. It can also be a slideshow presentation, with one slide per story beat. As always, it's a question of personal preference and established documentation at the company. There are other types of documents that can help you visualize your story outline better, in addition to the general outline, such as story flowcharts and character growth charts.

Story Flowchart

A story flowchart can visualize your **story beats connected by dependencies** and logic. This type of document can be a useful tool for games that have a lot of story dependencies, where player actions define what happens, and/or in which order it happens. Of course, this is a must for anything featuring interactive story telling (with branching stories and story dependencies), but it is also relevant for anything where players have a certain amount of freedom with how they move through your storyscape. If you have dependencies that are not all linear, a flowchart might be necessary. If you have a perfectly linear story, however, you can still create a story flowchart to depict the change of scenes/levels/tone more visually.

Character Growth Charts

A character growth chart can summarize the **personal growth beats** of individual characters over time, within the main story progression and (if applicable) the live story progression. The more seasons with character growth you have, the more obligatory a document like this becomes, especially if you have several characters that are supposed to change over time. This should refer to their individual goals and desires in each season, how those turn out, and how the season has changed them (if applicable). For a cast of several characters, a spreadsheet is recommended.

CORE FANTASY, THEMES, AND CONFLICTS

Defining the core fantasy, themes, and conflicts of your game will be crucial for making creative decisions (in terms of story, design, and visual direction) and to plan your future expansions. These literary devices can provide inspiration for new story arcs and content, as well as a means to keep a sense of thematic coherency across the entire lifecycle. Especially for a game that will provide new live content after the initial release, the core fantasy, themes, and conflicts are essential to keep your team on track.

Core Fantasy

Every videogame (live or not) offers the player a **core fantasy**, a thematic and experiential concept associated with a set of story elements, activities, and emotions. It's a promise for an archetypical experience and for the management of expectations, giving players an idea of whether they'd be in the mood for it. Think of being a powerful hero who saves the kingdom from evil, or a space adventurer exploring exotic planets to save mankind, or a pirate captain looking for treasure. A fantasy can also be that you're a scared everyman in a village filled with horrible creatures, trying to survive the day – or that you're a farm owner who peacefully grows your lands. Fantasy doesn't always mean *power* fantasy, after all. It can be a fantasy about power, survival, strategy, tragedy, despair, tranquility, collaboration, love, and whatever else you can think of. Usually, the core fantasy is something that your team assumes a lot of players want to immerse themselves in, and therefore, central to your marketing campaign. Defining your core fantasy helps in keeping your game coherent over a long period of time. But there's some wiggle room. Over the lifetime of your live game, you can cast a light on different aspects of the same fantasy, through the use of various themes and shifting narratives, as long as you keep an untouchable core intact. If you don't, you run the risk of muddling the game's identity and losing players after things have simply changed just too much. You also run the risk of your stories simply going nowhere, and players not knowing what to expect, which also increases the risk of them losing interest and dropping out of the game completely.

Themes

Secondly, there are the **themes** of your game. They should emerge naturally from your core fantasy, but will be unique to your game and your main characters. For example, in a pirate fantasy game, you can sell the concept of a feared pirate captain, with themes of power, crime, sea warfare, betrayal, and thievery. Or you can focus on a more collaborative interpretation, with themes of freedom, found families, teamwork, caretaking, and treasure hunting. The same core fantasy can explore very different themes. The bigger and more complex a game, the more themes you can explore, of course, but you should always try to keep things simple enough.

Conflicts

Thirdly, when you've got an idea of your core fantasy and core themes, you can think about the **core conflicts**. They should directly help to reinforce the fantasy and explore the themes, which still leaves us a lot of freedom regarding what exactly we want those conflicts to be. Is the conflict between a group of revolutionaries trying to liberate a country from a dictator? Is the conflict a will-they-won't-they of two potential lovers? Are you competing to be the best there ever was? These conflicts need to directly tie into the core gameplay or meta gameplay, if you want them to have maximum impact. In the context of live games, it's important to reflect upon the fact whether these core conflicts have the potential for *a lot* of content, too (although that will depend on how these conflicts will be used in the later live content updates, of course). But keep in mind that conflicts can and should very well change over the course of seasons. There should be a central conflict that remains the same, something directly tied into the core gameplay (such as power struggles between two factions), but narratively, we can have new ideas, new developments, and new core conflicts for the new season. Just make sure it doesn't become an entirely new experience that shifts away from the core fantasy.

To explore the connections between core fantasy, themes, and conflicts, I will provide a few examples. This doesn't mean that each fantasy can *only* be expanded with these themes and conflicts. They are meant as hypothetical examples, which can look completely different for your own game.

Example 10.1: – An Open World Action Game Set in the Golden Age of Piracy

Fantasy: Pirate Life

Themes:

- Freedom
- Exploration
- Friendship
- Lawlessness
- Outcast Existence

Core Conflicts:

- Law vs Crime
- Nature vs Man
- The Supernatural vs Man
- Battle for Survival
- Greed vs. Philanthropism

Example 10.2: A Visual Novel about a Forbidden Office Romance

Fantasy: Forbidden Romance

Themes:

- Love
- Family Issues
- Work-Life Balance
- Self-Actualization
- Business Life

Core Conflicts:

- Adventure vs Security
- Career vs Love
- Society vs Man
- Reason vs Emotion

Example 10.3: A Tactical Shooter about a Secret Government Agent

Fantasy: Secret Agent

Themes:

- Secrets
- Conspiracies
- Manipulation
- Resourcefulness
- Big Sacrifices

Core Conflicts:

- Obedience vs Rebellion
- Endangering Loved Ones
- Personal Sacrifices
- Truth vs Lies
- Control vs Agency

SETTING AND WORLDBUILDING

When you build a fictional world for your live game, you have to ask yourself: Can this serve as a foundation that will carry many stories to come? Your worldbuilding should naturally tie into what kind of conflicts your story will explore and inform the game's visual design and gameplay. When new features or events are developed, the worldbuilding will need to be kept in mind for any creative decisions – since all creative decisions should be an expression of the underlying lore. You don't actually need to explain all these hidden meanings to the player, of course, but when each decision stems from the same lore basis, it will create a sense of coherency and simply make more sense. This can also be seen as a chance for inspiration, allowing the team to draw ideas from a basis even when the team setup changes over time, allowing to keep the game coherent over a long period of time. This means that any additions to the worldbuilding should be recorded and easily available and accessible for everyone.

Depending on your genre and story vision, your worldbuilding will put a different focus on different aspects of the world. If your setting is a fantastical world completely unlike ours (for fantasy or science fiction), you'll probably have a lot more to cover when it comes to worldbuilding. But even when your setting is very grounded, maybe even a faithful recreation of a real place and time, it's helpful to gather and establish the worldbuilding directly relevant to your game. So let's take a look at an extensive list of **possible topics of worldbuilding**, from which you can pick and choose, depending on what feels most relevant to understanding and designing your specific project.

- Natural Laws *(physics, biology, chemistry, etc.)*
- Cosmology *(the structure of the planetary system)*
- Geography *(borders, biomes, inhabitants, routes, resources, etc.)*
- Ecology *(flora, fauna, and natural phenomena)*
- Architecture *(style, shapes, materials, functions, construction, current state, the history and changing purposes of buildings, etc.)*
- People and social groups *(social classes, subcultures, factions, etc.)*
- Religion and culture *(level of civilization, traditions, art, religions, groups, social conflicts, etc.)*
- Politics *(government structures, parties, etc.)*
- Crime *(level of crime, crime areas, popular crimes, law enforcement, etc.)*
- Economy *(structure and currencies)*
- Technology *(level of advancement and function)*
- Language *(real languages, specific dialects, slang, fictional languages, etc.)*
- The current state of the world *(important current natural, political, or social circumstances)*
- The history of the world *(important past natural, political, or social circumstances)*

Creating a world's lore can be created *top-down* or *bottom-up*. In the first case, we start with the broad strokes of the world and then start expanding on each individual aspect that will get more attention in the game, going from general to specific. Going from planetary systems to planets to continents to countries to cities to districts – for example. This makes sense for games that have the goal to create unique vastly explorable worlds, whereas, of course, only those aspects would receive more detail if they will be shown and explored in detail too. There is no need to define a planet the player will never even see.

The other approach, *bottom-up*, starts with details needed for the specific situations we will have. For example, you focus on creating the complexities of a specific city first (with its local geography, culture, political structure, commerce, and history) and then think about the terms of the country, and then the planet (if necessary). This kind of approach is good for character- and plot-driven stories, whereas the other is well suited for exploration stories with a focus on various cultures. In the end, both approaches can work for any kind of world though. The approach you choose is likely going to be a matter of how your project got started (starting with broad strokes or a specific moment), or how you function as a creative thinker. Both approaches are legitimate and can lead to a satisfying goal. With how videogames are developed, you're likely to have a bit of both for each aspect of the game anyway, where you, for example, are presented with a game mechanic that you then need to justify with lore, which then needs to be embedded in the grander scheme of things.

Also, not every game needs the same *amount* of worldbuilding, but all will need *some* worldbuilding. In a fantasy space opera world with new planets and alien races, where physics work differently from what we know, you're gonna need a lot of lore. For a realistic military shooter in a real setting, you still need to create lore documents that describe the setting as it will be portrayed, even if a lot of that will be based on research and real-life facts. What's the "real world lore" of the setting at the time the story takes place, geographically, socially, and culturally?

It's a narrative designer's/writer's responsibility to find a good balance between story depth and a good use of your development time. Which lore is likely going to be useful for creating the game you want to create (even if just for informing your creative decisions), and which would be irrelevant for development and invisible to players? You can't predict everything, naturally, since things will change throughout production. But it's about finding a good balance and trying to give details where needed, and leaving other things more vague (unless demand changes).

CENTRAL CHARACTERS

Creating a Core Cast

Many of the most successful long-running narratives are character-driven. Audiences return to see where their beloved characters go next, which decisions they make, and how that will affect them. These narratives therefore rely on interesting character casts that audiences fall in love with and continue to care about for a long time. So when you create your cast of characters (which is possibly going to get expanded over time), you have to ask yourself if your core cast is ready to have many adventures together, and whether they can remain *interesting* for a long time.

Therefore, your cast needs to fulfill two things:

1. Are there characters that audiences will become invested in, making them come back to follow their journey? (It doesn't need to be the same character for everyone.)
2. Are they well-developed enough to stay interesting for an extended time? Are they complex characters with trauma, flaws, dreams, needs, ideals, and many stories to experience? Is their lot in life a good source for drama (and/or comedy) and a variety of situations?

It's equally important to think about the cast's dynamics, and if it can serve interesting conflicts, resolutions, and changes. Think about different factions (or groups), friendships, romances, nemeses, and the possibility of shifting relationship dynamics. The conflict between characters can tie into the main themes of the game, as well as seasonal themes, but should also stem organically from the personality of the characters, and in how far their desires and flaws clash. You can use side characters to highlight personality traits and growth in main characters, too – so don't only focus on one main character, but how you could build them through the people around them, and how you can have several interesting arcs all over your story. Shifting your attention from character to character, and different dynamics, helps to tell new stories with the same cast in the same world.

When building a core cast, it's helpful to think about the following aspects:

- How **diverse is the cast**? What archetypes and personalities are used, and how different are they from one another? Will a large variety of players find at least one of them to get emotionally invested in? Do the characters each have unique ways of expressing their personality, in the way they look, behave, and speak, their interests and ideals, as well as the way they function in the game? It is worth thinking about diversity in ways of body type, culture, ethnicity, gender, sexuality, religion, and age as well.
- Is each **character complex and interesting** and a good potential member of an ensemble cast for character-driven storytelling? Do they have potential for conflict (both internal and external) and growth, a backstory that influences their actions and might be revealed over time, a (possibly) comedic element such as running gags and topics they get back to? What are their hang-ups, and how do they shape them? Can they captivate an audience with relatable human experiences? The more central a character is, the more complex they need to be.
- Do your characters represent different **ideological standpoints** in your game world? Do you have characters to represent different perspectives on important aspects of your world, and does that provide an interesting source for conflict, team-ups, changing affiliations, and growth? Do you have any factions that can have conflicts between each other (not obligatory, but often helpful)? This defines which themes and conflicts will be central in your narrative, as well as the emotions the experience will focus on.
- Do the themes that haunt your characters tie into the central theme of your story? Are they all an extension and consideration of a shared narrative core that defines your game's identity? Can those themes evolve over time?
- What are the **relationships between characters**, and where is the potential for conflict and changes over the seasons? Who might switch sides, fall in and out of love, start and end friendships? Have you meaningfully connected your core character cast by relationships among each other, making them friends, enemies, family, lovers, etc? Will the cast and their relationships allow you to tell countless interesting stories?
- Do your characters have **potential for drama**? What is their trauma to reveal, their wants they pursue, and their emotional needs they fulfill? This applies to both, individuals and groups. Are your characters going to be static (like in some comedic sitcoms), or will they grow over time (like in serial dramas)? Depending on the answer, you must either ensure they have potential for a long journey of growth (of consistent main characters), many different journeys of growth (with shifting focus between characters), or the potential for many different stories (of one or more characters, without getting repetitive or boring).
- Do your main characters have **potential for comedy**? Do they have running gags, quirky behavior, repeating themes and jokes made by or about them? Depending on the tone of your game, you might not want every character to be comedic, but even in the most serious of dramas, a little humor every now and then can go a long way.
- Do the characters in your cast have versatile **narrative functions**, and do they help to structure your game meaningfully? This applies to both each

character's function in the story (main character, sidekick, antagonist, etc.) and their function in the game (such as companion, quest givers, feature representatives, mentor/tutorial character, etc.). If you have several characters for the same function, they should bring a unique aspect to that function (such as a strong companion and a magical companion, or a gun tutorial character and a brawl tutorial character), otherwise, could you combine them and have a sleeker, more meaningful cast.

- Does the **player role** in the story provide an engaging experience? Do they step into the shoes of a character, do they have a relationship with the main cast, or do they belong to a faction? Is this role going to remain interesting for a long time? Will their role shift over time or do you plan to give them the option to switch between roles? Are they observers of interesting stories or actors in interesting stories (both of which are valid approaches, but influence how the game feels)?

All of this can be reflected in more than the way they're written, of course, and should be reflected in their visual designs, their animations, their voices, and possibly even the way they function in the game.

Creating Character Profiles

Profiles of individual characters, giving an overview of who they are and where they came from, to inform how they are written, how they act in the story and how they appear in the game (visual design, animations, sound design, behavior). The more central a character is, the more extensive the profile should be; a minor NPC often doesn't need more than a few sentences. The more you think about a character though, the more you can infuse that profile into the way they act, move, and speak, making them feel more alive and engaging. Sometimes games have specific category demands for characters, which need to be added as needed, such as running gags and comedic potential (for comedy games), symbolistic meaning (for artistic games), etc.

A **character profile** can contain many different elements. According to how central a character will be to the game, they need to be more or less complex. A central character benefits from a lot of thought, while a side character or minor NPC needs less depth. Here is a suggested list of possible elements in a character profile.

First Impressions

- **Game Function:** The function of a character inside the game's structure. A character rarely exists solely on a narrative level and usually ties to some gameplay element. They can be an avatar, a companion, a tutorial character, an NPC, a questgiver, a boss, a damsel in distress, and more.
- **Connected Feature:** Characters can be connected to a specific game feature and serve as its feature representatives. This way, players know who to address to access certain parts of the game, setting expectations, giving narrative depth to features, and enabling easier navigation in the game. A chosen feature needs to mesh well with the characterization of the representative, like a merchant being tied to the shop feature. Other examples would be a character being tied to all game tutorials, a questgiver for a specific type of mission,

a companion that can be used in certain puzzles, a party member focusing on long-range weapons, healing items, or magic attacks, or other features.

- **Story Role:** A character's story role defines their purpose on the narrative layer of the game, rather than the gameplay. This could be hero, love interest, mentor, antagonist, damsel, ally, and more.
- **Archetypes and Tropes:** This is the first impression of a character that audiences understand at first sight. Archetypes and tropes are usually expressed through how a character acts, looks, and functions in the game, and the first point of entry to understanding a fictional person. A character can combine more than one archetype or trope, but it's good to have a limited focus to set expectations quickly. A few examples would be anti-hero, hopeless optimist, fish out of water, lovable rogue, tomboy, mysterious stranger, well-intended extremist, etc.
- **Trope Subversion:** In order to make a character appear more unique quickly, and differentiate them from other characters of the same trope, you can add a surprising aspect of the character that seemingly contradicts their archetype. Like a cute girl who swears like a sailor, or a tough guy who collects cute keychains.
- **Physical Attributes:** A character is also defined by their physical attributes, which would include age, ethnicity, body type, eye and hair color, etc.
- **Disabilities:** Characters may have disabilities, either from birth or because of certain events in their lives. There are many different types of disabilities, such as physical impairment, vision impairment, deafness, mental health conditions, intellectual disability, and more.
- **Neurodiversity:** A character may be neurodivergent, which influences the way they think, focus, and behave. Examples for neurodiversity are characters who have ADHD, OCD, dyslexia, or are on the autism spectrum. If you choose to have a neurodivergent character, it's important to not resort to stereotypes or make this a character's primary personality – but to do research and involve people who actually have this specific type of neurodiversity that you'd like to portray.
- **Profession or Class:** The job, profession, or class of a character usually takes up a huge part of their daily life and often influences their role in the game or story. Examples would be plumber, knight, detective, special forces operator, treasure hunter, wizard, company employee, rockstar, etc.
- **Ways of Speaking:** Speech patterns and vocabulary can reveal a lot about a character's background and personality, and help to make them truly stand out from other characters. In a character's manner of speaking, you can reveal their personality, where (and when) they're from, their social class, level of education, subculture, age, and whether they belong to a specific in-group. All this can be reflected in their dialect or accent, sentence structure, slang or specific vocabulary, idiosyncratic language, and catchphrases. Different ways of speaking give off different impressions of a character, independent from *what* they're saying.
- **Quirks:** Characters can have unique quirks that show up again and again – may those be physical, behavioral, interpersonal, or other.

Personality

- **Personality and Attitudes:** A character's personality and general state of mind, including first impressions, contextual shift in attitudes, and unexpected personality contrasts.
- **Gender and Sexuality:** A character's gender identity and their sexual orientation.
- **Public Persona(s):** A character's public persona describes how they act in the presence of others – whereas different social contexts require different public personas, such as work, family, friends, lovers, etc.
- **Private Persona:** A character's private persona describes how they act when no one else is present.
- **Incognizant Persona:** A character's incognizant persona describes who they are at the core, which they're unaware of or actively suppressing.
- **Traumas and Fears:** Some traumatic events the character experienced may still shape their behavior and which might need to be revealed, faced, and overcome in the course of the story. Fears, on the other hand, can become an obstacle that prevents them from reaching their goals.
- **Wants and Needs:** There are specific goals a character *thinks* they want to achieve, but they aren't necessarily their true emotional need. Characters can be wrong about what would make them happy. That, on the other hand, would be their emotional resolution, what the character actually *needs* to achieve.
- **Strengths and Skills:** A character has a certain set of strengths and skills, which can be physical, mental, intellectual, spiritual, social, etc.
- **Weaknesses and Flaws:** A character has a certain set of weaknesses, which can be physical, mental, intellectual, spiritual, social, etc. Depending on the gravity of a flaw, they can have a greater impact on the character's life. There are **minor flaws** (which are just imperfections that don't affect the story deeply, such as scars or habits), **major flaws** (which are possibly a hindrance that impairs the character mentally or morally) and **fatal flaws** (which would be the cause of the character's downfall and possible death).

Opinions

- **Ideologies:** A character's set of beliefs in various areas of life, such as political, religious, philosophical, emotional, group-based, personal, etc.
- **Likes and Dislikes:** A character's likes and dislikes express their personal tastes and shape their choices and behavior. This can apply to food, drinks, music, activities, fashion, media, personality attributes in other people, and more.
- **Hobbies and Obsessions:** Characters may regularly engage in hobbies, or spend a significant amount of time on a special interest. This is then reflected in dialogue, special skills, or their behavior. Hobbies can be anything, from athletic activities to collections, entertainment, creative projects, areas of knowledge, and more.

- **Fashion and Self-Presentation:** The way somebody dresses says a lot about them, as well. A character's choices in self-presentation are reflected in their sense of fashion, situational clothing, hair, make-up, and general attitude – and can be an expression of their inner self or their aspired self.

Background

- **Biography:** A biography doesn't need to cover every single year from birth until the present, but it should lay out the relevant core experiences that lead them to where they are now. This starts with where they were born and how they grew up and then continues with core experiences as an adult. This backstory can then be reflected in current behavior, ideologies, trauma, goals, dialogues, etc.
- **Background and Culture:** A character's cultural background is defined by their region of origin, social environment, economic class, family circumstances, religious faith, and other cultural circumstances.

Interpersonal Relations

- **Group Affiliations:** People usually belong to several different groups in their lives, which defines them as a person in relation to the world. They can be affiliated with a workplace, organization, school, club, faction, social circle, or other.
- **Family Situation:** A person is shaped by their family situation and relation to different family members. Families can be big or small, tightly knit or spread apart, loving or hostile – and sometimes they're not even blood-related at all, but rather, an adoptive or found family. This can also change over time, and what was the situation in the past is not the same in the current time where the story is set.
- **Important Relationships:** The core relationships are most important to the character, irregardless of whether they have a positive or negative impact on them. This can be family relations, friends, lovers, mentors, or enemies.

Creating Relationships Graphs

In order to keep track of all the relationships and associations of your characters, it can be helpful to create character graphs. On these visualizations, you can add each and every character, and start connecting them to each other, marking the relationship in both directions. In addition to personal relationships with each other, you can visualize group affiliations by clustering them together, using color coding, or creating a separate graph. This way, it's easier to brainstorm and play with relationships between characters. You can discover relationship clusters (with social main characters and side characters) and might notice forgotten characters which could use a few more connections to others, which in turn, might inspire new plot dynamics in the future.

When it comes to live games, this will also come in handy when you create seasonal relationship charts (or graphs), recording shifting interpersonal connections between characters over time. These are valuable tools for narrative-driven live game storytelling, as it is a way how to track and plan how characters will evolve in relation to each other – a great source of drama! Think about people switching sides, befriending some, and betraying others.

AVATAR

The avatar is the character that the player is going to accompany and live through vicariously, so it's important to consider whether your avatar would be an interesting character to play for a long time. As a person, the avatar needs to hold potential for many interesting stories and conflicts. However, your avatar doesn't necessarily need to be one protagonist – you can offer a choice of several characters that can be freely switched between or a customizable character who's uniquely tied to the player. Depending on your game, one or the other choice might make more sense – as they influence the game experience and its meaning. For example, a massive multiplayer online game, where many players share the same space, needs more variety and will likely give customizable avatars, separated by classes or other categories, rather than one single protagonist.

I'd like to suggest a categorization of popular avatar variants:

- **No Avatar:** There is no visible protagonist, and the player interacts with the game as themselves. They have an omniscient perspective, acting directly on the game without having a representative inside of the world. This can often be found in casual and strategy games.
- **Companion Character:** The player doesn't have a visible avatar and directly interacts with the game as themselves, but they have a companion character inside of the game world. This companion is their representative and provides a perspective on the world, but the player doesn't control them directly. They just accompany their journey with their actions. This companion might break the fourth wall and directly address the player. This can often be found in casual and strategy games.
- **Embodied Character:** The player takes the role of a specific character with their own unique personality and backstory, and experiences the game roleplaying *as them*. Players have a certain level of freedom to guide the actions of this character, but choices are usually limited to what is in the realm of believability for the character, their skills, and their philosophy. This can often be found in single-player live games.
- **Customizable Persona:** The player creates their own character that serves as their own representative in the game (as a true avatar, so to speak). This representation may look like them or entirely unlike them, and can be played intuitively or in pursuit of creating a persona they can roleplay as. The predefined backstory of this customizable persona is usually minimal or non-existent, making it a pure tool for the player to interact with the game's diagesis. They might be able to choose attributes, such as a class,

which is connected to authored content, but the focus is on self-expression, rather than accompanying a written character. These customizations may influence gameplay as well, due to available actions, activities, and missions for specific character types. This can often be found in MMOs.

- **Customizable Cosmetics:** The player customizes their own appearance in the game, but it isn't tied to a persistent character identity. This isn't a character that they're building or roleplaying as, but simply a visual representation of themselves inside the game. The biggest difference to customizable personas is that these personas function as specific player-customized characters that can experience leveling and progress, while the customizable cosmetics avatar is a purely visual representation of the player in the game world. This representation can be changed at will and is purely cosmetic, usually unrelated to any gameplay and form of progression. This can often be found in Multiplayer Shooters and Battle Royales.
- **Multiple Playable Characters:** The player selects from a roster of characters, which all have a defined look, personality, and background – as well as gameplay, abilities, and skills attached to them. They define the player's experience due to how they play, and can usually be swapped out often and at will. They can have individual progressions, meaning that a player can level up several characters in parallel, rather than just one, and switch between them as they like. Often, champions can be customized with skins, but it's usually limited in a way that they still remain recognizable as themselves. Ideally, the skins reveal new aspects of their story or personality. This can often be found in Fighting Games, Character Collection Games, Hero Shooters, or MOBAs.

However, this doesn't necessarily capture the full range of possibilities when it comes to game avatars. When building creating an avatar for your game, they can fall into many different categories in how they relate to the game world, how they relate to the player, what role they play, and how they're expressing themselves. Your choices deeply influence the way players experience their impact on the game, and who they are in it. Most of the time, certain game genres already have established conventions of avatar types, as the game feel and experience is formed by the avatar provided. As you create a new videogame, you should analyze how other games of your genre handle avatars, but there's also the chance of shifting some of these attributes, and possibly creating a new experience that could act as a selling point and creative opportunity.

Each avatar will fall into one or the other category for every attribute on this list – and they can be freely combined.

An Avatar is either...

- **Diagetic** (with a visible representation inside of the game world – e.g., third-person-shooters, action adventures, or platformers) or **Non-Diagetic** (outside of the game world, either completely invisible or visible on a meta layer that doesn't exist in the same diagesis as the core gameplay – e.g., in simulation, strategy, and god games)

- **Directly Controlled** (embodies the player input immediately, controlled fully and directly – e.g., in FPS, action adventures, and platformers) or **Indirectly Controlled** (reacts to player actions after the fact, like following instructions – e.g. in simulations, strategy, and god games)
- **Without Personal Agency** (will only act on player instructions – e.g., FPS, action adventures, platforms) or **With Personal Agency** (will make own decisions if players don't give them instructions – e.g., in simulations, strategy or god games; or narrative games with timers and default choices if timers run out)
- **A Scripted Character** (players roleplay as an authored character, placing a focus on identification and empathy) or a **Blank Character** (self-expression through a blank slate avatar that can be played as the player desires, putting a focus on play)
- **With Defined Visuals** (character always looks as the game determines it) or with **Customizable Visuals** (player can change the avatar's look)
- **A Singular Avatar** (one avatar per player) or **Multiple Avatars** (several possible avatars per player, either at the same time or taking turns – e.g., RPGs)
- **A Steady** (permanent) or **Shifting** Avatar (can change over time, throughout a progression, or based on player choice)

Narrative Perspective

A game's narrative perspective defines how the story is conveyed to the player, both in terms of perspective, emotion, and level of information. It's the relation between the player, their avatar, and the game's diagesis, and how information about the diagesis is conveyed to the player, using avatars (or other narrators) as a filter. But first, it's important to define what diagesis means in this context: It's the game's inner world, with everything that happens *inside* of it. If characters are speaking to each other inside of the game world, other characters can hear it (making the sound diagetic) – if the game is playing a soundtrack to accompany a situation, which characters don't hear while the player does, then it *isn't* part of the game's diagesis (it's non-diagetic).

The player and their avatar(s) are two different, yet connected perspectives on the game's world, and it's important to define their relationship for your game, in how far they align or not. The player is the physical person in front of the game, and how they perceive it, while the avatar is a character inside of the game, who exists as part of the game's diagesis and as the embodiment of the player's will. The player causes the avatar to take action, in a more or less direct way, and as such it serves as a representation of themselves, but they are not the same person and don't necessarily have the same level of information. Just like a reader and the narrator in a book, or the audience and the main character in a movie.

A narrative perspective in a game can take a variety of forms, expressed through camera, avatars, level of information, depiction of the game world (including subjective distortions), the haptics of controls, voice overs or otherwise depicted thought, readable texts, user interfaces, and other such ludo-literary devices.

A game's narrative perspective is made up of the following aspects:

Point-of-View

The point-of-view determines which perspective the player is seeing, and which information they get in which shape or form. It answers the question: Which perspective does the player align with, how much information do they get, and how is the information portrayed? It could be, for example, the subjective perspective of their avatar, an external perspective that follows their avatar, or a more omniscient perspective that follows several characters and doesn't align with the level of information that their avatar has. But there are many more options. I'd like to suggest attributes of narrative perspective in videogames, based on literary narrative point-of-view, in combination with the concept of focalization as defined by narratologist Gérard Genette,[1] while rephrasing some terms to align with existing videogame UI terminology.

- **Singular** (one perspective character) or **multi-perspective** (several perspective characters)?
- **Limited** (only giving us the information that the avatar receives) or **omniscient** (showing us things that the avatar does not know about)?
- **Internal** (insight into the emotional world of the avatar, through voice over or similar literary devices) or **external** (focusing on the events that can be observed from the outside)?
- **Subjective** (influenced and distorted by the narrator's opinions, emotions, and delusions, which might result in an unreliable narrator) or **objective** (presented as a hypothetical objective truth)?
- **First-Person** (seeing through the avatar's eyes), **second-person** (seeing the avatar through other character's eyes – a very unusual camera) or **third-person** camera (looking over the character's shoulder or looking down on them)?
- **Diegetic** (perspective character is inside of the game world, such as a visible character avatar) or **non-diegetic** (perspective character is outside of the game, such as in god games, where the player is the perspective "character") or **meta-diegetic** (perspective character is outside of the navigable game world but still displayed inside the game – imagine a narrator who exists as an overlay, perceived by the player, but not the characters inside the navigable game world, existing in a realm between game and player)?

Player Role

The role of the player is defined by how they use the avatar to interact with the game world, and how they relate to them. They can adopt their perspective, literally stepping into their shoes, or they can keep a clear separation between the fictional character and themselves as two different people. There is also the possibility that there is no direct avatar in the game at all, and the player themselves become a character in front of the screen. On that note, players can be a meta character that influences or interacts with characters on screen, which may or may not be aware of them as a person.

There are several roles a player can play in the game, in relation to their possible avatar(s).

- **Roleplay as the Avatar(s):** Players take empathetic action as somebody else, and follow the journey of a defined fictional character or several characters. They drive the action forward, but in the way that matches the character's dramatic trajectory – even when the player gets to take choices, they take these choices as the character they're playing.
- **Roleplay as a Function:** Players roleplay as a function, rather than a defined character with a backstory. They are given a role in the game world, such as a town manager, a café owner, or a sports team manager, and act as this undefined character they can fill with personality themselves.
- **Roleplay as Self-Expression:** Players play as themselves or as a playful persona, by interacting with the game world through a blank slate character that can be customized through choices, gameplay, and possibly visual customization.
- **Visible Meta Character:** The player doesn't have a visible representation and directly controlled avatar in the game, but they are treated as a meta character themselves. The game addresses them directly, breaking the fourth wall.
- **Invisible Meta Character:** The player doesn't have a visible representation and directly controlled avatar in the game, but they are acting like an invisible guide to characters inside of the game (while not embodying them directly). The game diagesis does not address the player directly; they influence the development of events without being acknowledged as a character of the story. However, they take on an implied role anyway, such as a manager or a god-like entity. God games, management games, and casual games often fall into this category.
- **Non-Persistent Identity:** With games that have multiple skins to collect, there will be a dichotomy between the player as a persistent entity and the playable skins/characters as a fluid identity. This might create challenges for stories that want to include the player avatar as an actor, despite their look changing so much they're basically a shapeshifter. An option would be that they are recognized as the same person, irregardless of looks (can be explained within the game, or left open for interpretation), or alternatively, they embody many people who are treated as unique entities.

Depending on the game, some of these may be combined. Roleplay as function and self-expression, for example, are a popular combination. Additionally, visible meta characters and roleplay as self-expression has been used in dress-up games – where the player isn't the doll they're customizing, but they may be addressed by that character as a fictionalized meta character.

Form of Address

The third part of narrative perspective is how the player is addressed by the game, which we've already brushed upon in the role of the player. If the player is roleplaying as a specific character, this character is going to be addressed in the game, and the player isn't acknowledged as a person – if the characters use "you," it's directed at the avatar and not the player. If the player is taking the role of a meta character, this might go one way or another: They might be directly addressed with second person singular (as "you"), implicitly included with the in-game characters with first person plural (as "we"), or not acknowledged as a character at all, which means that the accompanying characters might just talk to one another. Note that this may change depending on context. In fact, it's very likely that you have several different ways of addressing your player in different contexts of the game. For example, within the story, characters may address the player as "You, the avatar who acts within the world," but when they open the meta shop, the player is now addressed as "You, as the player who purchases items with real world money." Meta layers, especially those that handle purchases, are usually a candidate for breaking the fourth wall and talking to the player as a player, rather than a character. This form of address therefore doesn't only depend on the pronouns that we're using, but also the way the game refers to the player and their role inside the game (as a character, a meta character, the player themselves, etc.).

Therefore, the most common forms of addressing the player would be the following:

- **Second person diagetic:** *"You*, as the avatar(s) inside the game world," for a more immersive experience that doesn't break the game diagesis. Can be singular or plural.
- **Second person meta:** *"You*, as the player(s) in front of the screen," when the player themselves needs to be addressed, e.g., for purchases, tutorials, and gameplay explanations, but also when the player is a meta character themselves. Can be singular or plural.
- **First-person plural inclusive:** *"We*, the characters and (implicitly) you as the player," when the player needs to be addressed in a more subtle and less immersion-breaking way than second person singular meta.
- **Non-inclusive:** The player and their avatar are not being addressed at all.

TONE, TARGET AUDIENCE AND AGE RATING

Tone Document

One and the same game idea can be executed in as many ways as there are people on the planet. Even if you think you and your team members are aligned in your vision, based on the story and core gameplay alone, chances are you're picturing very (or at least slightly) different final games. This phenomenon becomes even worse when teams change throughout development, and those who come after have an all-new interpretation of what the previous team members had in mind. This is where the *tone document* comes into place.

This is a document that clarifies your game's story genre, tone, target audience, and other matters of writing style. Keep in mind that a story genre is different from a game genre: A game genre is usually more focused on the game mechanics and gamefeel (such as first-person-shooter, action adventure, open world, or strategy), while a story genre refers to the type of story that is being conveyed (such as action, horror, or science fiction). A tone document also includes the intended target audience and age rating and, as a consequence, allowed topics and maturity levels of used language.

This document is an important tool for pitching the project, as well as clarifying the intended tone to your whole (shifting) team and therefore keeping better consistency across the game. The tone is usually made up of the **story genre** (thriller, action, horror, romance, comedy, adventure, slice of life, etc.), the **tone** (mature, light-hearted, tragic, provocative, comedic, adventurous, playful, melancholic, etc.), **target audience**, and other **dramatic devices** that might be relevant to understand the general story experience and structure (for instance, using an anthology structure, several playable avatars, unreliable narrator, surrealism, many flashbacks, etc.).

For the genre and tone, it's often helpful to suggest a few **comparable existing properties**, such as other games, movies, or books. They don't all need to be mainstream media, but it's always easier when the intended audience for this document (usually other team members or stakeholders) actually knows what you mean with your comparison. You can make things easier for you and your team by adding example screenshots and creating reference- and moodboards.

A **target audience** can be defined by the types of games they usually play (genre and platform), the types of stories they like to consume, whether they're fans of specific media (like a game series or TV shows), their player types, their motivation to play, their gender, their age range, and the game's age restriction. There are a handful of player-type taxonomies that help to define *player types*, and your company probably has their own as well. A popular and well-known example is **Richard Bartle's taxonomy of player types**[2]: Socializers, Explorers, Achievers, and Killers.

When it comes to defining which **player motivation** you want to cater to, **Quantic Foundry's Gamer Motivation**[3] system has defined different player motivations in the following categories: Action (Destruction or Excitement), Social (Competition or Community), Mastery (Challenge or Strategy), Achievement (Completion or Power), Immersion (Fantasy or Story) and Creativity (Design or Discovery).

It's always a good idea to research **age restriction guidelines** of your release countries and platforms, so you know which topics and language restrictions will allow you to receive the intended game rating.

ADDITIONAL STYLE DOCUMENTS

Lexicon/Glossary

Every game has a list of key words that will show up over and over again. Those can be related to the story (such as factions or locations), or the game mechanics (such as weapons, skills, or feature names). Therefore, it is essential to create a comprehensive (living) list of all the idiosyncratic terminologies in your game, to make sure that everyone on the team uses the same words. This is especially relevant for any in-game texts, but also useful for team-internal communication during development. It often happens that you rename game elements that are already established within your genre, to be something more appropriate to your game's world, but this makes it all the more likely that team members use the more genre-established term and later mix things up.

And while it's often the case that you'll go through development with internal names, which aren't meant to represent the final in-game terms, it's important to record both of them (likely in the same document), to facilitate understanding and make sure the final terms in the game are all what they should be. For example, a soft currency may be gold, credits, or bells. A playable character with unique gameplay may be a hero, a champion, or a survivor. A guild may be a team, army, or gang. As you see, all these example terms carry different meanings, despite referring to the same type of gameplay feature – and might be called something different during development. Keep in mind that they must fit your in-game universe, for the sake of immersion, coherency and as a little bit of extra narrative. And don't worry about changing this document over the course of pre-production (and production!), as long as it keeps up to date and your most recent changes will end up in the final release of the game.

In short, a lexicon should usually contain the internal name, the final in-game name, and a description of the term (and where it's used).

UI Guidelines

In collaboration with your UI team, you're at one point going to have to determine format and character count restrictions for various text displays inside the game. For example, if there's a tooltip pop-up, you're only going to have so much space, and it's a much better approach to have a defined character count before you write the bulk of your text, rather than seeing through trial and error that none of your written texts fit the boxes. Writing a few examples and making UI mock-ups with them usually helps to come to the right guidelines. And as common good practice, shorter is usually better. Common text displays would be dialogue boxes, speech bubbles, information pop-ups, weapon/item/skill names and descriptions, character/enemy/animal/area names and descriptions, collectible documents, tooltips and other interface texts.

NARRATIVE PILLARS

Your *narrative pillars* are the narrative features that are going to shape the core experience of the players. There will likely be more narrative features and systems, but those will be defined in the narrative design document or narrative system design document, rather than here. Think of it as the overview, which defines the most important core aspects of your narrative systems only. You should ideally narrow it down to your three to five *most important narrative pillars*. This will help build up the narrative systems around them, in order to expand and enhance them. Those pillars should align with the game's gameplay pillars, and put a narrative emphasis on core game systems and themes expressed through gameplay. Understand what the gameplay is trying to do in terms of experience, and then find narrative systems that support and enhance this. These narrative pillars are important for understanding the main idea of the game's storytelling structure and being able to pitch this idea to other team members and stakeholders, in a short time.

Your game's narrative pillars could be, for example:

- A dramatic mission-driven cinematic main story, humorous side stories, and a living world that can be freely explored. (Open World Game Example).
- Choice-driven visual novel dialogues, character-focused romantic paths and unlockable items with descriptions that reveal further information. (Dating Sim Example).
- Several playable characters with their own gameplay and multiple outfits, unlockable character stories with three cutscenes each, which are unlocked by defeating enemies as that character and fight taunts between specific characters that reveal their relationship with each other. (Beat'em'Up Example).

These pillars should clarify your main method of delivering the story, whether it's through explicit scenarios in a plot progression, implied scenarios through dramatic changes in the game, or through narrative-infused content – or a mix of all.

- **Explicit Scenarios** are dramatic story arcs with a progression, such as missions, dialogues or cutscenes. Similar to TV shows, they convey a dramatic plot in the form of episodic storytelling, or function as self-contained short stories. Players usually play an active part in driving these stories forward – either by playing as a character inside the story and driving the plot through their actions or by unlocking new plot beats for characters they accompany on their journey.
- **Implied Scenarios** are dramatic changes in the game with narrative implications, such as environmental, visual, or gameplay changes over time. They imply a narrative progression, but they're not dialogue- or plot-driven. Through observation of circumstances, players can infer changes within the world, may those be driven by the passage of time or their own actions.
- **Narrative-infused Content** is when game elements express narrative meaning in the way they are designed (functionally and aesthetically) and described. Such elements can be characters, environments, skins, items, gameplay, or any other part of the game. They can either expand the narrative of explicit or implied scenarios, or provide general lore revelations about the game's world and backstory.

NARRATIVE SYSTEMS

The narrative system of a game is the framework that defines *how* you want to tell the story, so, which formats you want to use for which purpose at which point in time. It's an architectural framework of narrative tools, their form, their dependencies, their triggers, their pacing, and their purpose. As will be illustrated in *Chapter 11*, we have a lot of tools to draw from. During the early development of your live game, you plan the state in which your game will be launched, serving as the basis of future expansions. This means that you should implement most, if not all, narrative systems of your game. You can, of course, add new systems during live operations, but this might create challenges in terms of balancing, pacing, changing the player experience too much, and keeping up with development deadlines. It is likely that new narrative systems, added after release, are connected to self-contained new features or expansions.

In order to record your narrative system design, you create a *Narrative Design Vision Document* first (for the general intention), and a *Narrative System Design Document* later (going into the details of all your features and systems). Eventually, you should lay out every narrative feature, system, and dependency. A *Narrative System Design Document* functions much like a Game Design Document, but only focuses on the narrative aspect of your project. This document could be a text document with images, of course, but this will quickly become overwhelming and hard to keep track of. It can be helpful to create a design document as a slideshow presentation, as this helps to keep things short and sweet, separates features and topics nicely, enables you to use ample visualizations, mock-ups, and graphs, and will be easier to present it to the team. Another popular choice is a virtual whiteboard that can be endlessly scaled.

For more detailed information about narrative system design and its documentation, see Chapter 11.

LIVE NARRATIVE INTENTIONS

After you've created the narrative systems of your base game, which will be ready for launch, you need to plan the framework of your upcoming releases as well. In order to estimate your production times and budget on the one hand, and your narrative opportunities on the other hand, this needs to be defined long before launch. These expansions can also include the introduction of new narrative systems (but this needs to be planned and tested carefully).

An example for new narrative systems would be to add character-based sequential unlockable missions, when this wasn't part of the game before.

An example for adding new seasonal content, based on your established base systems, would be releasing more characters with their own sequential unlockable mission when the feature already existed.

Popular ways of structuring your live narrative content are adding new chapters within an ongoing story, adding self-contained side stories or narrative-infused game elements that tell an implicit, rather than an explicit story, often aided by explanatory season trailers.

For more detailed information about planning and writing your live narrative design, see Chapters 12 and 13.

SUMMARY

- A **narrative vision document** creates the narrative foundation for a live game, and may contain:
  - Story Overview
  - Core Fantasy, Themes and Conflicts
  - Setting and Worldbuilding
  - Central Characters
  - Avatar
  - Narrative Perspective
  - Tone, Target Audience, and Age Rating
  - Additional Style Documents
  - Narrative Pillars
  - Narrative Systems
  - Live Narrative Intentions
- There are **story overviews** of various lengths and levels of detail – logline (short), synopsis (longer) and outline (the longest).
- **Story flowcharts** and **character growth charts** can be another useful tool to create a story overview.
- A **game's core fantasy** is the promise of experience you give to the players and remains static over time.
- A **game's themes** are the topics that are explored in its stories and gameplay (which can be shifted over the course of the game's live operations, and used as a means to structure seasons).
- A **game's core conflict** defines what drives its plot and action throughout its lifetime.
- When you **build your setting and world**, you should consider natural laws, cosmology, geography, ecology, architecture, people and social groups, religion and culture, politics (government structures, parties, etc.), crime, economy, technology, language, the current state, and the history of the world.
- You can approach worldbuilding **top–down** (start broad, then go into details) **or bottom–up** (start specific, then expand).
- When building a **cast of characters**, consider:
  - Diversity
  - If important characters are complex, interesting, and engaging
  - If characters have diverse ideological standpoints
  - Relationships between characters
  - The cast's potential for drama and comedy

- – The narrative function of each character
- – The role of the players
- Additional useful documents are **character profiles and relationship graphs.**
- The representation of an **avatar** can be...
  - – No avatar
  - – A companion character
  - – An embodied character
  - – A customizable persona
  - – Customizable cosmetics
  - – Several playable characters
- Additionally, it can be...
  - – Diagetic or non–diagetic
  - – Directly controlled or indirectly controlled
  - – With no personal agency or with personal agency
  - – A scripted character or a blank character
  - – With defined visuals or customizable visuals
  - – A singular avatar or multiple avatars
  - – Steady or shifting
- The **narrative perspective** defines the player's relation to the avatar and the game world. It consists of...
  - – Point–of–View
  - – Player Role
  - – Form of Address
- Defining your game's **tone, target audience, and age rating** is important for making creative decisions that support this direction.
- Additional style documents, like **lexicons and UI guidelines**, help keep things consistent over time.
- The **narrative pillars** give an overview of the most important narrative features that will shape the core experience of the player.
- Live narratives can tell stories using **explicit scenarios, implied scenarios**, or **narrative–infused content**.
- The **narrative system** defines *how* you want to tell the story, with which tools, and in what format.
- Your **live narrative intentions** define how you plan to expand the story over the course of its live operations.

REFERENCES

1 Gérard Genette, *Narrative Discourse: An Essay in Method*, Cornell University Press, 1980.
2 Richard Bartle, "Hearts, Clubs, Diamonds, Spades: Players who suit MUDs," April 1996, https://mud.co.uk/richard/hcds.htm.
3 "Gamer Motivation Model," Quantic Foundry, accessed April 20, 2023, https://quantic-foundry.com/wp-content/uploads/2019/04/Gamer-Motivation-Model-Reference.pdf.

BIBLIOGRAPHY

Ross Berger, *Dramatic Storytelling & Narrative Design: A Writer's Guide to Video Games and Transmedia*, CRC Press, August 27, 2020.

Tobias Heussner, Toiya Kristen Finley, Jennifer Brandes Hepler, and Ann Lemay, *The Game Narrative Toolbox*, Focal Press, 2015.

11 Narrative Tools

In this chapter, we'll take a look at the many exciting tools you can use to build your live game's narrative packages. They are the same you'd use to build your base game, but we will put a special emphasis on their potential for expansions and seasonal content that comes after the initial release. Consider this a toolbox of inspiration, and a way to remind yourself of your game's narrative opportunities. Depending on your project and narrative intentions, some of these tools will be central to your narrative design, while others are only minor or don't even appear at all. Which is which will be based on the project's genre, game design and your creative decisions. As a general rule, it makes sense to choose narrative tools that can support and work in tandem with your game systems, rather than exist separate from them. Whatever is core to your game's player's experience should be supported with the according narrative systems.

STORY AND PLOT AS NARRATIVE

Starting with the most obvious, you can tell your game's story through the use of story and plot in combination with gameplay. They can be expressed through a series of cutscenes, interactive scripted events, narrative-driven missions, visual novel dialogues, discoverable documents, and more. The idea stays similar: Using drama and screenwriting in order to tell a story that you can follow (or embody) by playing the game.

When it comes to live games, the most ambitious form of this would be to create **seasonal stories** akin to a TV show. This ambitious concept offers players a series of episodes, grouped in season arcs, which are (normally) attached to game seasons. These story arcs can potentially be sequential and continue to follow characters of previous seasons while introducing a new overarching story arc that allows new players a new point of entry.

Instead of one seasonal story, you might want to choose to have several different **parallel stories** that players can pursue, too. They can be attached to parts of the game, such as characters, areas, or roles. They can show a similar structure to a seasonal story, but usually have more streamlined focus, since they share a space with other stories that ran parallel with another point of view. This is relevant for games that might want to have progressions tied to characters, roles, game features, or factions. In content release packages, you can add new parallel stories and their attached content.

There's also the option of adding new **side stories** which are short stories tied to the game world, but stay independent of the main story arc. Those can be considered as spin-offs, having an even narrower focus. They are optional stories that players get in addition to a main story or parallel stories.

You will see more about main stories, parallel stories, and side stories in the later section, *Progression Design*, which naturally overlaps with the topic.

DOI: 10.1201/9781003297628-15

But story as narrative in a live game can also be more simplified than that, such as a **story context** for new releases that functions as an introduction to the new conflict, themes, and settings for the season or content release, without making use of any plot progression at all. This often takes the shape of a season or content release trailer, a short video to introduce the themes and game content, as well possible conflicts and central characters. Trailers aren't the only way to give context, though. It can also be depicted through the use of other marketing tools or the visual, functional and textual depiction of added content. The plot evolution isn't happening within a season in this case, but from season to season – though the connections can sometimes be fairly loose, with a lot of room for interpretation.

Another option is the release of **document packages** – new character biographies, letters, logs, collectibles, or whatever else you chose to expand your lore with. They can be attached to a chronological progression or more of a collection rather than a sequence, like in Dead By Daylight. It can even be a bit of both: A collection of several sequential documents can tackle different types of stories, such as a series of letters from one character, combined with a series of reports from a detective, and a handful of local legends taken from old books. Story as narrative can, therefore, take a plot-driven and/or a story-collection approach.

For more detailed information about writing the plot of a live game, read Chapter 13.

ADDITIONAL TEXTS AS NARRATIVE

There are texts in games that are not plot - or story-driven, but rather, interface texts, names, descriptions and other documents. Your narrative can be expressed in the way things are named and described – feeding into the general mood, revealing lore and expanding the player's understanding of the world. This can be as small as the naming and description of a weapon or a skill, or as expansive as descriptions of locations, enemies and animals. Texts and documents can be a source of seasonal narrative, too. When you release a package of items, weapons, or skins, their naming and descriptions can tie into the seasonal story, or expand the game's story in other ways. You can also add new documents that expand the game's lore, such as descriptions of regions, creatures, enemies, and more.

PROGRESSION DESIGN AS NARRATIVE

Pick the first classic video game story you can think of. Chances are, it's about achieving a goal by becoming better and traversing locations to reach it – personally and geographically. Video games are usually driven by progression systems, and narrative drama emerges naturally while players play through them. Progressions are inherently dramatic, as they imply a goal and a way to get there, even if they're not purposefully embellished by explicit narrative features, such as cutscenes. Consequently, designing your progression is likely going to be one of your core narrative features, no matter which type of game you're making. A progression can be tied to unlocking narrative units, such as cutscenes, new objectives, barks, or documents, but it can also stand on its own, telling a story through its objectives, systems, and player actions alone. After all, a goal plus obstacles plus taking action equals drama.

Being an interactive medium, a video game can have more than one single progression, especially when you have a live game with many different features, seasonal content, and live events. And a progression is usually composed of smaller units, either a series of quests or missions, or milestones along the progression. In live games, progressions are usually tied to a feature, to make it meaningful and reward players when they interact with it.

Progression designs are defined by their **importance, necessity and accessibility.** They can fall into different categories for each of those elements:

- **Importance:** Main, parallel, or side progression
- **Necessity:** Obligatory or optional content
- **Accessibility:** Permanent or temporary availability

MAIN PROGRESSIONS

Your main story should be attached to your main progression and core gameplay because this is the content that most players are going to see. You want players to see the central story where they're going, and not somewhere off the beaten path, where they'll never find it. Of course, you can and should have interesting narrative on the side as well, to encourage exploration, player freedom, and nonlinear experiences, but this is a matter of both cost-effectiveness (invest the most time and money into the content that is seen by most players) and readability of the narrative (provide the most important narrative to the most players). If you need players to see it, put it on a progression tied to core gameplay and/or main progression. The same applies to making the most important narrative content obligatory and permanent, rather than optional and temporary – although a seasonal live game may choose to make all main progressions temporary (seasonal), in order to create a constantly evolving story. In a live game, this main progression could be tied to the seasonal game pass, another seasonal main progression, or permanent onboarding missions (or several of these options).

PARALLEL PROGRESSIONS

You can also have more than one main story progression, by offering several parallel progressions with similar narrative weight. This can either be employed *instead of* or *in addition to* a main progression. A parallel progression can be tied to locations, playing as specific characters, fulfilling missions for specific characters, or playing specific modes – just to name a few examples. This allows for some player freedom in regards to in what order they consume the provided narrative in, and can shed narrative light on specific aspects of the game world (locations, characters, groups, sides in a conflict, etc.). This influences the structure and meaning of your story and can serve as a literary device. If your story is about the many perspectives on war, having several progressions that focus on different affected characters and point of views can help you tell that story. Several progressions also allow us to reward several different game aspects (such as modes or features) independently, in order to encourage a varied interaction with all features of the game. This also provides a level of freedom to players, allowing them to choose which features to interact with (and getting rewarded for all of them), which progressions to start with and which order to play them in, such as various roles that can be leveled up. Parallel progressions also allow players a fresh narrative start and a new entry point into the narrative – in live games, this can become more and more relevant, because you might *not* want to add all your new content at the end of one single story progression, and only cater to end-of-content players this way, leaving the rest standing in the metaphorical rain. New parallel progressions can be a new starting point accessible for everyone.

Examples in live games would be progressions tied to playing as specific playable characters (Identity V), classes (Red Dead Online), or groups (D4DJ).

SIDE PROGRESSIONS

You can also create side progressions, such as side missions/stories, spin-offs, event stories, time-limited content or live events. Especially for live events, which players only have very little time to complete, a self-contained side story tied to a temporary side progression can be an interesting part of your live strategy. Side stories can serve as self-contained short stories (or several connected short stories) that narrow their focus on a specific part of the game world and narrative. They can serve as an optionally available expansion of an element mentioned during a main progression, or something otherwise hinted at in the game world. This narrative expansion usually reveals more about side conflicts of your main character, specific characters, regions, events in time, or even game features. They can even be *"what if"* scenarios. This enables you, as the narrative designer, to deepen your worldbuilding and characterization beyond the dramatic pacing of your main progression. Players can actively choose to pursue deeper knowledge of the game world where their curiosity takes them. Side stories are often optional, and not obligatory for the main progression, and can therefore differ in tone, structure, and focus as well. They can be more lighthearted, strange, or comedic, for example (but don't have to be). The Yakuza (*Ryu Ga Gotoku*) games are famous for going that route – while the main progression is a serious crime drama with only occasional humor, the side missions are often playful, absurd, and comedic.

HOW PROGRESSIONS CAN CONVEY NARRATIVE

Now that we got ourselves an overview of the dramatic uses of progressions, let's take a look at how progressions can convey a story. On the one hand, they can be connected to obvious devices for plot-driven storytelling, such as cutscenes, barks, and other story milestones players unlock and experience along the way. But ideally, you'd be able to work with both layers of a progression: The narrative units attached to the progression *and* the progression's design itself.

Progressions are inherently dramatic because they present a conflict, a goal, and a series of actions taken towards that goal. But the design specifics of a progression also influence how players perceive and categorize the game world and their own actions within it – what is the narrative framing for their actions, and what do they result in? If you take all design aspects of your progression as a whole, they express something about the themes and conflicts in your game, and their characters' roles in them.

The following elements influence the **narrative implications of a progression system**, and should be purposeful design choices:

- **Theme** (e.g., revenge, heroism, grief, following your dreams, fighting for love, etc.)
- **Conflict, Goal, and Purpose** (e.g., rescue the princess, kill the big bad, become stronger, discover all regions, help random citizens, collect all weapons, win someone's heart, etc.)
- Is it a **Main Progression** (obligatory), **Parallel Progression** (alternate path, simultaneous with main progression), **or Side Progression** (optional)?
- **Objectives and How to Progress** (e.g., finish main missions, discover specific places, craft objects, gain XP with a specific character or in a specific region, win matches, etc.)
- **Connected Gameplay and Actions** (e.g., general gameplay, specific mission types, specific game features, collections, using specific characters, playing in specific areas, etc.)
- **Progression Markers and Feedback** (e.g., cutscenes, barks, dialogues, new objectives, visual effects, etc.)
- **Rewards and Results** (gameplay rewards (items, cosmetics, characters), new missions, new areas, new gameplay, game & story consequences, etc.)
- **Challenge Level and Progression Speed** (Is it challenging or easy? Quick or slow? How long will it take until it's finished? Is this a focused mission or something you do on the side?)
- **Connected Character** (e.g., playable characters, companions, NPCs, enemies, etc.)
- **Connected Game Features** (e.g., roles, classes, weapons, game modes, etc.)

EXAMPLE PROGRESSION SYSTEMS

In order to get a better grasp of how these elements could be combined, and how that might look in-game, let's take a look at **a few established example progression systems.**

- **Player XP Progressions:** You unlock beats of the progression through *Experience Points* gained by playing the game, winning matches, and/or completing a list of objectives – not tied to specific playable characters or features, but only the player's general game activity. This implies that players have a variety of ways to progress simply by playing the game, making this a popular candidate for main progressions. This type of progression is often found in match-based live games and is often tied to seasons (such as Battle Passes or Season Passes). *Example:* Dead by Daylight.
- **Feature Progressions:** You unlock beats of the progression through Experience Points gained by playing a specific part of the game only. Similar to Player XP Progressions, they're usually more useful for parallel progressions (several stories for different features) and side progressions, especially when it comes to time-limited live events that are only available for a limited time. *Examples:* D4DJ and Candy Crush Friends.
- **Quest Progressions:** You unlock beats of the progression by completing a specific set of tasks, with some level of chronological dependencies (meaning, you have to play specific quests before you can move on to the next ones). This

type of progression can be useful for linear narrative progressions with narrative-driven gameplay, for example, player onboarding, seasonal content, or a new story or location to discover in a DLC expansion. These quest progressions can be tied to a specific location or quest type as well, so that players can discover several parallel stories as quest progressions, sorted into different categories. *Examples:* Red Dead Online, Destiny 2, and World of Warcraft.

- **Character Progressions:** You unlock beats of the progression by *playing* as a specific character (avatar) or completing objectives *relating to* a specific character (NPC or companion). If tied to playing as a character, it can either make use of pre-made heroes (or champions) with their own inner life and story to tell, or the player's own customized characters. If it is tied to playing as a specific character, the progression can explore their individual story (who they are, their conflict, their goals, their desires, etc.), and with several playable characters, you can have parallel progressions that work this way. With customized characters, the written story may depend on an aspect that the player has chosen for their avatar, such as personality, race, class, or job. *Examples:* Genshin Impact and Mighty Quest Rogue Palace.

- **Location Progression:** You unlock beats of the progression by playing in a specific location. This can either be tied to the missions within a specific area (such as a village, region, or realm) or include any kind of side activity too. These locations usually come with their unique set of aesthetics, characters, and stories, as well as a self-contained arc. In Far Cry 5, for example, every XP you gain within one of the regions fills up a region progression bar. Main missions give you the most XP, but side missions and additional activity fills up that bar as well, giving players a certain level of freedom. Throughout the progression, there are three milestones which trigger that the player will be abducted by the *"Herald"* of the region, throwing them into a cutscene and unique mission – when all milestones of a region have been triggered, and the final boss fight of the progression has been won, the region counts as completed, and the story arc with that character as finished (ending in their death). Players can jump from region to region and don't have to complete a progression before they begin another – they can progress in parallel. *Examples:* Far Cry 5.

- **Role Progressions:** You unlock beats of the progression by playing as a specific class, job, role, or morality alignment. To better differentiate role progression from character progression, it's important to understand that role progressions may allow you to play the same character while adapting another role over the course of the game. A role would usually contain a set of gameplay, character abilities, activities, and missions and often also unique visual attributes such as outfits – as well as a story progression immediately tied to the meaning of this affiliation. These roles can either be purposefully chosen or gained through gameplay (like a morality system that unlocks "good" and "evil" role progressions).

In Red Dead Online, players can purchase and unlock *roles* with their own abilities, items, missions and activities attached to them, such as Bounty Hunter, Trader, and Moonshiner. Additionally, onboarding missions (called Honor Missions) separate you into two possible parallel progressions, as either an Outlaw or a Gunslinger, depending on your moral choices during those onboarding missions. *Examples:* Star Wars: The Old Republic and Red Dead Online.

- **Real-Time Progressions:** You witness beats of the progression by participating in the game over a period of time. This progression is uniquely relevant to live games and not tied to player actions, but rather, time passing in real-time. A season progresses whether the player plays or not, so at specific dates, new tasks or events may become available, such as live events or time-limited events, that drive a story forward. They do not depend on the player completing anything – they just need to wait and be around for it. As a narrative designer for live games, you can decide to drive a progression like that, like a TV broadcast, tied to the passage of time. You can find this type of progression in live events (where players participate in an event as it takes place), like in Fortnite season finales, but also in other types of games. On the other hand, some mobile games include waiting periods, where the passage of time unlocks a new episode of content, rather than progressing by playing the game. This can be found in time management and strategy games, but also some narrative-driven and seasonal games, where your new episode becomes playable after you wait a certain period of time. An interesting example for that is the dating sim Mystic Messenger, where new story chapters (chatrooms, text messages, and phone calls) unlock at specific times of the day, making the player participate in a 12-day-long story in real time. When they enter a chatroom, they make choices that influence the story, and they can only progress by interacting with the timed content. *Examples:* Mystic Messenger and The Ssum: Forbidden Lab.

To summarize, progressions can provide a big variety of ways in which stories can be unlocked and experienced by players and can provide satisfying big chunks of seasonal releases. These new release packages can add new progressions, tied to new features, new areas, new playable characters or NPCs, new roles, and more. This can either remain a permanent addition, providing a new entry point into a story, or a time-limited addition for the season or a live event.

QUEST DESIGN AS NARRATIVE

Quests (ideally) aren't only tasks and chores that the player ticks off on a list. They are conflicts that need to be solved by the player, and as they take actions to progress towards a goal, they inherently experience drama. But in this case, the player are a core-essential part of driving this plot forward. Action is narrative, which means that the actions and goals we suggest to the players are also a part of narrative (even if we stripped away any kind of obvious 'narrative framing' such as quest givers or cutscenes). Quests can have several different narrative intentions and strengths. They can be a game designer's tool to guide players to do something they'd find enriching, encouraging exploration of worlds, learning and mastery of gameplay, or narrative revelations that deepen the emotional bond with the game's characters. Quests can take many different forms, but they should be a reflection or extension of the game's themes, core conflicts and narrative intentions. Even when they're side quests.

Purposes of Quests

The general **purpose of quests** usually falls into one or several of these categories:

- As a **Tutorial** tasks that introduce the player to new gameplay
- To provide training towards **Mastery** offering challenges that encourage the player to master the gameplay
- As **Game Progression** guiding the player towards the game's completion, or by giving out rewards that make the player stronger or otherwise better
- To encourage **Exploration** pointing out and rewarding additional ways to interact with the game and the exploration of settings in the game world
- For **Narrative Purposes** (expressing something about the game world and its characters)

Narrative Intentions of Quests

No matter what purpose a quest serves, it always has a narrative layer. Even if its main purpose wasn't to be plot-driven, a quest's design, narrative design and framing is still going to convey a narrative intent. Therefore, you need to consider its **narrative intentions**[1]:

- **(Short) Storytelling:** A quest can be a short story in itself, telling us something about the protagonist, the game world, a specific character, a specific event, or anything you want. It can be treated as a short story embedded within the grander arc of things, and you can use it to expand your game's universe in the shape of a short story that either works as a self-contained unit or is part of a bigger progression (both main or side). A quest always contains a set-up, a goal, and objectives along the way – functioning as a dramatic arc with three (or more) acts.
- **Exploration:** Quests can also be used to guide players towards exploring aspects of the game world, either physically, emotionally, or in relation to gameplay. When physical exploration is encouraged, players are guided to **locations** to engage with local environmental storytelling, possibly even gaining additional information about the visuals through their own actions, barks, cutscenes, or documents. In relation to **gameplay**, explorative quests can encourage players to engage with character abilities and game systems in a way they might not have done before. This either helps them to understand the narrative meaning of these features (game systems have inherent meaning through their implications about the world and the avatar) or allows them to see in a new light, making them more narratively complex than before.
- **Characterization:** Quests can also serve as a way to characterize the game world, its characters, and the avatar. Through its use of theme, conflict, and its solution, we find out something about everyone involved and the kind of environment they are in. Think of stealing cars in a crime-ridden urban world. Think of killing monsters in scary dungeons. Think of crafting cute clothes to gift to your neighbors. Quests inherently tell us something about all involved characters: Where are they now? What do they want? What

actions are they taking to get it? And what does that tell us about them? The solutions that characters resort to say something about who they are, after all. Is the quest focused on violence, exploration, strategy, stealth, collaboration, assistance, decoration, etc? A quest should always express something about the questgiver, playable character, *and* the world they're in. Even when there's no personified quest giver – actions have inherent narrative drama.

- **An Extension of the Game's Themes**: Even if they're a self-contained experience, individual quests need to match or extend the themes of the game as whole. They can tackle sub-themes, subplots, or related themes – but should never be at odds with it. That doesn't mean that they can't have a different tone and focus, especially when it comes to side quests or quests grouped under a specific feature, but there is such a thing as straying too far from the game's core identity. A game usually has a few main themes that it strives to explore, through story and gameplay – often connecting specific game loops with specific themes. Such themes can be collaboration, wonder, friendship, purpose, faith, technology vs. humanity, man vs. nature, etc. These themes should be found in the main storyline and feed the core gameplay loops. But the individual quests, the moment-to-moment game experience, should also reflect these larger story themes. For example: The Uncharted series has three distinct types of gameplay, defined by specific tones and themes, that are represented in different game loops: *Exploration* (when you walk through exotic locations), *Action* (when you fight against enemies) and *Mystery* (when you solve environmental puzzles). Every quest falls into one of these categories, and as such, an expansion of the game's themes of awe, exploration, mystery, curiosity, and greed.

WRITING QUESTS

The next question is how to write a good quest. As a self-contained narrative experience, it needs to have a three-act story structure (at the least). *Conflict, action, resolution.* Longer quest progressions will, of course, have more steps than that, but they usually fall into the *action* part of this separation. This is because *conflict* is the set-up before the player takes on the challenge, and the *resolution* is the result and reward after the player succeeded.

1. **Conflict:** The briefing phase. This phase can contain quest givers talking to the player, but might also just be a new log entry, or an introduction of a specific goal. In this phase, the player needs to become aware of a conflict and that they're the one meant to solve it. This includes the current state of the world, the central conflict, and the steps that need to be taken in order to solve this conflict – or at least the goal and the *first* step. This part should also include emotional stakes, who this quest concerns and why. Think about the avatar's personal stake and emotional involvement, as well. These set-ups can be of varying emotional intensity, depending on your game, and where in the game they show up. Sometimes low-stakes quests can be a way to relax after a high-stakes quest, or a side quest that allows players to wind down. A quest about just picking up some berries is less suspenseful and

urgent than, for example, finding a lost child in the woods, lest it will be eaten by wild wolves. Unless the berries are set up to have high emotional value of course (as the last wish for a snack of a dying old woman, for example). In short, clarify to the player what the conflict is, how they're meant to solve it (first steps and final goal), and why they should care, including implied consequences and rewards for doing or not doing it.

2. **Action:** The gameplay phase. This is the part where the player takes action to solve the conflict. They go to places, find things, deliver things, solve puzzles, kill enemies, and so on. This plot point is executed by the player, and driven by player action and gameplay. It might have multiple steps, which might act as smaller tension arcs inside of this phase. During the action, players might be further guided through barks, triggered moments, updated mission logs, cutscenes, and more.

3. **Resolution:** The reward phase. After completing the quest, there needs to be a resolution. The players need to become aware of the meaning of their actions in this world, to feel like they had an effect on it, to ensure a sense of agency. Why else would they have done it? This can be as extensive as a cutscene showing the effects of the player's actions, and how it solved the problem – or as small as a pop-up showing the player their rewards. Quests can also have longer-lasting effects in the game world, on the avatar itself, or feedbacked in the story or the environment. They need to see the result of their actions *somehow*, even if it's just an audiovisual effect or seeing a dead enemy on the ground.

NARRATIVE DESIGN FOR QUESTS

And lastly, it's important to be aware of the narrative design tools at your disposal when creating a quest. The story arc isn't the only narrative aspect of a quest, after all. You can infuse narrative meaning through other elements, such as:

- Who is the **quest giver**? How do they look and act? What's their place in the world? How are they related to the quest? How does the quest giver change our perception of what we're asked to do? Have we been asked by a shady criminal, an innocent child, or a whimsical magic bear?
- Where are we accepting this task? What is the **location and the framework** for accepting the task? Did we find a clue in a cave? Are we taking a wanted poster from a sheriff's office? Are we following mysterious text messages sent to our phone?
- What is the **gameplay** of the task? Which actions will we take? How does this express the questgiver's and avatar's personal views on how things should be solved in the world?
- Do we have **choices** regarding how to solve the objective? The choices offered to us tell us as much as the choice that we actually pick. It implies something about the playable character, the game as a whole, and the world it's set in. For example, if we can be stealthy or run in guns blazing, it sets the thematic tone of cleverness vs. brute force, which should, ideally, be part of the main story's themes as well. If we can decide to kill monsters or recruit monsters, it sets the thematic tone of violence vs. friendship. If we

can decide to rescue or leave prisoners on a mission to prevent a terrorist attack, it sets the thematic tone of hard decisions made during warfare.

- What is the promised **reward** of the task? And what is its meaning in the game world, to the questgiver and to the avatar? After all, it makes a big narrative difference if you're promised mountains of gold, some delicious apples, or the fellowship of a new party member.
- What does the **visual and sound design** tell us about the nature of the quest? Are there any narrative implication about the quest's origin, nature and purpose? What is the tone, the mood, or any cultural, historical, or artistic affiliations?
- What are the **consequences of our actions**? How have the world and other characters changed after we have completed the task? For example, If we defeated an evil monster, maybe the villagers are now peacefully walking around the village again, instead of hiding in their homes. Or after you cleared some corruption of the land, flowers start to bloom again. Or after you've committed an immoral act, the people of that town will start to treat you with suspicion.

In summary, to create a story-driven quest, you should imbue it with a game purpose (such as tutorial, mastery, game progression, exploration or narrative) narrative intention (such as storytelling, characterization, exploration, or as a reflection of the game's main themes), give it a 3-act structure (conflict – action – resolution), and make use of as many narrative tools as you have at your disposal. Quests aren't only tasks with a bit of flavor text added to them. The story is conveyed through the player's actions and all other design elements of the quest – so much so that a traditional *questgiver dialogue* isn't even obligatory for a quest to have narrative meaning. Also, quests are often part of a bigger progression, which means that a set of quests often come together to exist within a larger meaning, and can gain more meaning as a whole than they have on their own.

ENVIRONMENT AS NARRATIVE

Environmental storytelling, as a term, is often used in a specific way. Popular examples will refer to the creation of mise-en-scène arrangements that tell the tale of a specific scene that has happened before the player has arrived. It's important to remember that this isn't the only way in which environment can tell a story because it limits the actual possibilities of environmental narrative. Game environments are inherently narrative-driven, in their visual design, architecture, navigability, and props. They are created with purpose and can provide players with insights about the game's world, its rules, its past, its characters, their actions, and values. Visual design choices should imply a place's most recent function and history, taking into account human planning, after effects of events, and natural influences. This often takes the form of narrative layers, which build upon one another, and can combine many different time periods into one current snapshot (a building might have been a church in the past but is a hideout for bandits now, for example). The environment of a game is generally crucial for the contextualization of gameplay. Whatever the player does, its purpose and interpretation will be influenced by where they do it – the context. Especially for games that are more gameplay-driven, this becomes a crucial way of storytelling and worldbuilding.

The layers of environmental narrative can be categorized in the following way:

- **Environmental and Geographical Factors:** An environment's foundation lies in the setting before any outside influence – its natural state and geographical conditions, such as geology, flora, fauna, and weather conditions. Any human influence and construction comes after these natural givens, and they are a direct reaction to what the environment has given them, and what they, themselves, can make of it. Also consider how these environmental factors have influenced the setting over a long period of time, and how they are visible now – for example, a wet environment might have caused abandoned buildings to build up mold and rot away. A hot desert environment might have buried a building half-way underneath sand, and worn away at paint. These environmental factors may have changed over time, but there are still visual hints at the past.
- **Man-Made Structures and City Planning:** When your environment contains structures created by man (or other beings of your game universe), they must be a reaction to the natural and social circumstances. Hot, humid temperatures demand another architecture than cold, dry temperatures, and your worldbuilding should strive to create logical holistic settings where everything seems like a logical consequence of the given factors, needs, cultural and technical advancements. Then, there's the social purpose of a building, a function they're meant to fulfill. This might even shift over time: What used to be an old sports stadium may now be used as a hideout from zombies, for example. All of this can be made visual in the current design and state of the building. When you design a building, consider their function, and the circumstances of construction – visuals (such as architecture and aesthetics) can reveal something about the people who constructed it, which time period they're from, as well as their culture, ideals, circumstances, and budget. After that, consider how the building has changed over time – how old or new is it? Is it in use, abandoned or restructured? A building might also be a patchwork of different time periods, echoing destruction, renovation and expansion of existing buildings. A building is never just a building, but it tells a story of culture, history, function, usage, and environmental factors.
- **Social Erosions:** Not all structures were purposefully built by humans, but end up being a part of a culture's environment anyway, just due to the daily lives of the people who live or lived there. An example would be desire paths, these well-trodden paths through forests and plains, taken so often that they're now a permanent, visible fixture. These paths were never planned, but created socially, because they were a shortcut or otherwise desired road that people took until they were forged by 1,000 feet walking across them. Human activity can have a visible influence on nature, architecture, objects, and more. If something has been used often, or been in an extreme event, it will carry this influence with it, unless it gets renovated at some point.
- **Personal Decorations:** A character can be characterized not only through design, action, and dialogue but also through their direct environment and how they choose to shape it. Most commonly, a character's personal room can say a lot about them. Where is their living space – A dingy urban apartment?

A spacious modern mansion up on a hill? And how do they choose to decorate it? Anything from decorative objects to posters and photographs allows the environmental artist to build an impression of who that person is.

- **Situational Remains:** Like in cinema's *mise-en-scène*, a set design can tell a story all by itself, by revealing an event of the past through the display of its after-effects. This type of environmental storytelling is a snapshot of a specific moment in time, rather than a result of long-term factors. Through the use of objects and set dressing, a story is being told. For example: A dinner table set for two, food only half-eaten – one of the chairs is toppled over, and there's a gun shot at the opposite end of the room. This arrangement tells a whole story of what happened here. It can be as simple as putting more trash on the dangerous side of town, or as complex as visual clues that reveal an entire criminal mystery. Situational remains can be great for social and personal narrative, and can even tell short stories through little constructed scenarios.

- **Suggested Mood and Usage:** If you take everything that makes a game environment, including spatial and navigational design, shape, color, sound design, and lighting, as well as connected gameplay and interactivity, you create a mood. An environment can create emotion, meaning, and desire for specific actions just through spatial design alone. Narrow alleyways can create a feeling of danger and alertness while suggesting the player action of stealth. Navigating a dark cave with some suspicious scratches can make you feel curious and nervous, while a few horizontal jagged edges on the wall invite you to climb it and take a look. When you've fought through a dungeon and arrive at a fountain, lit in a cool, calming blue, while the music becomes peaceful and sweet – you know you're invited to rest and recover, possibly finding a health item. An environment gains an additional identity layer through its emotional presentation, and therefore, contextualizes the player's relation to it.

Changing Environments

When it comes to live games in particular, an environment doesn't even have to remain static. It can **change over the seasons**, showing a progression of the world as if it is its own character, either due to outside influences, the passage of time, or even the actions of players in previous seasons. There is potential for implicit narrative, just through changes in the environment alone.

When you want to use environment as a means of storytelling in your live narrative, it can take two distinct forms: **Adding new places** with their own stories, or **letting existing places evolve**. Environments can change over time, no matter if the players are there for it (through playable seasonal activities or live events) or witness the change abruptly with the new content release.

- Areas can **appear, disappear, or move**. Think of an HQ that has been destroyed, a camp that has been relocated, a space ship has been moved, an island that has sunk into the ocean, or even more fantastical reasons like a shift in dimensions. The entire map may even shift due to a catastrophic event. It's also possible to add entirely new areas as a way to group new DLC expansions, stories, and gameplay in a specific location.

- A shift can also be connected to a **change in the ecosystem**, either with nature changing due to its regular weather and seasons (spring, summer, fall, winter – or whatever alien seasons you might have on your game's planet) or out of the ordinary, with natural catastrophes or external influences.
- Individual **locations can change due to the events** that have taken place around them, either on purpose, or on accident. It can be anything from a form of destruction as the aftermath of a conflict to a redecoration or renovation effort of characters. This way, locations can also serve as an expression of progress (e.g., players upgrading their home base) or the echo of a great story milestone.
- More specifically, **locations can be re-purposed** and change due to a shift in their function or ownership. For example, when a building is taken over by a specific faction and has been adjusted to fit their own needs, culture, and aesthetics. This can nicely tie into gameplay changes, modes, and features, which are connected to a specific location. A few more examples: An old train station is now a rebel outpost. A recently collapsed tree is now a nest for small animals. An old airport is now a battle royale arena.
- **Locations can also decay or grow**, either through natural influence, or the actions of characters. For example: A few abandoned cars are now overgrown with moss. A snowy mountain is melting. A faction's HQ has gained a new floor, after a season of construction.
- And on a most temporary level, **signs of recent human, animal, or other activity** can change props and details in a location. This wouldn't be a large change, but rather small changes that imply an event that has recently taken place. For example: A shop has been broken into and looted. An empty room now shows signs of a recent party, with plates, bottles, and trash littered about.

As you can see, there are a lot of ways you can express worldbuilding and narrative events through both static and shifting environments. Even if you're working on a project that doesn't have unlockable story progressions, if you plan on changing your map over the seasons, there is a lot of potential for narrative in that. If you can have both plot and environmental storytelling, they should complement each other, express parts of the same narrative whole, and create something even bigger together.

GAME DESIGN AS NARRATIVE

Something that is exclusive to video game narratives is telling a story through gameplay and game systems. A system can tell a story about the world, its dynamics, relations, and worldviews (of society, the avatar, or narrator). Player actions are a form of *experiential story,* as they engage in an activity to solve a conflict and reach a resolution. It expresses beliefs about the world's social and natural rules, as well as the avatar's perspective on it. After all, our options tell us how the avatar, or their quest givers, thinks such problems should be solved. And the game's systems and their reaction to the player's actions imply narrative meaning as well – the story of how this world works. Game systems are a form of storytelling, and should be treated as such. They express themes, systems, characterization, and express a worldview.

Game Mechanics are the rules by which the player can interact with the game. A mechanic is always tied to a conflict and its resolution and expresses something about the protagonist and their relation to the game world. In a live game, new mechanics can create new ways to play the game, often accompanied by complementary elements such as progressions, areas, or modes where these mechanics are encouraged. Game mechanics that are tied to characters, like their move sets, abilities, and perks can be used to express something about their personality, skills and state of mind. (*For more information, refer to the section: Characters as Narrative.*) Game mechanics that are tied to a specific location, like a level or a region in an open world, express something about their attributes and how the player's avatar reacts to these attributes – for example, movement speed is slower on planets with higher gravity, and so on. In General, each game mechanic attached to specific parts of the game will be part of the characterization of that aspect, may that be a scene in the game, a character, a location, or something else.

Game Systems, on the other hand, describe the laws of the world, and the dependencies and interactions between its actors. Game systems imply a worldview on how things work in life, and define the way players interact with the world, and how their actions are reflected back at them. Adding new game systems in a live game can provide new spaces for emergent gameplay too, with enemy systems, fire systems, dynamic destruction, etc. This can also result in emergent narrative, where the game systems create moments of narrative meanings through their dependencies and interactions between their actors.

Lastly, there is also the possibility of **emergent social narrative** between players. By giving players new ways to interact with one another, and new ways to interact with the game, they can receive an expanded vocabulary of interaction and self-expression. The focus here wouldn't be to create authored content, but to provide more actions relevant to roleplay. Whatever possible actions we provide define the possible space of actions, after all, and expand the potential of emergent player narrative. Some examples would be to offer new emotes, a feature to team up in guilds or to have a photo mode for group photos.

NARRATIVE SYSTEMS AS NARRATIVE

Narrative systems are a subcategory of game systems, which define the logic and dependencies of *how* narrative triggers in your game. The systems are what comes before the text, as they describe the logic, format and intention (how), rather than the final content (what). They deeply define the player's experience of a game story, as they are the framework of how they will be able to unlock and consume it. They can be divided into different variants (whereas all can appear in the same game):

1. **Game Systems** with narrative meaning. They express a perspective on the world through their rules and logic. What do we imply about the world, the player's role within it, and this game's ways of resolving conflict? *Mentioned in the previous section.*
2. **Narrative Systems** that define triggers, dependencies, and formats of narrative units. These systems shape the narrative experience of the player by defining the dramatic structure, defining the focus on specific types of

narrative, and meaningfully connecting player actions to them. Depending on how your narrative system interlinks with the game design, you influence how players perceive the game and their role within it. Narrative systems should be chosen in a way that they go hand in hand with your narrative intentions (what is your game about?) and game intentions (what will the player do?). To give a few examples: If you want your game to have a focus on unique authored playable hero characters, your narrative systems should be designed to emphasize their unique stories and personalities, possibly by attaching personal story progressions to playing as each of them. If you want your game to have a focus on a living world, your narrative systems should be designed to emphasize meaningful interactions with the world and its inhabitants. If you want your game to have a focus on factions, your narrative systems should be designed to emphasize the personalities, actions, and stories of said factions. If you want to focus on an uninterrupted action-driven core loop, you should only place non-disruptive barks in it, and move cutscenes or readable documents to, for example, a meta layer.

3. **Systemic Narratives** that generate narrative through the use of systems. Here, the systems *generate* the narrative experience based on a defined logic, rules and dynamics, rather than just describe the triggers of various authored narrative units. This can be highly interesting for live games that try to create big amounts of content (or even "endless" amounts of content), beyond purely authored content, as well as games with social player-to-player interaction.

   – Procedural Narrative Systems Allow the creation of narrative experiences based on a pre-defined logic and a pool of possible options, with a certain level of randomization. Narrative designers define the intention, format, and logic of these experiences, feed the required options into the system, and then use the procedural system to create a big amount and/or uniquely randomized narrative experiences inside the game. Procedural narrative systems can be for any part of a game. For example: Generated character biographies based on a list of attributes, each with a list of possible options. Generated world events, based on a selection of event types and possible variables. Or even generated plots, based on pre-defined story beats and possible options that follow.

   – Emergent Narrative Systems are systems that allow players to experience emergent narrative through experience and observations of game systems, rather than a generated story with intention. This can be, on the one hand, focused on making the game world more alive through PvE (player-vs-environment) and EvE (environment-vs-environment) interactions, by creating a system of interconnected actors who listen to input and have an output and react depending on how they clash with other actors. For example: An actor can be the weather system, which triggers the output "rain". Another actor is an NPC standing outside, who listens to input and picks up the condition "rain". The NPC is now running indoors to avoid getting wet and will have barks that reflect the frustration with the weather. The player has now observed a small narrative that was created by interaction between game system, as an emergent story. Narrative systems can also be focused on player inter-actions, PvP, instead of PvE or EvE. They can allow players to cre-ate emergent stories with other players, through the tools and systems they are given by the game, such as social, collaborative, or competitive game systems.

When creating a live game, adding narrative systems can provide a big variety of narrative experiences that don't all need to be authored and extended. By offering emergent and/or generated narrative systems, players have more things to experience when all authored content has been consumed. It's also a way to imbue interactions with other players and the environment with narrative meaning. You can also expand or change these narrative systems over time, releasing new systems for the players to play with – possibly related to a seasonal theme, a new mode, or area to play in.

CHARACTERS AS NARRATIVE

Characters aren't only actors inside a story, they hold narrative value in themselves and can embody the story of who they are and where they came from. In a video-game, characters can come in the shape of playable avatars, companions, NPCs, ene-mies, and more – so when you release a content package, new characters can act as narrative content, just by themselves. They embody a role, personality, background, and relations to each other and the world. (*For more detailed information about writing a character profile, refer to Chapter 10, the Central Characters section.*)

To express the narrative of a character, we can make use of a variety of ludonar-rative devices. What's important to remember is that a character's story isn't *only* to their actions inside a plot-driven progression – the way they look, act, and func-tion inside the game already expresses a lot about them. If anything, videogames don't even necessarily require a plot to express the personalities and backstories of their characters at all – and characters can be a form of character-focused world-building all by themselves. Especially in games that are character-focused, such as character-collection games, fighting games, MOBAs, or hero-based shooters, this new content type can be an interesting way to expand your world's narrative in a way that aligns with the focus of gameplay. You can then add new charac-ters as part of your seasonal content, expressing their narrative through them-selves and the package that comes with them (such as cosmetics, game features or progressions).

The following ludonarrative devices can be used to express a narrative about a character, may that character be playable, a companion, an NPC, or an enemy:

- **Cinematics:** A character's story arc and personal growth can be explored with them as an actor within a plot. Through the way they act and talk, audi-ences get to know who they are, their ideals, their trauma, wants, and needs – and how experiences change them. This mirrors cinematic storytelling in mov-ies and TV shows and can take the shape of cutscenes, motion comics, dia-logues, or other forms.

  For more information, refer to the section: Story and Plot as Narrative.

- **Character Design:** A character's visual design is usually the first impression audiences get, even before they do or say anything. This first glimpse at the way they look and dress already reveals a lot about their personality, tastes, cultural background, skills, and role. As games are visual medium that often require quick recognition of a character's meaning, working with established archetypes, visual shortcuts, symbolism, and visual conventions is key. This can further be expanded with new outfits and customization options, which can reveal another hidden side of the character. No matter if they are costumes or believable outfits, they should ideally tie into the character's personality or backstory. *For more information, refer to the section: Cosmetics as Narrative.*

- **Game Mechanics, Function, and Abilities:** No matter if a character is playable, a support character, an enemy, an NPC, or a feature access point: Their function and gameplay mechanics express something about them as a person. If they're a playable character involved in battle, this can be reflected in their move sets, abilities, perks and the way they control. An NPC providing free health items implies another personality from an NPC providing health items at exuberant prices in hopeless situations: One is a caring philanthropist while the other is a greedy sleazebag. A final boss with three fire-themed phases implies another personality from a boss that employs shadows and doppelgänger illusions of themselves: One is a domineering hothead while the other is a sneaky trickster. (In order for characters to not remain cardboard cutouts, this impression can be subverted by letting other narrative elements contradict the assumption, of course.) When you consider attaching characters to specific parts of the game, as feature representatives (such as gun merchants, exploration quest givers, healer party members, etc.), always consider whether that matches their personality, or how this application changes the type of person they are. It should never be at random, but part of their narrative whole. In short, the way a character is used in the game, and how exactly they work when it comes to mechanics, functions and abilities, is part of their personality and serves as a form of storytelling.

- **Attached Quests:** No matter if they serve as quest givers for specific kinds of objectives, or whether they're a playable character with a series of objectives tied to them, quests can serve as a form of character-bound narrative that expresses their problems, goals, and way of thinking. The objective of a quest should be tied to a character, inasmuch as the proposed solution expresses the way they approach their problems. A fisherman NPC might ask you to chronicle the variety of fish in a lake, a concerned villager might ask you to kill the monster that has been terrorizing them, or a healer hero might have quests about protecting and saving people. New seasonal packages may also contain new quests attached to specific characters.

- **Character-Driven Progression:** Progressions can be tied to a specific character, playable or non-playable, that unlock more narrative about them along the way. Such narrative can be anything from new objectives to cutscenes or text documents. As part of seasonal content, a newly added NPC might have a series of missions and dialogues that you can then progress through, or a new playable hero might have a sequence of unlockable dialogue and cutscenes, tied to how much players play as them.

For more information, refer to the section: Progression as Narrative.

- **Encounter Location:** The location of a character influences their context, and therefore, how they're perceived by the player. Especially when it comes to NPCs, where they can be found says something about them. Their location can imply where they live, what locations they're drawn to, or where life has taken them at that point. They might be attached to a predetermined place, or show up near specific types of locations, such as safe rooms, water, types of enemies, shops, etc. What are the attributes of that location, and what does that imply about the character? For example, are we in a toxic swamp but they can breathe just fine? Are they a fish person in a pond? Are they an outsider living in the woods? When they're connected to a specific location, they can serve as an extension of it, giving more insights into the location's lore based on their other narrative elements, such as design, barks, and quests – just as the location's lore can give us more insights about the character.

- **Animations and VFX:** You don't need words to understand a character's personality, because actions say more than a thousand words. The way a character idles, walks, gestures, emotes and attacks has endless possible variations, which can express their background, skills, style, age, gender expression, personality, and current state of mind. Through the visual storytelling of acting, animations can express a character's whole personality. A serious middle-aged military man, a playful teenage trickster, an elegant elderly healer – even if they were serving the same function, such as playable character, companion or antagonist, they would all move differently. Fighting games are great studies for this. You will notice that characters differ in how they walk, move, block and take damage. They're each animated with unique movements for attacks based on their fighting style (a boxer has different moves than a capoeira dancer, for instance), and usually express a strong first impression of their personality: Lively, controlled, flirty, creepy, playful, defensive, elegant, etc. These animations can be enforced with visual special effects, such as particle effects, lights, glows, etc. The shape and color of these effects can serve as an extension of the animations, too.

- **Sound Design and Barks:** Characters often have a selection of sounds tied to them, may that be the sound of their footsteps, their grunts during attacks, or specific barks that mark moments of gameplay. These sounds can emphasize their physical presence (age, weight, gender, body type, etc.), but also express their personality, as well as their gameplay function. Especially barks, short sentences for contextual feedback, provide a glimpse into the background of a character and need to be written with a good balance of personality and clarity (of what they're indicating). Voices and vocal performances influence how these texts are then perceived, and are another valuable piece in the puzzle of a character's general impression. These barks and sounds can also be released as their own package, such as a commentator voice package for MOBAs, or new barks for NPCs that tie into the story development of the season.

For more information, refer to the section: Audio Design as Narrative.

- **Character Biographies and Additional Documents:** Characters can come with their own biographies, available in-game or externally, on a website or in other marketing materials. It doesn't need to be the only type of additional text tied to a character – some games choose to add profiles, anecdotes, short stories, or other character-specific information too – some of which may be available with the character, while others may be a type of unlockable. They can be part of a seasonal content package as well, expanding new or existing characters with additional insights.

COSMETICS AS NARRATIVE

As an expansion of the opportunities of character design, cosmetics can express something **about a character**. Rather than only serving as costumes, they ideally reveal something new, such as cultural background, aspects of their personality, affiliation with a group, hobbies, past associations, and more. Think of cosmetics as alternate outfits from their wardrobe, which are still meant to be uniquely tied to them. Some games are more loose with those associations than others, but even if the cosmetics are clearly costumes or even alternate universe versions of the characters, they should ideally tie into who they are as a person. This applies to anything related to a character, such as customizable weapons, pets, vehicles, and more.

Cosmetics aren't exclusive to specific characters though. They can also be more **player-oriented customization** options, which are meant as a form of **self-expression.** Here, the narrative of them should tie into the game's world and, possibly, their context of release (such as a specific event). They can visually relate to specific characters, factions, regions, or more – and that visual connection makes a potential statement about their gameplay attributes, too. Cosmetics can also tie into the theme of the current season – a pirate season brings pirate cosmetics, a cyberpunk season brings cyberpunk cosmetics, and so on. As such, they allow the players to weave a narrative about themselves and how they want to be perceived inside the game world. This is part of a game's context, which deeply influences how players perceive their actions.

ADDITIONAL VISUALS AND UI AS NARRATIVE

The UI and general visual direction of a game are also part of its narrative, as they refer to a visual language implying genre, art style, time period, and more. Seasonal narrative meaning can also come in the form of *changes* in the general visuals of the game. More specifically, changes in UI, splash screens, loading screens, home screens, hubs, maps, screen layout, and more. As an example: The seasonal theme is winter holidays. Therefore, the loading screen and splash screens now have a festive winter illustration, the home screen is covered in snow, the interface has been changed to a cool blue, and the assistant NPC is now wearing a Santa Claus outfit.

AUDIO DESIGN AS NARRATIVE

Audio design and music enhance a game's moment-to-moment storytelling and expand the story beyond what is already seen. Sound can underline the drama of what's happening inside of the story in several ways: Either as intra-diegetic sound (what characters can hear, such as environmental ambient sounds), or extra-diegetic sound (what only players can hear, but which expresses the story as well). Extra-diegetic sound takes a more stylized role in terms of indicating meaning. This can be in the form of functional sounds related to gameplay, which make the player aware of a game event, or musical themes that are connected to story elements. A game's score is likely to be full of themes for specific purposes in-game – a battle theme, a romantic theme, a theme for the antagonist, or even themes that indicate a relation to somebody, or someplace. On the other hand, we have intra-diegetic sound, the ambience that characters inside the game would also hear. Through the layering of background sounds (such as howling wind, animal noises, creaking houses, ocean waves, etc), sound can build entire soundscapes that express the game world, its characters' perception of it, or even say something about the location or characters we're dealing with.

Sound and music are a storytelling medium, and should be treated as one part of the narrative design.

But this doesn't only apply to the music of your base game. Changes in audio design over the seasons can create a story progression. These sound changes can be based on player action or automatic, such as a shift in score, sounds, and ambient music. For example, a location on the map suddenly has another background ambient score, because it is now destroyed and haunted. Or there are festive jingles on the main screen during the winter holidays. Or a character's theme is sounding darker than before, using instruments that are also present in the antagonist's theme music.

This new audio content can also be unlockable or purchasable, such as new sound packages, alternate soundtracks, background, narrator packages, barks, and more.

SUMMARY

- **Story and plot** are narrative tools.
- A live game's plot can be expanded with seasonal stories, parallel stories, or side stories.
- Seasonal stories can also be told through **changing narrative contexts**, without a plot progression (such as seasonal themes or world changes).
- **Document packages** can expand the game's lore.
- **Additional texts** are a narrative tool.
- They can be self-contained stories, additional information, descriptions, or names for things.
- **Progressions** are a narrative tool.

- They can be main, parallel, or side content, obligatory or optional, permanent or temporary.
- Progression design is composed of theme, goal, and purpose; type of mission (main, parallel, or side); steps to progress; progression markers; rewards; challenge level; progression speed; connected characters; connected game features; and connected gameplay.
- Established progression types are player XP progressions, feature progressions, quest progressions, character progressions, role progressions, and real-time progressions.
- **Quests** are a narrative tool.
- Quests can serve the purpose of tutorial, training for mastery, game progression, encouragement to explore, and/or narrative.
- Quests can have the narrative intention of storytelling, exploration, characterization, or as an extension of the game's themes.
- To write a quest, you need conflict, action, and resolution.
- Quest design is composed of a quest giver, location and framework, related gameplay, possible choices, reward, interface, and sound design, as well as consequences.
- **Environment** is a narrative tool.
- Environments are composed of geographical factors, man-made structures and city planning, social erosions, personal decorations, situational remains, and suggested mood and use.
- In live games, environments can change over seasons, telling a story over time.
- Environments can appear, disappear, or move; have changes in their ecosystem; changes in their locations due to past events (such as repurposing them); decay or grow; and show signs of recent human, animal, or other activity.
- **Game design** is a narrative tool.
- It can express the game's narrative intention, characterize playable characters, and show the game's worldview
- This includes game mechanics, game features, game modes, and game systems.
- Game design is inherently dramatic because it implies a conflict, goal, and the player's steps taken toward solving it.
- **Game systems** are a narrative tool.
- This includes game systems, narrative systems, and systemic narrative (procedural or emergent narrative systems).
- The narrative meaning of systems comes from dependencies between actors, how the player can interact with the system, and how the system reacts to it – this expresses a worldview and the avatar's take on it.
- Procedural and emergent narrative systems can help create an "endless" amount of content and unique player stories.

- **Characters** are a narrative tool.
- A character's personality and background can be expressed through their character design, game mechanics, functions and abilities, attached quests, character-driven progression, encounter location, animations and VFX, sound design and barks, character biographies, and additional documents.
- **Cosmetics** are a narrative tool.
- They can be used to expand the visual characterization of a character, their personality, and background.
- Character-unrelated cosmetics can expand the narrative about the game world, its themes and events and serve as a narrative opportunity of self-expression for the player.
- **Additional Visuals and UI** are a narrative tool.
- The visual direction can undergo seasonal changes as a form of storytelling, such as changes in UI, splash screens, hubs, maps, and more.
- **Audio Design** is a narrative tool.
- It can expand the moment-to-moment storytelling through mood, references, and symbolism. Changes in audio over time can also serve as a form of story.

REFERENCE

1 Lee Sheldon, "Games: Charting New Territory" in *Character Development and Storytelling for Games*, Course Technology, 2nd edition, April 3, 2013, 234–247.

BIBLIOGRAPHY

Ross Berger, *Dramatic Storytelling & Narrative Design: A Writer's Guide to Video Games and Transmedia*, CRC Press, August 27, 2020.
Tobias Heussner, Toiya Kristen Finley, Jennifer Brandes Hepler, Ann Lemay, *The Game Narrative Toolbox*, Focal Press, 2015.

12 Planning Your Seasons

CONTENT RELEASE FRAMEWORK

So you've created the narrative foundation of your game. You've decided what kind of story you want to tell and how you want to do it – but this is only the first step towards a successful live game. Now you need to plan the seasons that *follow* your initial release. Naturally, it's unrealistic to plan the next 5 years in detail, since you don't know how long your game will remain live for, how players will receive the game, and whether you might need to adjust the trajectory of your plans along the way. It's important to keep flexible developing live games, but rushing into things without a plan is impossible and can easily end in a disaster – both in terms of production and narrative. Therefore, you need to create a plan for a few future seasons while staying adaptable. This will help production and keeping on top of things. Your budget, time, schedule, and content plans will have to work out together, lest you risk missing deadlines, disappointing players, and going over budget. But it's also crucial for making narrative plans. After all, you should know where your story is going, even if you don't have all the details laid out yet.

A **content release framework** describes the content packages you plan to release as part of the live service, and the intervals at which they are meant to release. This document clarifies the following questions: What's the schedule for new content? What is the new content, and how is it structured? Is it permanent or temporary? Planning this roadmap is crucial, not only for production cost and team planning but also for managing player expectations, and knowing what kind of story material you'll be able to work with for future releases. You need to know your narrative's structure before you can think about the details of the story you're going to tell with it, after all.

Your **content framework** needs to define the following:

- Your **Seasonal Narrative Vision**, and your various types of **Release Packages**
  The narrative structure and creative direction of your content packages – this defines how you plan to tell the seasonal narrative
  - Types of content
  - Permanence of content (live, time-limited, or permanent)
  - Narrative purpose and structure of content
  - Dependencies and accessibility of content
  - **Release Schedule**
    A timeline for content releases, which includes seasons and events throughout each season – this defines the pacing of your content

RELEASE PACKAGES

The content types of your release packages will define *how* you tell your live story, which, in turn, influences what kind of story you can tell. Are you adding a new plot-driven progression? New characters and items? Time-limited events throughout the season? and should be something that was already defined as part of your narrative vision for the live operations. Now that you're planning your upcoming seasons, you need to clarify the shape and scope of your release packages, as well as the rough narrative content for the first few seasons. You don't need to lay out all seasons to come (as this would be an impossible task), but as many as needed to prepare your production cycle comfortably, plus, as many as you need to plan your long-term story. In *Chapter 11*, we've laid out different options of content types, which will be the building blocks that these release packages are made of. They don't always have to look the same way inside the same game either and can change over time and the seasons. The longer a game goes, the more you can experiment with your packages.

Here are a couple of **examples for release packages**, to serve as inspiration. You could feasibly combine those in the same game as well!

- A **new role** with unique gameplay and a new progression to complete. This progression is driven by character-specific missions and rewards players with unique items and unlockable story moments.
- An entirely **new area** on the map, coming with new environmental story-telling, new NPCs, and new enemy factions. The NPCs are questgivers with new quests, exploring the story and meaning of the new locale.
- A **change in the map,** explained by a narrative event in the finale of the last season. This change brings a new tie-in gameplay mode that highlights the map's new functions, and unlockable cosmetics matching the new environmental theme.
- A new **gameplay bundle,** with a new game mode, a new XP progression for that mode, and unlockable cosmetics that fit the mode's narrative theme. There is a trailer for this bundle, which introduces the main theme and conflict with the help of three fitting main characters.
- A new package of **chapters** that are added at the end of the current story progression. As new end-of-content gameplay, it provides a continuation of a currently existing plot, by adding a new season-style story arc. Additionally, a new **parallel story** has started, which takes place in the same game world, allowing beginners to consume this new content, too.
- A new playable **side story** that focuses on a minor character. The quest-driven chapters can be unlocked in chronological order, and only need an upfront currency investment to access them, as well as ownership of this specific playable character. Playing these chapters/missions unlocks the ones that come after.
- A new set of **characters,** each with their own design, play style, weapons, and backstory. They also have a character-based progression with rewards and a unique self-contained story. They shine a light on a new aspect of the game world that was previously unexplored, and the characters are directly related to it.

- A new **social location** with new methods of player interactions, such as emotes, photo opportunities, and mini games. A space for roleplay-based emergent gameplay, where players are meant to interact and experience their own emergent stories.
- A **seasonal change** in the game that re-skins the UI, the loading screen, and maps to fit the theme. There are several live events in which visually fitting cosmetics can be unlocked through playing a new seasonal game mode.
- A new set of **lore documents,** hidden at the end of several treasure hunts – which is a new gameplay feature encouraging exploration.

RELEASE SCHEDULES AND PACING

When you release a season, you don't simply launch your content whenever it's ready. You schedule releases for the best possible pacing. You want to stay relevant and keep players entertained, but not overwhelm them (or your production schedule) too much. It's all about striking the right balance.

You influence the pacing of your game's live content by deciding on the launch dates and lengths of your seasons, and possible events to occur within a season. Additionally, you design how quickly players can progress through new content, either by the amount of content, or how much time needs to be invested to unlock the individual pieces of the content. This is a question of progression balancing. Not all players play the same amount each day, or with the same skills, or invest the same amount of money, which means that you have to cater to a variety of players with your pacing and schedule decisions.

You want to **engage different types of players.** There are two **extremes you want to avoid:**

1. **Fast players run out of content too fast**, become bored, and stop playing the game. They might complain that the game doesn't have enough content, jump to another game, and then don't return because they decided it's not worth their emotional investment anymore.

   → **Solution:** Having too little content may be mitigated through multiplayer experiences or other interesting repeatable actions that players can use to entertain themselves before new content drops happen. Additionally, you can release additional challenging content that is just for those hardcore players, which takes much more time and skill investment to complete, with a perceived air of prestige or premium items to unlock.

2. **Slow players don't get the chance to play all the content** before new content is added, and they either lose access to something they wanted to play or get overwhelmed with too many things to do. They might lose emotional investment because they feel like they can't keep up with it anyway, or they don't see enough of the seasonal content to get attached in the first place. Even if new content remains in the game permanently, they might get too overwhelmed by the amount of choices, and not knowing how to approach, let alone conquer them.

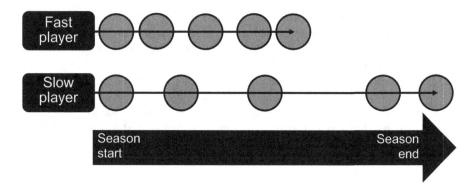

FIGURE 12.1 Comparison of content completion speed in fast and slow players.

→ **Solution:** Having too much to do during a season can be mitigated through giving players several smaller pieces of content (or content progressions), which allows them to pick and choose which stories they want to see and complete first, even if they can't get through all of them. Alternatively, you can balance your main story to be achievable for most players, even if they are slow, either by making it easy, tying it to the passage of real time, or allowing the option to purchase boosts that make you unlock things quicker or immediately. There's also the option to make content permanently accessible (which needs to be balanced against the entirety of your game), whereas here, creating a well-structured user experience becomes even more important to not overwhelm them. For that, you need to create easily understandable progression structures, limit how many progressions players can have at once, and/or give them an accessible overview for all progressions that are active/available. Alternatively, you can create gates for various pieces of the game, so that not everything is available at once. This can be limited through XP or level progression, being in specific locations, or other dependencies, limiting a player's moment-to-moment options to avoid that they feel overwhelmed. (see Figure 12.1)

On development side, the challenge is to **deliver as much content as needed to satisfy your players**, when it comes to your pacing and content release sizes, while still being able to **reliably achieve that development goal over a long period of time** with the team and budget that you have. Don't plan too ambitiously and then run into missed deadlines or overworked employees. Do not plan for crunch. Good live game scheduling means being aware of your resources, dependencies, and team abilities, and plan sensibly, leaving some breathing room in between releases. You never know when you might run into production issues – might that be technical issues, creative complications or sickness. Good pre-planning and streamlined processes help you to work more effectively and comfortably, without having to force workers to work overtime or cut corners where you shouldn't.

These **factors influence the pacing** of your season:

- **Season Length:** How many weeks or months does your season last?

- **Release Schedule for Individual Content Drops:** Is everything dropped at the start of the season? Are there individual packages spread across the season, such as weekly episodes, specific time-limited, or live events? How long are these individual content drops available for – are they permanent or temporary additions?
- **Progression Balancing:** How long will it take players to get through each piece of content? How much playtime would go into it if you're a high-skill or low-skill player? Are there any dependencies with other features? Can players speed up the progression, and how would that influence their game experience?
- **Content Accessibility:** Who will get access to which content? Are there parallel progressions, or one that needs to be played in chronological order? Are there different player groups with different access to content, for example end-of-content players, or players that completed an onboarding experience first? Are there other dependencies, such as content relying on a previous progression? Is there premium content that needs to be purchased to be accessed (such as a DLC expansion, season pass)? How will that influence various player experiences?
- **Repeatable Content:** Is there content that can be repeated often, and entertain players for an indefinite amount of time? This can be purely gameplay based, but also in the shape of narrative content with replay value, such as narrative systems for emergent gameplay, procedurally-generated narrative, interactive stories with multiple branches and outcomes, etc.

Before you release your first season, a lot of this is guess work, estimations, and trying to anticipate the pacing of casual and hardcore players. Try to create example walkthroughs of your season with anticipated behavior of various types of players, to better understand how much content you need, how you may want to spread it out, and how that experience would feel for each player. Doing this might also give you some ideas for monetization, if you plan to monetize speeding up processes (buying ranks of battle passes, instead of having to gain XP manually, for example). After you've released your first season, you can gather player data and feedback in order to adjust your pacing after the fact.

Here are a few more things to consider when you plan your pacing:

- **Critical Path:** This is the shortest route the player must go to reach the end of the content or season, without any sidetracking, side missions, or distractions. Going this path, they might miss some content you've created but reach something that can be defined as an ending of content, such as the last rank of a season pass, the last mission of a set of missions or the game's ending credits.
- **Golden Path:** The Golden Path is the hypothetical optimal route for the best possible game experience. This means that it's by definition longer than the Critical Path, and the experience you, as a designer, deem the most enjoyable and true to your vision. Being aware of this Golden Path can help you create incentives for players to play parts of your content you deem

enjoyable and important – either by making them aware of it, attaching rewards to it, or making it otherwise accessible or attractive.

- **Player Freedom:** When players have the freedom to stray from these paths, you have to consider possible alternate routes and how rewarding they would be. When you give players a lot of freedom to stray, there is a chance of them losing sight of the critical/golden path and feel like they're not progressing in a satisfying way, or that there is no interesting content. So balancing player freedom and design intent with guidance, reminders, and access to information is key.

Different players will have different ways to interact with your game, and therefore, take different paths through your progressions. They differ from one another by how much time they spend in the game and how they behave in the game. You must plan for a variety of them (taking into account your target audience), to estimate your required scope and strategic release schedule. Some players will sink all their free time into playing your game, to progress as quickly as possible as soon as new content has been released. Others will take things slower, and take their time. Some will pay to progress faster, some try to play it without spending a single cent. Some players are highly skilled, others will need many attempts to complete objectives. They're all unique. Anyhow, you wouldn't want most of your seasonal content missed by the majority of players, but you also wouldn't want to give so little content that hardcore players aren't satisfied. There is no one perfect strategy – it all depends on the size of your project, team, and your target audience – so it's important to plan, check, and revise. The good news is: A live game allows you to revise your schedule strategy over the seasons, based on your observations from real players.

The following list contains **differences in player behavior** that might **influence the personal pacing** of your content releases, and should be planned for during your planning phase:

- **Achiever vs Explorer vs Completionist:** Will they only stick to the critical path, explore whatever they find interesting, or try to complete every piece of content available?
- **Low vs High Time Investment:** How much time will they invest in the game day-by-day?
- **Low-Skilled vs High-Skilled Players:** How quickly will they complete objectives and master challenges, based on their game skills?
- **Paying Players vs Non-Paying Players:** Is there paywalled content, such as a premium season pass, playable characters, mission packs, or DLC expansions? And how does the pacing differ between non-paying and paying players? Is there a way for paying players to speed up their progression, and how does that influence their experience and the non-paying player's experience?
- **Beginners vs Players with Previous Progression vs End-of-Content-Players:** Does some of your content have dependencies on previous progressions, and is only accessible if another milestone has been reached

before? Will the new content feel different to players, depending on their level of progression?

- **Individual vs Social Players:** Does your progression rely on multiplayer interaction, and if so, how will the experience differ for players who prefer to play alone (if the option is available)?

PLANNING PERMANENT AND TEMPORARY CONTENT

PERMANENT VS TIME-LIMITED VS LIVE

When you design your content release framework, one question that needs to be answered for every piece of content is how *permanent* it will be. Live games have the unique property of being *live,* which means that they are a living medium that continuously receives new updates and can change over time. Playing an MMO on day one will be different from day 30 and year 5. The permanence of each piece of content can range from **permanent** (persistently available from the moment of release), over **time-limited** (such as seasonal content or time-limited events available during a specific timeframe) up to **time-specific/live** (happening in a specific moment in time, with a pre-scripted timeline tied to real time passing).

Why would we not simply keep every piece of content permanent, as soon as it's added? We could, of course. But that would imply a constantly growing library that balloons the download size of the game and might become overwhelming for players. It's possible to do so, and some game genres actually release a lot if not most of their content as a permanent addition (such as MMOs and visual novels), but it might not be feasible or a good idea for your specific project. Plus, you might find it interesting to make use of the unique storytelling and marketing potential of time-limited and live content.

In general, how much of your content is permanent will influence the type of experience you offer with your game. Is your project a growing world, expanding permanent content over time, creating an increasing library of content? Or is your project a living world, with things changing over time, creating an evolving library of content?

Each permanence has a different strength and application and can be used to tell different types of stories.

- **Permanent:** This includes the base content that is available at launch and any future expansions that will remain **permanently accessible** from their moment of release (Expansions). Players can progress through this content whenever they want and on their own terms, in other words, it's asynchronous for all players. This type of permanence is especially useful for onboarding, main stories, and long-term motivation. The narrative can focus on plot, character growth, and relationships.
- **Time-Limited:** This is content that will only be available **for a limited time**. This limited time can span several weeks or months (Seasons) or a shorter time frame for additional events inside of your season, spanning from hours to weeks (time-limited events). Players usually have time to progress through

this content in their own time, within the designated time frame, so it's asynchronous to some extent. This type of permanence is especially useful for seasonal arcs, time-limited events, and long-term, as well as mid- and short-term motivation. The narrative of seasons can focus on season arcs full of plot, character growth, and relationship dynamics – especially an endless variety of changes over time. The narrative focus of time-limited events is smaller and should depict self-contained short stories that focus on characters, events, or details. They can have topical relevance (such as real events, seasons of the year, holidays, etc).

- **Live (Time-Specific):** This is content that will only be available at a **specific point in time**. The pacing is pre-scripted and tied to the passage of real time (Live Events). These events work like a live performance or a tournament. They're synchronous for all players, experienced at the exact same time, and will continue independently from their personal input. Games might choose to have several instances of the same event for several time zones, to reach all their players. This type of permanence is especially useful for live events and short-term and social motivation. The narrative can focus on plot, character growth, and relationships – especially an endless variety of changes over time. The narrative focus of live events should be limited and should depict self-contained short stories that focus on characters, events, or details. They can have extreme topical relevance (such as real events, seasons of the year, holidays, etc.), as well as mark special points in the game season (such as finales) (Table 12.1).

Each of these categories has different uses, advantages, and connected risks. Usually (but not always), your project wouldn't only have *one* of them, but apply different levels of permanence to different types of content. If you combine them, you can

---

TABLE 12.1
Comparison between Varying Permanence of Content

	Permanent (Base Game, Expansions)	Game Season	Time-Limited Event	Live Event
Length	Permanent	~2–6 months	~1 day–2 weeks	30 minutes–2 hours
Motivation	Onboarding, long-term	Long- & mid-term	Mid- & short-term	Short-term & social
Best use	– Onboarding – Main stories	– Season arcs – Side arcs – Plot- and relationship-focus	– Self-contained short stories – Character- event- or detail-focused – Topical/seasonal relevance	– Event stories – Self-contained super short stories – Social/player stories – Topical/seasonal relevance

make use of their unique strengths and mitigate their risks with other aspects of your game, to end up with an engaging whole. (see Table 12.2).

Permanent and temporary content can be split into different release types: Permanent content can be base content, expansions, and content generation systems, while your time-limited content can be a season, time-limited event or live event. Let's take a closer look at each type.

Permanent – Base Content

The content that your live game is launched with.

Good for: Onboarding and permanent (main) stories. This is the content that allows you to give a standardized first-time-user-experience, no matter when they start to play the game. It's therefore crucial in providing a guided experience until they're sufficiently onboarded and convinced that they want to keep on playing. If your game focuses on non-seasonal content, this is where your first big batch (or the entirety) of the main story goes. Onboarding for seasonal games can either be a short onboarding, or a long main campaign that can be played in parallel to live content.

Permanent – Expansions

Permanent, new additions to the base content. They can be new arcs or self-contained stories, as well as narrative-infused content without plot progression (game features, characters, items, etc).

Good for: Onboarding and getting players invested in the game world, as well as setting up the goal for long-term motivation. Expanding the permanent experience available for all players, no matter when they play. Also, extending player retention and attracting players to the game. These can either be lapsed players that are drawn back in, or new players that were convinced by the new content to give the game a try.

Permanent – Content Generation Systems

While not necessary, there is also the possibility of providing game systems, with the **launch** of your product **or as a later addition**, which **generate more content** automatically or through the actions of players, without the development team having to design/write each individual experience. Over time, you would perhaps add more tools and functions to those systems, as well as content.

- **Emergent Narrative Systems:** Emergent narrative describes when a game provides tools that don't provide pre-scripted events, but rather enable player stories: Narrative experiences that are driven by player action and interaction with the game's systems and other players. This can often be found in simulations and open world games, as well as games that are designed to be social. This means that they have a playground for narrative experiences, defined by world system units, their relation to each other, and the possibilities of interaction that the player is given. Emergent narrative systems can be split into two distinct varieties:

TABLE 12.2

Comparison between Risks & Risk Mitigation of Time–Limited and Permanent Content

Permanence	Advantages	Risks	Ways to Mitigate Risks
Time–limited	– Drives moment–to–moment motivation and user engagement – Can pull churned players back in – Marketing potential (especially if accessible for all players) – Greater potential for a social spectacle – Can shift the thematic focus from season to season, and explore the story from various perspectives (Seasons) – Can narratively highlight a specific aspect of the game world, such as characters or events (Time–limited Events)	– New players jump into the middle of a story and are lost/unengaged – Ongoing production costs for content that is scrapped after a specific time	– Create permanent onboarding campaigns to introduce new players into the live content – Allow regular easy entry points into the story, such as the beginning of a new season – Make information on the past seasons accessible – Make main story progression permanent, while time–limited content is composed of self–contained side stories – Make time–limited content self–contained arcs that can be joined at regular entry points (such as season beginnings) – Strike a balance between permanent and time–limited game additions
Permanent	– Enables a standardized story progression, experience no matter when players join the game – Growing library of content as a selling point for players	– Ballooning file size – Lots of content might be hard to navigate and overwhelming – New content may only be available for end–of–content players – New content may be less interesting for potential new players (due to the inaccessibility)	– Tech solutions (e.g., only download the parts the player is about to access) – Add new starting points/progressions so that new players can also access new content, such as new parallel stories (such as new roles, new parallel paths, or new stories), short stories, etc – Guide player experience, so they're aware of options but not overwhelmed

- **Roleplay Features** allow players to express themselves, their (character's) personality and roleplay a narrative with features that aren't necessarily needed to progress inside the game. Emotes, gestures, and actions can hold a symbolic and roleplay value, which allow players to immerse themselves in a narrative fantasy, even though they might play the game without ever using these systems, too. In multiplayer games, especially MMORPGs, those can become an important layer of social interaction. Examples for roleplay features would be skins, emotes, progression unrelated interactions with the environment or other players, progression unrelated mini games, environments designed for social gatherings, etc.
- **World Systems** allow players to interact with a virtual world, influence it, and provoke reactions with narrative meaning. These reactions can be shown through animations, game systems, or even barks or similar elements. Additionally, the actors in these world systems may influence each other, independent from the actions of the player, and the player then walks into generated scenarios that naturally emerge from the systems between actors in a system. Emergent narrative comes from observed behavior and dynamics, in this case, but can also be enhanced with narrative features such as barks or other observable behavior.
- **Procedurally-Generated Content:** If you want players to have a large amount of content to explore, which you don't need to design individually, there is the option to develop systems for procedurally-generated content. This could be missions, battles, regions, planets to visits, and more. This means that the narrative designer would design the possibilities and limitations of content, rather than handcraft individual pieces of content. That applies to both, text-based content (such as generated missions that combine pre-written randomly created objectives, characters, and the context) and world content (such as planets with a randomly created fauna and a list of possible encounters that can be found there). It's even possible to change these systems over the progression of seasons, shifting the range of possible experiences that players will encounter during each season. For example: A new season can introduce new navigable spaces, or change available spaces. This can be to shift your narrative and emotional focus, and simply change the available possibilities of generated content, or to simply expand your game world.
- **Player-Generated Content:** Another option to create a large amount of content is to provide players the tools to create their own content. Here, again, the narrative designer decides the available possibilities and range and guides the resulting content through the options provided. If you give players level editors for FPS levels, then they're going to create FPS levels (and anything else they might discover they can do with the provided tools). Despite providing the limitations and tools, this still takes a lot of agency from the narrative design team and is usually best suited for games (or features) that have a narrative vision that matches this approach. The structure is part of the message, after all, and providing these tools for generating

content should be part of the narrative meaning. Additionally, there will be a need for curation, to provide players with good experiences and filter out anything your company wouldn't want to be associated with.

Usually, player-generated content would only be a part of the entire narrative experience, and limited to specific game features. There are other live games, however, that aim to provide a creative platform to players first and foremost, and here, this is central for new content. The responsibility of the narrative designer would be more about expanding tools meaningfully over time, to enable players to create more types of content or create it more easily or meaningfully.

Good for: An ever-growing pool of content that doesn't require authorial scripting of individual content, enabling players to partake in content creation, or discover player stories through roleplay options and a reactive world. The narrative designer defines the playground, the options, and the dynamics – and therefore functions as an author of the scope and vision of the experience, rather than the specifics of the plot. There is a limit to this type of content, however, since it doesn't allow for pre-scripted narrative experience in the same way as other content types. Dramatic arcs, growth, and well-built tension can become hard to pull off – and if there are tools for it, they are in the player's hands. Emergent narrative features can, however, be a great enhancer to other narrative features, for example: Emergent narrative inside the new area of an open world, making the region feel alive and brimming with stories, or narrative roleplay features that fit the seasonal theme, or allowing player-generated content as part of the game's general narrative vision.

Time-Limited – Seasonal Content

Seasons are used to structure significant new content packages that are added at a regular interval (usually a few weeks to a few months). Parts of these packages can be permanent, while other parts might be limited to that time. This can be a seasonal story arc, which the player can complete within the duration of the season, or other types of content available for that time. The release schedule can be bingeable, everything unlockable with the start of the season, or have a timed release structure – where episodes or partial content is released over the course of several weeks instead of dropped all at once. They're often tied to a progression of missions or milestones, such as new missions, a battle pass, or new game feature progressions – which usually come with rewards and XP as well.

Good for: Long-term and mid-term motivation, motivating players through the season, attracting new players with big changes between seasons.

Time-Limited – Time-Limited Events

Time-limited events are content that is only available for a limited time (usually a few days or weeks). It allows players some freedom of choice regarding when they want to engage with said content, within the given timeframe, but if they don't complete it, they miss the rest and will be unable to access it thereafter. These events are often tied to a progression and a reward, such as new characters, skins, weapons, XP, and more – which are for the player to keep, even after the event has ended. They're best used for self-contained short stories about characters, events, places, or other details of the world – an independent diversion from the main progressions. They're an opportunity for small spin-off stories that expand an aspect of the game world that the main story already introduced, for topical stories that refer to current events (such as annual seasons, holidays, a game anniversary, etc.) or collaboration events with other brands.

Good for: Short-term and mid-term motivation, and to keep players engaging with the game on a regular basis so that they don't miss out on content they want to see.

Time-Limited – Live Events

Live events are content that is only live for a specific point in time, going through a pre-scripted progression in real time. Players experience these events synchronously and have to be present as it happens, usually sharing the experience with other players, although there might be several instances of the same event for different time zones. The live event will usually happen with or without the individual presence and input of each player, since its progression is based on the passage of time. This has been done for special social events, such as in-game concerts (Fortnite, Roblox, The Sims 4) and season finales (Fortnite).

Good for: Short-term motivation, marketing, and social experiences. Due to the extreme limited availability and potentially social experience, they're good for word-by-mouth marketing and people discussing the event prior to or after it happens. Live events can mark a special occasion, such as a new season, a celebration or a concert/performance[1] (see Figure 12.2).

Narrative Roadmap and Season Overviews

Now that we have an idea for the framework of our releases, we can make plans for how the story itself will develop from season to season. Before the launch of your

FIGURE 12.2   Various content permanence in a game season.

project, it's important to plan further than your first season. You should make a narrative roadmap for a longer period of time, to lay out where your seasons are going to take the players narratively. This will make development a little quicker, seasons more coherent, and helps you plan some season-spanning story ideas. It's important to not be near-sighted, although there is no hard rule how many seasons you should plan in advance (especially because longer seasons give you more time before your next batch of content needs to be ready). I'd recommend to at least think until the end of the first big arc and then have a rough idea of what happens next. Try to plan the key aspects of several seasons ahead of time, and have at least a rough idea of the seasons that lie even further into the future. Usually, planning the entire first year of your live game before launch is a good idea. That doesn't mean that everything is set in stone, by the way. Stay flexible to react to player insights and changes in gameplay content release plans.

This narrative roadmap defines the seasonal progression of the key story aspects – from season to season, and not only within a season. For each season, create an overview, and how it will change from the previous to the next season. The further into a future a season is, the rougher the outline can be.

A **narrative roadmap** for season-to-season storytelling should provide overviews of the following aspects (if relevant):

- **Mood and Gamefeel:** Based on seasonal themes, which experience do we want the players to have in each season? What is the general mood and the gamefeel of each season's features and modes?
- **Topics and Themes:** Before going into depth, it's sensible to start with a season's general theme and topics. This will often be used by marketing to communicate the new selling points to the players as well. Most if not all live games will heavily theme their content releases, since it helps to quickly set expectations for a game experience – but it's also useful for inspiration and production constraints, as well as making sure that your seasons keep on providing new and unique content to players (instead of always doing similar things).

    A season's **theme** is the big picture: The overarching shared subject matter of its story, visuals, and content. The theme should be recognizable at first sight, contextualizing the new content with clear visual shorthand. A season's theme could be *pirates,* and so pirates are part of the story, gameplay, and visuals. It's a great way to market the game to your players over and over again – it sets expectations for story content, new gameplay, characters, and items. This is more than just slapping a coat of paint on whatever you wanted to release though: Make sure your topic is directly reflected in your story, your gameplay, and other game content you intend to release. If the theme is pirates, make sure to feature pirate topics in your story, and give players gameplay relevant to the theme – such as robbing merchant ships, finding treasure, water-based modes, etc.

    A season's **topics** describe the subject matters that will be explicitly explored in the story, which usually defines the core conflict and topics of discussion. A season's topic could be *"freedom,"* and so we witness characters fighting for their freedom, or exploring what freedom means to them. Topics are usually more abstract concepts that are narratively interesting and filled with drama. A topic does not need to be reflected in the visuals, and might not even be central to marketing (though it can be), but it's always central to the narrative experience and the writing progress. This refers to both the story elements, as well as gameplay elements. We must not forget that what players get to do is also part of the narrative experience: Actions sometimes speak louder than words.

For each season, clarify: What are each season's main themes and topics, and what are its secondary themes and topics, expressed in e.g. limited events or side content? Also, what is the reason for this evolution, and is it set up in a previous season? For example: If season 3's topic is rebellion and revolution, was there a plot development in season 2 that set up this theme sufficiently, for example, by being about an authoritarian evil organization taking over the world? Or, was there a season finale in which a natural disaster flooded the entire map, introducing the theme of water in the subsequent season?

Is the change of themes and topics related to real-time events, such as a holidays-themed season during December? The evolution of themes and topics should ideally provide a good basis for themed game content, such as modes and cosmetics, and give players a thematic variety from season to season. Themes are usually the core part of marketing and are used for keeping players around and to attract new players.

- **Goals and Conflicts:** A season's conflict indicates a main goal, and the conflicts that need to be solved in order to reach it – both in terms of gameplay and story. This means that this defines the trajectory of the season, and where it will end up (no matter if the initial goal is reached or not). The narrative and gameplay core conflict may differ slightly, but should ideally align. It's crucial to think about the player's role in this as well: How are their actions tying into solving the season's conflict? For example: If the main conflict is about defeating the monster of the season, how do their actions translate into working toward that goal? Besides your key conflict, you can also have side conflicts, attached to side progressions, specific characters, or other elements separate from whatever your main content is. Examples for conflicts would be: Defeating an antagonist, faction VS faction, rebuilding something broken, winning over a love interest, winning a competition, gathering resources to be able to do something, discovering something hidden, revealing a mystery, liberating a prisoner, etc.
- **Player Role:** What's the player's narrative role in each season? Does it change over time (e.g., do they go from desperate survivor to powerful hero)?
- **Main Cast:** Each season needs a set of **main actors** who will drive the action forward and get the most attention – the protagonists, antagonists, and side characters. Depending on your project, you may use the same main cast across many seasons, but that doesn't mean you can't shift the focus between groups of characters. Additionally, you can change the antagonists, locations, or key objects. An actor in a story doesn't need to be a human

actor, either – a location, for instance, can show conflict, action, and growth, as well. For example, think of a planet that changes over time under the influence of a war, and in turn, its changing nature acts upon the people on it. So, your main cast can be composed of the following:

- **Season Representatives:** Characters who will be used in marketing to represent the season and aesthetically tie into its theme, often but not necessarily a main character. Might have other additional purposes in your game, such as a questgiver, narrator, playable/unlockable character, etc.
- **Main Characters:** Characters who drive the action of the season, or get the most attention
- **Side Characters:** Characters who get secondary attention and accompany the action
- **Main Antagonists:** Characters who oppose the player in their goals and are considered the final boss or biggest menace of the season
- **Side Antagonists:** Characters who oppose the player in their goals, but are considered sub-bosses or a minor menace of the season
- **Main Locations:** The main setting of the season
- **Central Objects:** Important objects of the season, such as MacGuffins (a central object that characters search or fight over, thus kicking off plot and conflict)

    Some of these may be recurring, while others can be entirely new. Additionally, somebody who used to be a main focus in a previous season may become less central in the following season, and in turn, minor characters might become the focus of a later season.

    For each of those actors, you should clarify their personal role, relevant topics, motivations, shifting relationships and personal growth within the season (and from season to season).

- **Character Growth:** Characters can change over the seasons, based on what they experience and how the story progresses. If your project chooses to include this type of seasonal storytelling, consider each character's seasonal stakes. What are their wants, needs, and conflicts this season? Do their attitudes, opinions, and behavior change? This change can happen within a season, or from season to season – just make sure it stays coherent. Be mindful of the **personal goals, growth, and change** these key players might go through and document these changes for all seasons. They can serve as a blueprint before you even start writing, to make sure you know where you're going. For an individual season, that usually means defining each individual character's **agenda and goal**. Where they start, what conflict and topic they will deal with, and where they will end up. Take note of the differences between wants and needs here as well: A character might actively want one thing, but actually need another, and the change experienced within the growth of a season might not include reaching their goal but a completely different new state of mind or being. This change can be about their feelings, attitude, ideals, role, affiliations, goals, personality, or self-perception. Or even their physical state.

Not every character needs to change all the time, and this will also depend on the strategy of your live game narrative. But even if you have persistent characters who don't grow and don't change, it makes sense to define their arc for the individual season, even if it doesn't imply a permanent change for them. If you do plan to have growth across the seasons, it's important to note the change over seasons, too. You can even make "personal growth plans" for a character across several seasons, and document that to make sure you keep it in mind while writing each season. Take note that growth and change might not only apply to your characters but also to objects, locations, or factions.

- **Character Relationships:** Your actors might also experience a change in interpersonal relations with the other characters. Characters who used to be friends are now foes, others have a budding romance, or a mentor has disappeared. Consider: Which relationships will be focused on in which season? How do relationships change? To keep track of something as potentially complex as this, a character matrix can be useful, where core relationships are tracked and summed up over the seasons, marking when they are central and when they experience change. **Interpersonal changes** can be a central drive of your narrative, akin to soap operas or TV dramas, focusing on shifting dynamics and relationships between characters and factions. This doesn't only have to be about romance, but can also shift between statuses such as:
  - Strangers
  - Teammates or coworkers
  - Friends
  - Found family
  - Lovers
  - Rivals
  - Nemeses
  - On the same side
  - On the opposite side
  - Reluctant collaborators
  - Manipulator
  - Mentor

  You can go into more detail than that, of course, logging interpersonal conflicts, aligning or opposite goals, shared or conflicting values, etc. – whatever is relevant for the season's narrative developments (see Figure 12.3).
- **Factions:** Deeply related to the evolution of character relationships, you might also want to explore the evolution of factions in your seasonal story. If your world has factions and groups, this means that members may join or leave, the inner politics and hierarchies may change, and they might have a different agenda from season to season. What can start out as a heroic group may turn out to be an extreme group driven by vitriol and misguided intentions, making them new antagonists when they used to be allies to the faction of the playable character. Also mind the relationships between factions,

B \ A	John	Nick	Mary	Stacy
John		Dislikes	Dislikes	Collaborators
Nick	Likes		Neighbors	Aware of
Mary	Romantic interest	Neighbors		Strangers
Stacy	Collaborators	Suspicious of	Strangers	

FIGURE 12.3   Example character relationship matrix.

and in how far their goals and ideologies clash in each season. Factions can join forces, merge into one, or split up into a whole variety of splinter groups. Especially when your drama is driven by inter-group conflicts, like in war or vigilante settings, the evolution of factions can provide an interesting foundation of your seasonal plot.

- **Evolving Storylines:** Depending on your level of changes across the seasons, you need to track the evolution of storylines that carry over into the next season. When you show change within a season, you'll likely have to continue that change in the season that follows to keep a narrative consistency, unless the arc is wrapped up and doesn't have a permanent effect on anything that follows. On the other hand, these changes can be smaller, such as a character having a new job, a character growing older, or characters referring to a big event that has happened in that season. Also, not all plot threads need to be wrapped up within one season. If anything, it's easier to keep your audiences curious about what's coming next if you don't. An open topic or narrative thread can be picked up in a later season, either as the starting point to a new main arc or as part of a side arc. Depending on your narrative roadmap, some stories may be told through changes from season to season, rather than having a progression within a season. For example, if you have a game season without plot, but only gameplay and cosmetic content and season trailers, a narrative evolution can happen through the difference in these elements from one season to the next.
- **Evolving Worlds:** The evolution of your world, if you plan to employ it, is part of your seasonal narrative as well. This is a live game with a living world, after all, and even if you don't have a season plot akin to an ongoing TV show, you might still create implied narrative through the changes of the world players exist in. This includes map expansions, adding new maps, and changes on existing maps. These changes can either be feedback to an event that has happened, a change of the thematic focus, the introduction of a new narrative, or the implication of a story through visual design and changes from one season to the next. What has been a ruin in one season might be rebuilt in the next, implying the action of an actor in the story. What was

once part of the land has now become an island, implying a change in nature or even a natural catastrophe. A settlement might be destroyed after a beast attacked. What can change about an environment is its environmental and geographical factors, its artificial structures, social erosions, decorations, and situational remains from human or other activity.

But the map isn't the only aspect of a world that can grow. The evolution of a world can also be expressed through changes in its game systems, environment systems, NPC behavior, barks, sound design, music, and more. Ideally, they all work together, inasmuch as your project has the budget and systems for it. For example, if a camp has been destroyed, the local sound design can be quieter and more eerie than before, previous NPCs are gone and are exchanged with a new enemy type, and the NPCs could have barks that refer to the event that has happened.

For more on evolving worlds, see Chapter 11, section: Environment as Narrative.

- **Other Evolving Narrative Content:** Whatever narrative tools you choose to tell your seasonal story, make sure to lay out and consider the narrative implications of those changes. If something hasn't been mentioned here, that doesn't mean you shouldn't track it. If you see an opportunity for seasonal storytelling in your project, which would bring changes over the seasons, make sure to track it.

CHAPTER SUMMARY

- A **content release framework** consists of a release schedule, the narrative vision of your seasonal content, and your various types of content packages.
- **Release packages** define the way that you tell your story during live operations, so they make up the core of the experience.
- When **planning your schedule**, be mindful of **different player types** and how quickly they consume new content
- This is influenced by player motivation, time investment, skill, money investment, state of progression, and sociability.
- Content can be released as **permanent, time-limited, or time-specific** (live).
- **Permanent content** enables a standardized progression and creates a growing library of content.
- On the negative side, it creates larger game file sizes and might be overwhelming or have content invisible to the majority of players.
- These risks can be mitigated by creating permanent onboarding, allowing several entry points, making information of past seasons

accessible, making a main story permanent, making time-limited content self-contained or striking a balance between permanent and time-limited additions.

- **Time-limited and live content** can drive moment-to-moment motivation, increase short-term engagement, and has marketing potential.
- On the negative side, ongoing production costs are significant, and players might jump into the middle of a story arc and get lost.
- These risks can be mitigated with tech solutions, several starting points for different content, and a guided player experience to make players aware of their options but not overwhelmed.
- Permanent content can also include **content generation systems**, such as emergent gameplay systems, procedurally generated content or tools for player-generated content.
- A **narrative roadmap** should provide overviews of mood and game feel, topics and themes, goals and conflicts, player role, main cast, character growth, character relationships, factions, evolving storylines, evolving worlds, and other evolving narrative content.

REFERENCE

1 "The State of Mobile Gaming 2023: An Analysis of Mobile Gaming Market Trends and Top Titles in the U.S., Europe, and Asia," Sensor Tower, March 2023, p. 34.

13 Writing Your Seasonal Plot

After we've decided on the methods we want to employ to tell our seasonal stories, it's time to actually write them. Depending on the narrative tools you've chosen, your project may include a story progression that continues over the seasons, akin to a seasonal television show. This chapter will offer strategies how to **structure such a seasonal plot progression**. This will not only help us write dramatic arcs for game seasons but also **any kind of story progression** you might choose to add to your game.

As video games aren't the first medium to try their hands at seasonal storytelling, other media will serve as our inspiration. To understand how to write a season for a live game, we will take a look at the methods of writing for television shows and see how we can apply our learnings to games. Additionally, we will take a look at seasonal story opportunities unique to live games, that go beyond TV structures.

In order to gain a better understanding of the narrative overlap between live games and TV series, let's first compare their structures side by side (Table 13.1).

TABLE 13.1

Comparison between TV Shows and Live Games

TV Shows	Live Games
– A **sequence of episodes and** (possibly) **arcs**	– A **sequence of episodes and** (possibly) **arcs**
– **Seasonal/episodic release**	– **Seasonal/episodic release**
– Pre-determined pacing, a **passive audience**	– Interactive pacing, an **active audience**
– **Pre-determined progression** per season (watching episodes in order) *(Note: If a TV show receives transmedia projects, such as specials, spin-offs, and other tie-in media, audiences can choose to consume them in any order.)*	– Possibly **several interactive, nonlinear, and/or parallel progressions**
– **Live broadcast:** Release is **time-specific,** broadcasted, and repeated at scheduled times	– Release can be **permanent, time-limited or time-specific**
– **Streaming** and on-demand: Release is (more or less) **permanent,** either through streaming or download	
– **Home media:** Release is **permanent,** and usually comes after live broadcast or streaming releases	
– **Plot-driven or character-driven** content	– Can include **plot-driven or character-driven** content, but doesn't have to
	– **Nonstory narrative content** is a central storytelling method (gameplay, environment, visual design, etc.)

DOI: 10.1201/9781003297628-17

As you can see, what's unique about video games is that they are **interactive**, which means **pacing depends on player actions**, and they can have **several progressions** within the same product. Content can be released **permanently or for a limited time or even as a live broadcast (time-specific)**. Also, they additionally make use of **nonstory narrative** to express a narrative – beyond cinematic dialogue, cutscenes, or traditional audiovisual dramaturgy. This includes using context, gameplay, game systems, environment design, and visual design in general but also micro copy like names and texts. Transmedia content, such as trailers, can set up narrative context without plot, as well.

But when it comes to writing a live game's season, or rather, features that have a **plot-driven dramatic arc** (such as a narrative progression of dialogues or missions), TV shows are the best role model we have. Even if your project doesn't employ this narrative method, these lessons can also be partially applied to the changes from season to season, which are another method of expressing a progressing narrative over time.

DRAMATIC STRUCTURE IN GAMES

But first, let's take a look at drama in videogames in general. Not live games, not even narrative-driven games, but just games as a medium. The dramatic structure in videogames follows its gameplay structure or at least that would be ideal for optimal alignment between narrative and gameplay experience. Since games are an interactive medium, drama and tension are created through audience action, meaning **gameplay** (how a player interacts with the game), the game's level of **challenge**, in all its frustrations and victories as well as additional emotional and narrative **contextualizations** on top of these actions. This fact creates a few dependencies between your narrative drama and your game drama – if you want your narrative and gameplay tension to align, for a synchronized holistic game experience, you need to understand the tension curves created by game loops and challenges over time. Since game design and narrative go hand in hand, it's not so much about asking your game design team what they did and then add some narrative later, but rather, figuring out the *vision of the complete dramatic experience*, and then game design and narrative design construct it together, with each of their crafts working in tandem.

There are a few key words relevant for understanding the dramatic structure of games:

GAME LOOPS

Game loops are loops of actions that repeat throughout a videogame, creating an ebb and flow of actions and effects. A loop defines the set of actions undertaken by the player, over and over again, usually with a reward or resolution at the end, before a new loop begins. More complex games often have several game loops that take turns. In live games, these game loops are often separated into **core game loops and meta game loops**, whereas the core loop is the *action phase* and meta loop is the *debriefing phase,* defined by reward claiming, upgrading, and strategic preparation before the next core game loop session. A meta progression is also usually persistent (such as character leveling or mission progressions), whereas the core game loop is often

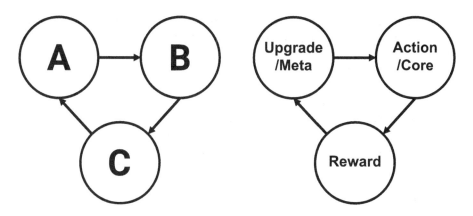

FIGURE 13.1   Game loops.

reset each time – except for the strategic improvements applied during the meta layer. The core layer is usually action-driven and fast-paced, while the meta layer is usually reflective, strategic, and not time-sensitive. This means that longer narrative units may be better off in the meta layer, in case you have a fast-paced or even multiplayer-driven game (such as MOBAs, Battle Royales, Multiplayer FPS, or even Rhythm or Puzzle games) (see Figure 13.1).

Each game loop should follow a small dramatic arc, since it contains a set-up (intention of outcome), an action, and a resolution to that action. Now, a game isn't only a sequence of tiny arcs and then the game ends. Over time, the tension is meant to build up to something greater than the sum of its parts. You don't want a player to feel the same throughout the same game, without a sense of improvement and increasing challenges, just as much as you don't want an audience to feel like a story isn't building up to something (this is where *context and challenge* come into play, more on that later). In fact, game loops can be considered analogous to movie scenes, while the challenge curve can be considered analogous to the dramatic structure of the whole movie. This means that a game loop already defines our smallest dramatic structure unit, which should be accompanied and **contextualized** by a **narrative framing.**

Each game loop has an implicit **conflict-action-resolution** arc, even without any narrative added to it: What am I trying to achieve through my actions and why? What am I doing, as a player, to achieve these actions? And then, finally, how are my actions resolved, and what is the impact I had on the world? This can be as simple as: I want to defeat these enemies to be able to cross the area. I defeat the enemies. The area is cleared and I receive a reward for it as well as an open path to the next area.

By adding a narrative context, these game loops gain an emotional meaning and enable the player to experience the story through actions. This does not mean that we need a dialogue set-up for every small thing we do, naturally – narrative context can be created through previous explanations, or setting, worldbuilding, visuals, naming, feedback, barks, etc. The goal of clearing an area from enemies feels very different when you're a spy killing security guards in a government building, compared to when you're an outlaw in the Wild West pulling a big heist in a rich town.

Changing the player's experience of the gameplay through narrative information, given in the form of story, visuals, sounds, naming, mechanics, etc. is called **narrative contextualization**, or framing.

So, to summarize:

- **Game loops** provide the smallest dramatic arc in games and should receive some kind of narrative contextualization
- **Core game loops** can often be time-sensitive, and may not be best suited for longer narrative units, unless they mesh well with the pacing of the action
- **Meta game loops** are usually not time-sensitive, and well-suited for longer narrative units, but may end up feeling detached from the action of the player

But there are likely going to be other tension loops that envelop the smallest game loops. Something bigger, such as **missions** (a set of actions required to complete a goal), **game levels**, **game regions,** or **other progressions**. These loops should also be accompanied by a **narrative contextualization**, but this time, it makes sense to also add a **clear narrative arc**. The relevant context comes with the three steps of a game loop and can be portrayed with dialogue, text, visuals, game mechanics, sound feedback, and whatever tools you have at your disposal.

CONTEXTUALIZATION OF GAME LOOPS

Narrative contextualization is the concept of adding a narrative framework to the elements of the game, and the actions that transpire during gameplay. When applied to a game loop, contextualization is the narrative framework that gives the dramatic arc its meaning. Therefore, the narrative contextualization is what creates the narrative layer and arc of a game loop. Contextualization isn't only about having an NPC be a questgiver that explains everything though. Contextualization is also about the narrative meaning of game elements, as mentioned in previous chapters *(see Chapter 7 and Chapter 11),* since a story can also be told without texts and cutscenes, and can be given with visuals, names, sound feedback, etc.

When it comes to game loops, the narrative framing is the narrative layer of the individual dramatic steps. In adherence to the structure of a game loop, the narrative questions of each step usually boil down to the following:

1. **Conflict**
   Instructing the player of their required actions to complete the game loop.
   - What is the goal of their actions?
   - Why are they supposed to do it? What are the reasons and emotional stakes?
   - What are the consequences going to be?
   - What rewards can they hope for, what effect will they have on the game world and their own avatar?

2. **Action**
   Actions taken to achieve the end of the game loop.
   - What are the individual steps they have to take?
   - What conflicts do they run into along the way?
   - Who and what is involved?
3. **Resolution**
   After the player has completed the required actions and game loop.
   - Depiction of the true consequences of the player's actions, based on what was anticipated in Step 1.
   - Are they being rewarded?
   - Has their character changed? Has the world changed?

This is a dramatic 3-arc structure,[1] aligning with the steps of a game loop. They can function entirely without words, too, if the player understands the individual steps anyway, with the help of visuals, gameplay, or microcopy. Not all of these loops need to tell a big epic story, either. Some game loops are small, and the tension is simple. Usually, this is only the smallest unit of dramatic storytelling in a game and will be embedded in much larger pieces.

Curiously, the same structure applies to quests that can, by themselves, have individual game loops inside of them. You will find that we're building a nesting doll of dramatic arcs filled with smaller arcs filled with smaller arcs. You'll see that this is a recurring thing in dramatic videogame storytelling (if you weren't already aware of it anyway).

To give **a few examples** of **narrative arcs of game loops**:

Example 1: The Temple Room Puzzle

1. **Conflict:** There is another locked temple room in front of us, and we need to get inside. The architecture and level design suggests that this is where we can find treasures and continue our game journey. We're motivated by curiosity about the temple and promises of rewards. Sculptures outside might even suggest a personal relevance to a culture that our avatar has personal investment in.
2. **Action:** We solve a room puzzle that speaks of intricate architectural prowess of the culture which built this location.
3. **Resolution:** The room opens up. Our curiosity to see what's inside is satisfied, and there are rewards for our success, too.

Example 2: The Fish Collection

1. **Conflict:** We now own a fishing rod that enables us to fish. Rivers and ponds promise us many different kinds to find – driving our curiosity about the environment. There's an NPC who promised us information about the local animals, if we collected all the types of fish at least once.

2. **Action:** We locate the right fishing location, use various lures, and finally pull the right fish on land.
3. **Resolution:** With each fish, we see our collection growing. After we've repeated the loop often enough and caught all the fish, the NPC tells us the promised information.

Example 3: The Battle Arena

1. **Conflict:** We are fighting for our survival in a battle arena. Our goal is to become the strongest fighter. By fighting, we are promised rewards and ways to grow even stronger. We're playing as a specific hero, who is fighting for dominance over other defined unique characters.
2. **Action:** We fight and defeat opponents, to the best of our skills.
3. **Resolution:** With the experience, we've grown as a fighter. We can improve our weapons with the rewards we've earned. We can enter the next match better prepared.

CHALLENGE CURVES

A game isn't just a sequence of short narrative loops with a 3-act structure. Just creating a series of those, one after the other, would give us a sequence of small tension arcs that don't build up to anything, with no rising tension. In this case, players are more likely to tire of it (unless we're dealing with a cozy low-stakes game). Therefore, we have to take a step back and look at the game as a whole. Before we add any plot-driven story elements on top of our game (such as cutscenes or mission progressions), there is a bigger dramatic structure inherent to games: The rising level of challenge in gameplay. However, narrative should align with, support and enhance the dramatic arc of the gameplay itself, instead of trying to to its own thing.

So, does that mean our game just gets harder over time, in a straight rising line? Not quite. This would keep the perceived level of tension the same, and that could result in fatigue in boredom as well. The answer lies in the previously mentioned **flow theory**[2] by Csikszentmihalyi, a psychological concept describing the state of complete hyperfocus while executing an activity.

In order to achieve this state of flow in games, one must design difficulty curves that try to keep the player in a perfect balance between feeling challenged enough that they don't get bored, but not too challenged to be overwhelmed. However, over time, a person's skills will improve, meaning that they need a higher stimulation/challenge to feel the same way. People want to *feel* that they're getting better sometimes, too. And for that, they need moments of perceived competence, interrupting the tension of challenge.

This means that games are (ideally) designed with an ever-rising difficulty, composed of smaller challenge curves; players get into a pleasant rhythm of challenge, growth, power, and relaxation. Players face a new challenge, have to improve to be able to overcome it, and then they can ride the wave of feeling powerful until the next challenge begins again. This can be a level, a world, or a chapter. Those are usually made up of game loops. These small challenge curves can be called micro-flow

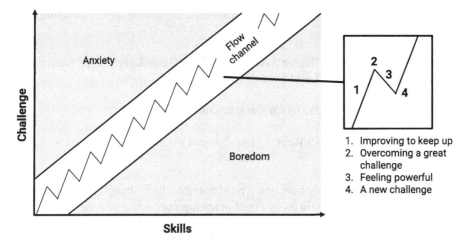

FIGURE 13.2 Challenge progression over time for optimal flow.

(short-term), whereas the sequence of the micro-flow states creates the macro-flow, staying with the game for a long time. This means that there is a flow channel of the ideal, satisfying challenge progression – and instead of a constant rising curve, it looks more like a rising wave, as defined by Jesse Schell.[3]

The drama of your narrative should align with that: The tension arcs of your game loops, embedded in the arcs of levels, embedded in the arcs of regions, and embedded in the arc of the whole game (and how many sub-arc sequences you add in between).

The *story* arc needs to raise the stakes over time, too, parallel to the game's dramatic curve (see Figure 13.2).

MICRO AND MACRO NARRATIVE

The term micro narrative describes narrative in its smallest units, observed in moment-to-moment narrative experience as players go through game loops, and the individual elements of a game. Macro narrative is the big picture, the story that is being told over the entirety of the game. The concept of micro and macro narrative is that a game's narrative themes should be reflected in the smallest as well as in the biggest dramatic layer of a story. And these two need to align, mirroring one another, to create one pleasing coherent experience. Otherwise, you'd create a conflict between your players' actual lived experience and the story and themes the game is going for. Movies function in the same way: Each scene should relate to and expand on the themes of the entire film, giving it depth and layers, rather than feeling disconnected and random.

In a game, these layers aren't movie scenes (small) and the whole movie (big), but game loops (small) and the entire game (big) – whereas both have steps in between, such as arcs (in a movie) and levels (in a game). What you do from moment to moment should directly relate to the bigger themes of the game, so that the player's actions tie into what the game is exploring as a whole.

This layering of themes can look several ways, depending on the structure. For example:

- Full Game > Game Region > Active Mission > Game Loop
- Full Game > Game Level > Game Loop

Or also like this, when we're looking at live game content:

- Full Game > Season > Week > Time-Limited Events > Game Session > Game Loop

A game doesn't always only have one type of narrative loop, though, for example, an action adventure can contain loops about defeating enemies, exploring exotic locations, and solving puzzles. But they all tie into the bigger fantasy of being an artifact hunter in a foreign land, and the bigger story arc about his adventure there. The micro narrative is, therefore, providing puzzle pieces that express the bigger picture (the macro narrative). If you don't pay attention to how your small arcs relate to the bigger story arc, the end result can easily feel disjointed, contradictory, and dissatisfying. In the worst case scenario, the game's intention becomes either unclear or completely defeated.

SEASONAL STORYTELLING IN TELEVISION

Television has been broadcasting long-form storytelling for much longer than videogames. Their episodic structure mirrors the episodic nature of game missions, levels, and regions, while telling an overarching story over the course of a season (like a game, in its entirety). In that regard, writing for television is relevant to videogames as a whole, but even more so when it comes to live games, where we're trying to tell a story that will continue over many seasons. Therefore, our greatest role model for dramatic structure is the TV show. We're going to take a look at different seasonal structures, approaches to continuity, the relation between episodes and seasons, as well as genre-specific season structures. These learnings can help us write the (seasonal) story progression(s) for our live game.

WRITING FOR TV

A TV show is fundamentally different from a movie in terms of pacing, character growth, and structure. Due to the long-running nature of a series, characters continue to act, talk, and change for hours on end, instead of going through *one* dramatic arc of change over the course of a 90 to 120 minutes long movie. Therefore, the focus is on depth and complexity of characters, revealing more and more about who they are as a person, rather than a constant and drastic change in every single episode. This means that they approach character and growth in a fundamentally different way from cinema – and something that we need to apply to live games, too.

Additionally, these bigger stories of (possible) change aren't told through scenes, but through episodes, which each act as their own self-contained story, and eventually add up to something bigger. Depending on the format of a series, the focus is on episodic self-contained stories within a story world, or the dramatic continuation of an epic plot told through self-contained episodes that make up that bigger arcs, or sometimes something in between. Either way, TV series are inherently composed of nested story arcs – just like videogames.

TV shows also have space to focus on more than one character, but instead a whole cast of main characters, supported by side characters and cameos. While the main characters are the focus and center of a TV show (often depicted in A-plots, see the upcoming section *Writing an Episode*), the side characters are often going through their own stories (in B-plots), reinforcing the themes of the episode, revealing a new perspective on the conflict, emphasizing the personality of the main characters or, simply, experiencing their own adventures.

Additionally, due to the distribution model of TV shows in the past, they had to accommodate the possibility of audiences jumping in at any random point of the season (*this* is highly relevant to us, as live games struggle with the same problem). However, nowadays, people don't have to wait for DVD box releases anymore, since streaming services like Netflix enable audiences to binge a season in chronological order. It's no wonder that this technological change has seen a lot of highly continuous serialized shows with high production costs. This doesn't mean, however, that we can't take inspiration from a variety of TV show structures, depending on the structure of our game.

RELEVANCE FOR LIVE GAMES

The length and structure of many video games lend themselves to taking inspiration from TV shows, rather than movies, but this is doubly true for live games. The player is going to experience an on-going in many continuous sessions, after all, and not in one single sitting. An episodic nature is inherent to the design of videogames anyway – just consider level- and mission-structures, which separate gameplay experiences into self-contained scenes and arcs. But live games intend to go on for even longer, and just like TV shows, have to struggle with keeping the audience's attention for a long time to come, while accomodating for late joiners as well.

Since games are an interactive medium with the possibility for multiple progressions and multiple methods of storytelling inside of one game, they require a slightly different structure from a TV show, if considered as a whole. They are multi-track, multi-progression, and multi-interaction media formats, as opposed to the linear chronology of a TV show that has an episodic structure. They can even function without any narrative progressions within a season, but just a story told through the changes from one season to the next (such as themes and gameplay releases). However, parts of a live game can look very similar to a TV show, in particular its **plot-driven progressions**. These progressions can have a narrative layer consisting of a sequence of missions, a series of cutscenes, a collection of unlockable documents, or something along those lines. They might be exclusive to a season, and serve as the season's plot – which makes the comparison to television even more poignant. They can, however, also be permanent additions that continue the existing plot – structuring ongoing permanent content in contained arcs (like in the mobile games Episode or Chapters).

When writing these specific parts of a season's narrative content release, these plot-driven progressions, the dramatic structure of television shows gives us a great idea of how to do it – and we can lean on their decades of experience working with a similar fictional structure.

CONTINUITY – SERIES, SERIALS, AND ANTHOLOGIES

TV shows are traditionally separated into various formats, depending on how they handle continuity. A show can be one continuous story, chopped up into episodes, or consist of individual short stories that just share the same cast and setting. They are defined as an **episodic series** (often found in half-hour sitcoms and cartoons; they're also called *procedurals,* especially in the context of case-of-the-week structures for law shows), a **serial** (often found in one-hour dramas) or an **anthology** (reserved for anthology series). These differentiations imply not only how they approach continuity, but also character growth across episodes and seasons. Length is usually also a factor, whereas series are more likely to be short (30 minutes) and serials are more likely to be long (1 hour), but this is no hard rule and usually more related to the genre, rather than the show type.

These different formats answer the questions:

- Are episodes self-contained or sequential?
- Will characters grow over the course of the seasons? How important is it to witness that growth?
- Do audiences need knowledge of previous episodes to understand what's happening if they jump into a random episode?

The following table will lay out the approaches of these different TV show formats (Table 13.2).

As you can see in the table, seasons often have key episodes which take on a special role: **Season beginnings and season finales**. They're used to introduce and resolve the bigger dramatic arc of the season if the show chooses to have one. They are often used as markers of significant events, and for episodic shows, they might be the only moments that introduce a change in the seasonal progression of the show – leaving the other episodes self-contained and with a less urgent need to be seen in chronological order. This is something we can use as inspiration for live seasons, especially if they have no "episodes" to speak of.

APPLIED TO GAMES

These different formats of continuity can directly be applied to your live game. When planning your game season, decide on your level of continuity between seasons. However, since your game can have multiple progressions that may be played in any order, you can even apply several different approaches to continuity to different progressions of your game.

- Will characters grow over the course of one season or story progression?
- Will character growth carry over into future seasons or other progressions?

TABLE 13.2
Comparison between Different TV Show Formats

	Episodic Series (Non-sequential)	Episodic Series (Semi-sequential)	Serial (Sequential)	Anthology
Continuity	– Episodic reset – Self-contained standalone stories, audiences can jump in at any time	– Episodic soft reset (some changes are carried over to following episodes, but audiences won't be disoriented if they watch a random episode) – Self-contained standalone stories, audiences can jump in anywhere – May contain a special season beginning and a season finale, which introduce and resolve a conflict that is vaguely relevant throughout the season, but usually not the center of attention	– Sequential Narrative – Each episode directly continues the previous episode, possibly adding a cliffhanger at the end of an episode hinting at what comes next – A dramatic arc across the season, which is introduced in the beginning, has several dramatic developments throughout, and is resolved by the end of it	– Self-contained stories, audiences can watch them in any order – Episodes have a shared creative vision, such as genre, topics, themes, characters, or settings – May contain a shared framing device, such as a narrator on a meta story
Watch order	– Watchable in any order	– Watchable in any order, but contains changes across the seasons which can only be understood and appreciated when certain key episodes are watched in order	– Episodes need to be watched in order to properly understand and enjoy the plot	– Watchable in any order

(Continued)

TABLE 13.2 (Continued)
Comparison between Different TV Show Formats

	Episodic Series (Non-sequential)	Episodic Series (Semi-sequential)	Serial (Sequential)	Anthology
Character growth	– No growth – characters stay (mostly) the same – Learnings are self-contained to episodes – New lore instead of changes: New situations reveal new information about the world and its characters, such as personality traits and dynamics between characters	– Slow growth – characters stay (mostly) the same – Learnings may carry over into later episodes and be referenced later (in callbacks, flashbacks, jokes, or general changes) – Bigger changes are rare and often (but not always) limited to season finales/beginnings	– Focus on character growth – Significant changes throughout a season, which carry over into the following seasons, too	– New characters or conflicts for each episode – Growth is contained to individual episodes and doesn't influence any of the other episodes
Change over seasons	– Usually only a shift in themes, which doesn't need to be understood in the context of other seasons	– Often a shift in thematic focus, introducing a new setting or core conflict (which doesn't need to be understood in the context of other seasons) – Character learnings may carry over, and big changes usually introduced during season premieres or finales	– Significant changes from season to season, which build on each other	– Seasons are independent, like the episodes, but may choose to introduce new concepts or themes
Popular genre	– Comedy, animated	– Comedy, animated	– Drama	– Any
Example TV shows	– SpongeBob Squarepants, Seinfeld	– Rick and Morty, The Nanny	– Breaking Bad, Game of Thrones	– Black Mirror, Twilight Zone

- Do players need knowledge of previous seasons to understand what's happening in any given episode? Is every season self-contained and a new entry point (with a new cast, new goal, etc.)? And if not, how do we give players the required information?
- Are episodes self-contained or sequential? (e.g., self-contained short story missions vs. a sequence of missions)

To give an example, I'll paint you a picture of a hypothetical (ambitious) game that includes **all three formats** in the same game.

- A **seasonal main story** progression, which includes character growth. Not every mission directly drives the story forward, and players have some freedom to choose the order of missions in the middle. There is a season premiere and a season finale, which are timed live events. Character changes carry over to the next season. These changes are briefed in the next season's trailer, no matter if a player had reached this point or not. (→ "Semi-Sequential Series")
- There are also **character-driven missions** that are sequential and need to be played in a specific order. Playing as a specific character unlocks missions in a sequence. They tell one story arc about the character being played. The next season adds a new progression that continues the character's journey with a new arc. (→ "Serial")
- Additionally, there are self-contained **side missions** attached to a variety of NPCs. They do not require any previous knowledge and don't cause any change in the seasonal story. They function like short stories. (→ "Anthology")

Keep in mind that applying continuity to a game with various progressions or temporary progressions also comes with its challenges. Ask yourself: Can players access a part of the story that comes after another part before having played that previous part (like an old season and a new season)? Can they still understand the story, no matter which order they play them in? Or will you limit their access in order to avoid this (by creating dependencies between progressions, for example)? Make sure to plan for all your dependencies and try to limit continuity errors or confusion.

WRITING AN EPISODE

A-, B-, AND C-PLOTS

An episode can usually be separated into several parallel plot progressions, between which we cut back and forth. Instead of just one conflict, TV shows usually combine several parallel conflicts in the same episode, to be allowed to give focus on multiple characters and keep viewers curious and engaged. When one plot-string is interrupted to switch to another part of the cast, they remain curious about how it will continue, while not getting immediate satisfaction. Those plots take turns and take up screentime; however, the writer sees fit and they often tie into similar themes, complement each other, or cross over at some point.

They can be described as the main plot, the side plot(s), and additional narrative that refers to events that have happened outside of the current episode, continuing long-term narratives or simply referencing previous events.

- The **A-Plot (main plot)** is the primary focus of the episode, dealing with its main characters and the current core conflict. It drives the momentum of the episode and has the most amount of screentime. It's usually introduced and resolved within the same episode.
- The **B-Plot (side plot)** is the secondary storyline (or several secondary storylines) often headed by characters who are less central, either in general, or in this episode specifically. It often thematically mirrors or enhances the A-Plot, offering new sides, perspectives, and aspects of the conflict. It can, however, also be entirely separate from it, and just a way to give side characters something fun to do. It's also usually introduced and resolved within the same episode.
- The **C-Plot (also called "runner")** is a continuation of something that has happened in previous episodes or even previous seasons. They're ongoing references or stories with a long-term pay-off. In the case of series without long-running arcs, C-plots can also be running gags that neither tie into the A- or B-plot. They can be highly meaningful or just a callback for the sake of a joke.

With that said, shows can have more than A-, B-, and C-plots in each episode, especially when they're a full hour long. In that case, this usually means that there are several B-plots, which focus on different sets of side characters and side conflicts.

Applied to Games

Since we're creating an interactive, nonlinear experience, videogame can separate A-, B-, and C-plots into different progressions and locations inside of the game. But you can also create a TV-inspired progression that integrates all of these elements into the same progression. Anyhow, since we're working with another medium, it's worth it to consider using its unique ways of storytelling in a way that utilizes the medium's unique strengths and fits your project. Because of that, an A-plot could be the seasonal main progression, while B-plots could be inserted as side progressions, such as optional character-focused or time-limited progressions, while the C-plot might surface within both of these, as well as the visual and gameplay direction of the season.

An Episode's Structure

Each episode is divided into several acts, which define the dramatic purpose of its contained scenes. Originally, this separation was based on the amount of commercial breaks. This is why short episodes (24–30 minutes) are traditionally 2-Act and 3-Act structures, whereas longer episodes can be anything between 4-Act and 6-Act structures. The dramatic curve remains the same, just either more condensed or spread out.

In a **3-Act structure**, commonly used for 30-minute comedies, an episode is divided into three acts. They are similar in length and possibly framed by two additional much shorter scenes in the beginning and in the end (namely *teaser* and *tag*).

- **Teaser/Cold Open:** Some shows choose to add a teaser before the actual first act, which is a high-intensity moment to hook audiences into the show to make sure they stick around for the rest of the episode. It establishes the tone, setting, and characters like a sales pitch. This scene throws the audience into the middle of the action, a dramatic moment, or a funny joke. It either teases what the episode is going to be about (usually if dramatic) or stands completely independent from the rest (usually if comedic). The intro sequence of the TV show often follows *after* the teaser.
- **Act I: Conflict:** The central conflict is introduced with an inciting incident and establishes the character's initial plan how to react to it. Audiences find out what's at stake if the protagonists fail this challenge.
- **Act II: Action:** The characters embark on a course of action in order to solve the conflict, but they face new obstacles along the way. At the end of act 2, the story should have taken a new, unexpected direction.
- **Act III: Resolution:** The characters come up with a solution, overcome the final obstacle and resolve the conflict in some way (may that be good or bad).
- **Tag:** A tag is an *optional* mini-act which takes place after the dramatic resolution and before the credits. It serves as a wrap-up, final comment, or epilogue of the story. It shows the after-effects of the plot and how everything has returned to normal (or a new status quo). Alternatively, it sends the audience off with a last standalone joke or running gag (which is usually the case for comedy). This scene can also serve as a **cliffhanger** to tease the next episode or hint at unfinished storylines.

In a **5-Act structure**, commonly used for 60-minute dramas, the steps of the progression are more detailed but retain the same basic principles.

- **Teaser/Cold Open.**
- **Act I: Exposition:** An overview of the current state of the world, the main characters, the antagonists, and other needed context. The central conflict is introduced with an inciting incident. For an ongoing TV show, the exposition can be very short, and the inciting incident takes the main stage.
- **Act II: Rising Action:** The conflict escalates as the characters work toward achieving their goals. On their way, they encounter a series of obstacles and possible antagonization from other characters or situations. They're discovering what would be the worst possible outcome of the conflict, putting more pressure on them. At the end of the act, they think they have found the solution – but this will usually turn out to be false.

- **Act III: Climax:** The story's midpoint, where the tension reaches its peak and the characters are at their lowest point. This can be a turning point, a twist, or a major throwback for the protagonists, which may change how they will tackle their problems. The solution they thought they had found in Act II turns out to not work, so they need to find a new approach.
- **Act IV: Falling Action:** The final actions that will ultimately lead to the inevitable resolution. There are additional complications, escalations, and learnings for the protagonists. Audiences may already see the ending coming from this point on (or think they do) and only wait for it to realize itself. In a 4-Act structure, Acts IV and V are combined into one.
- **Act V: Resolution:** With new strength or knowledge, the protagonists manage to resolve the conflict, which brings the story of the episode to an end. The goal has been achieved, or not achieved, and we see the effects of that development. The characters have survived or even learned something from the challenge. If the show doesn't choose to have a *tag,* Act V may also leave audiences with unresolved questions, a cliffhanger or teaser for upcoming episodes, which makes them curious for what's to come.
- **Tag.**

As general rules, each act should begin and end on the A-story, whereas B- and C-stories are weaved in where applicable. Also, all main characters need to be in all acts – an act shouldn't only be about the A-, B-, or C-plot exclusively.

Also, note that ad breaks used to be located between acts, which means that writers had to make sure that audiences would stay around to see how the story continues. Because of that, each act should ideally end on a cliffhanger, question, or unresolved issue.

APPLIED TO GAMES

You can directly apply 3-act and 5-act different structures to the episode equivalent of your story progressions, whether they are part of the main or side progression. What you define as the dramatic equivalent of an episode will depend on the narrative design of each individual project – this could be a group of visual novel chapters, a group of missions, a series of unlockable cutscenes, or something else. If what you define as an "episode" is short, a 3-act structure is likely better suited for your storytelling. If it is longer, a 5-act structure makes more sense.

Your "episode" may not consist of three or five narrative pieces, but rather a separation into another number of missions, chapters, or cutscenes. This doesn't mean that you can't use the structure of a TV episode as a basis – you'd simply assign several narrative units to each act. After all, an act has several scenes, too. That way, one act could consist of two to three scenes, and still create the dramatic tension of a 3-act or 5-act structure.

The concept of a teaser and tag is the most unusual part of the structure if we're trying to apply it to games directly. Usually, they're not used in videogames – which doesn't mean that you can't think about adding them. They don't have to be the same format as the rest of your episode, they could be, for instance, a trailer or a cutscene.

Additionally, let's take special note of the use of cliffhangers and unresolved information when writing for TV. TV writers structure episodes with teasers at the end of each act, which would be followed by an *ad break*, so that audiences would continue watching. This can be applied to whatever story structure you're using for your game as well. However, since we don't have ad breaks at the end of each act, it makes sense to place cliffhangers more appropriately, before longer segments of gameplay or the player's freedom to take a break from this progression. For example, each mission might end with an open world gameplay break, where players can potentially go somewhere else. Or each visual novel chapter might end with a timed break, where players need to wait for new energy to be able to continue playing. This means that each unit of narrative should end with a cliffhanger, unresolved issue, or burning questions. This way, players will be more motivated to continue this story progression.

Note that 3-act and 5-act dramatic structures aren't the only ones that can be applied to games. TV shows are a mainstream medium designed to be easily digestible for a wide audience – and live games are usually aiming for mass market compatibility, as well. But that doesn't mean you can't research and apply other dramatic structures that fit your game's vision better.

WRITING A SEASON

CONFLICT

Conflict is at the core of a seasonal arc and the potential of character growth. This is usually driven by conflicts **between characters** (and their opposing viewpoints), **characters and the outside world**, and/or **characters and their inner world.**

Especially in drama shows, the latter is usually at the core of the personal character growth, on top of them going through external conflicts and challenges. A protagonist's inner conflict usually emerges from friction between their different personas (mentioned in *Chapter 10*): The public, private, and incognizant persona. Who they are in the presence of others (depending on social context), who they are when nobody else is present, and who they are at their core. Eventually, they are put into situation where that dissonance becomes so stressful that they are forced to go through change or break under the strain. (For more on that topic, refer to the later section *Writing Seasonal Character Development.*)

KEY MOMENTS

Seasons are the vehicle for changes and plot developments that are bigger than those of each individual episode, since they are the sum of all those episodes coming together. Depending on your show format, series, serial, or anthology, those changes are either non-existent (anthology, non-sequential series) or central (semi-sequential series, serial). If you are going to have changes, a season should start in one place, experience change, and end in another place – even *if* there is no visible evolution throughout the season, the switch from one season to the next is usually accompanied by some big change that differentiates the previous season from the next.

This applies to the **general conflict** of the season, as well as **individual character arcs** (though not all characters need to change in all seasons). A season either goes through similar steps as mentioned in *Writing an Episode,* or at least these two to three **key moments of change**:

1. **Season Premiere:** Episodes 1–2. This episode or double episode introduces the new core conflict and themes of the season and shows us most central characters involved in it. The audience might get a first idea of the steps that will be taken to solve the conflict.
2. **Optional Mid-Season Twist:** In the middle of the season. A drastic development, set-back, or plot twist that changes the audience's expectations regarding how this conflict will be resolved. Maybe the ending that audiences anticipated is proven to be impossible, now or in general.
3. **Season Finale:** Last 1–2 Episodes. The seasonal conflict is finally resolved, either by success, failure, or an unexpected diversion. It is also possible to postpone the resolution of the central conflict to future seasons, but the finale at least takes the characters into the next direction and allows them to reach a new insight or sub-goal.

Between your first episode and finale, there can be as many twists and turns as your story demands. If it is a serial procedural drama, you might want to have a new twist every episode – and a cliffhanger at the end of it, indicating which new conflict the next episode might cover. If you're writing a comedy show, you might only have big moments in the premiere and the finale, with maybe 1–2 developments in between (or none at all). As long as your conflict is resolved (or has seen a significant new change or twist) by the end of the season, it works.

When it comes to sub-conflicts, relating to individual characters, the change of the season might also happen somewhere in a random episode. In general, change isn't reserved for the beginning, middle, and end of a season, but can happen at any time, it's just that either the beginning or end or both *need* to establish the identity (core conflict and themes) of your season. What you do in between is a matter of your individual project choices.

Applied to Games

If you have a primary progression in your live game season, either through a main progression or live events that are tied to the passage of time, you can consider adding changes in a Key Moment I (Season Premiere), an optional Key Moment II (Mid-Season Twist) and Key Moment III (Season Finale), whereas there can be as many beats in between those as makes sense for your project. For the moments of your seasons tied to real time, which is the chronological start, middle, and end of availability, these key moments can be useful in the shape of meaningful time-limited or time-specific events that mark changes that are meant to happen to all players simultaneously – independent from player-driven progressions. The shift from one season to the other, is when change will happen anyway, and these premiere/finale moments are a way to introduce them narratively, while a mid-season twist can add more complexity and tension. Anyway, since you can have several progressions in the same game, you may apply these key moments to each progression individually as well, with as many steps in between as needed. Depending on the length and complexity of your narrative progressions, you may also want to apply other dramatic structures. Anyway, keep in mind that adding persistent changes to optional progressions might become more complicated when you want to refer to these changes in moments that players might see before they completed said progression – this can be avoided by not referring to these changes in any other place, or creating dependencies that prevent continuity errors.

WRITING SEASONAL CHARACTER DEVELOPMENT

VERTICAL CHARACTER DEVELOPMENT – PERSONAL CHANGES

If a character is meant to change in a big way, TV shows usually take an entire season to get them from point A to point B. This may as well be one step on a longer journey that leads to something even more extreme. But if you want to employ character change in your story, you establish the character's current state of self in the beginning of the season, let them experience the things they need to change, and have them end up another person (at least to some extend). Vertical character development is chronological, which means that a character cannot go back to how they were before after this season: This is our new normal. This character change can be driven by a variety of character conflicts. Here are some examples:

- **External vs. Internal Goal:** The character pursues an external goal, their wants, but realizes that this isn't what they need. They may or may not achieve the external goal, but it's more important that they recognized that this isn't what they needed, and perhaps even realize or achieve what they need instead.
- **Downfall:** The character engages in bad behavior, caused by their personality, environment, compulsions, or addictions, and gets worse and more desensitized over time. This causes them problems and gets them deeper into trouble.
- **Redemption Arc:** The character engaged in bad behavior in the past, and now tries to become a better person. They have to make things up to other people, adjust their behavior, and/or work through their own issues.
- **Trauma:** The character experiences something traumatizing, such as the loss of a loved one, violence, hopelessness, etc, and comes out a changed person.
- **Trauma Recovery:** The character was traumatized, and now has to recover from it and become whole again. This doesn't mean that they revert back to how they were before, but discover a new self.
- **Assumption of Power:** The character pursues and gains some kind of power, may that be physical, political, economic, financial, social, psychological, or something else.
- **Loss of Power:** The character has lost power they used to have in their life, may that be physical, political, economic, financial, social, psychological, or something else.

The effected changes can be about a character's identity (both self-perception and how others perceive them), their place in life (job, family, purpose, status, etc.), their ideals and goals, their behavior, their emotional world, their skills, and more.

HORIZONTAL CHARACTER DEVELOPMENT – NO PERSONAL CHANGES

It's important to note that your characters don't need to go through changes all the time. In fact, the change can be minor, or not exist at all. There is the chance of making your character more complex, rather than having them change, and revealing more about their past, their personality, and their different social personas (which are the different ways they act in different social environments and scenarios, such as work, family, friends, or on their own). You dig deeper, broadening our understanding of them, rather than taking them to new places. This doesn't have to be something that happens at the end of an episode or season either, but can take place at any given point of the story. But if you reveal something new about a character in an episode, chances are that episode will be perceived as adding something new and interesting to the series, which might be the starting point of new types of stories that build upon this new aspect of a character. There is no limit to how complex a character can become – you've got their whole past, hitherto unseen personality traits, and an endless amount of possible new scenarios that might bring out something new in them.

APPLIED TO GAMES

Either of these approaches can be directly applied to your live game. Alternatively, you can go for something in between as well: Rare and slow vertical character development with more frequent horizontal character development. Each of your characters can be treated differently, with the more central characters experiencing more development (possibly vertically) and the less central character experiencing less development (or more horizontally).

However, there is one aspect unique to live games: Even though your player's avatar is technically the most central character of the game, this doesn't mean that they need to go through the most change. Avatars can be their own person that players roleplay as, which allows for more change – but they can also be a blank slate avatar for the player's self-expression. Additionally, multiplayer environments such as MMORPGs create the issue that every player is hypothetically the main character in their own game, but not *the* main character of the whole game. This means that they either play their own instance of the story, or they become a part of a group along with other players. This means that this character change might have to be applied to a faction, rather than a person. Or the change is within the world and its NPCs, not the avatar itself, making the avatar more like an active observer and agent of change, rather than the true protagonist.

If your player embodies a written character, they can be treated as any other character when it comes to change and development – but remember that *choice* and interactivity might play a role in the nature of that development as well.

So, consider giving players options to drive the change of their avatar. For vertical character development, this could mean story choices creating story branches, influencing variables, changing attributes of their personality, etc. – and for horizontal development, this could mean choices and available content that shows the character in a new context that reveals something new about them, or, gives them the option to act in a way that makes them reveal something new about themselves as players.

WRITING A LIVE GAME SEASON

We've taken a look at how to write a plot-driven story progression for your live season, but that doesn't include everything we can do with it. Your live game may have **more than one progression**, but rather act as a collection of progressions, each with their own dramatic arc. Those progressions can be more central and less central to the main story of your game though (having different weight, focus, and length), and can take the role of A-plots and B-plots. Together, they then create what would be one television season, with players having more control over which storyline they follow first. A videogame can separate different plot lines of a TV show and give it their own space, progression and access points. Anyhow, it can be helpful to structure these individual progressions similar to a movie (if self-contained) or a TV season (if it's meant as the live season or sequential), with their *episodes* (which can be chapters, a mission or set of missions, dialogues, documents, etc.) structured in a 3- or 5-act structure, just like a TV show episode.

Anyway, if you want to have persistent seasonal changes (and from one season to the next, you'll likely want some thematic changes), it makes sense to take inspiration from **seasonal key moments (premiere, midpoint, finale)** in television. These moments must be attached to real time in some way, due to a game's season being tied to real time too. They can be designed as time-limited or live events but also expressed through new content releases alone, such as the beginning of a new season, the release of content, or a new trailer video. Additionally, narrative changes can be within the game itself, such as changes in gameplay, creative direction, or the layout of the map – and the player-synchronous update of these game elements is what expresses a narrative change. Your seasonal main story can therefore be a progression that **depends on player action** (permanent or time-limited to the duration of the season), or on the **passage of time**, whereas the main story progresses no matter if players are around for it or not (new chapter releases, changes inside of the game, or live events).

No two live games are structured the same, which means that you have to see which structure makes sense for your narrative systems, budget, and vision. This exploration of television writing is providing insight into tried and trusted conventions **for mainstream audiences** – there is no hard rule against being more experimental than that! But if you adhere to an established structure that audiences immediately feel at home with, you can focus more on the content of your story and have an easier time delivering information to players fast (which is usually what you want – they want to get back to playing the game after all). No matter the extent and complexity of your individual story progressions, these 3-act and 5-act structures, in combination with different approaches to continuity in television shows, will help you structure your narrative units meaningfully, and create tension and curiosity.

The key is to treat your seasonal story as a **nested narrative** of narrative segments embedded in larger progressions, embedded in even larger progressions, which are then told in sequence to other larger progressions. Also, use key moments for persistent changes and create dramatic arcs (inspired by television and other fiction) within each layer of the narrative.

WRITING SEVERAL PROGRESSIONS

What makes a live game different from TV is that it can contain more than one progression, each with their own focus, length, permanence, and format. They can refer to one another and have dependencies. So, one part of writing your dramatic progression for the season is to also understand the narrative systems and design of the entirety of your available progressions – together, they create the seasonal story, with main and side content.

Keep in mind: The way you can express a seasonal story evolution is not limited to episodic dialogues that you unlock over time or at the beginning of the season. It can also be in documents that players unlock, in the way your map changes over the course of the season, different gameplay features that go live across the season, live events at specific points in the season, and more. So, even if you don't plan to have a sequence of cutscenes, drama can also be structured with other tools of narrative design.

Here are a few questions that can guide **designing and writing** your **several seasonal progressions:**

- **Season Arcs, Season Changes, or Story Collections?** Live game seasons don't necessarily need to provide a sequence of story arcs to create dramatic change and thematic shifts. It can also create an implied story through the changes in the game, from one season to the next (such as visuals, sound, gameplay, etc). They can also drop new packages of narrative content, such as lore documents, characters, areas, descriptions, and more. This would be an increasing story collection that creates an indepth view into the world as it exists, rather than focusing on plot-driven change. Story collections are more akin to an anthology TV series structure, with self-contained episodes that don't (or barely) refer to each other – although some story collections may unlock sequentially, while others can be read in any order the player wants. The same project can employ both of these things, too. So the question is: Are there going to be sequential story arcs, implied story through game changes, or a collection of narrative content with (or little) narrative sequentiality? Or a mix of all of these options? Different approaches are useful for different types of content, and a mix can offer you the best of all worlds.
  - **Season Arcs** (Analogous to serials and episodic TV series) provide a sense of urgency and presence, allowing the player to be in the moment and act upon the story in the now. Since they take place in the current time, they can create bigger tension, cliffhangers, and a feeling of player agency. They are the actors in these stories and feel a sense of agency.

- **Season Changes** Are additional dramatic changes in the game that aren't a cutscene, mission or dialogue-driven story progression, but still imply dramatic change in the world. They are implied seasonal storytelling, using narrative design elements beyond explicit plot. Elements like thematic shifts, available gameplay and elements, changes on the map, or visual direction can create a sense of a living world and give more impact on player actions (especially if they are narratively tied to something the player has been involved in).

- **Story Collections** (Analogous to anthology series) can provide a deeper insight into the lore and background of the game world, as well as its characters and (past) events. This puts the player in the role of a detective, rather than the action hero. They are explorers in these stories, driven by curiosity and a desire for completionism. You can also consider making story collections about "current" events, though it will have a slightly more passive and investigative feeling than when players are "in the moment." There may be some sequentiality between elements (a series of documents that tell parts of the same story, for example), but they aren't arcs the players actively take part in.

• **Main Arc, Side Arc or Additional Narrative?** When your game is intended to have a strong seasonal narrative, you might want to offer players a plot-driven seasonal arc just like in a TV show, with the whole season spanning a dramatic plot with a conflict in the beginning and a resolution in the end. But in addition to that main arc, we can also add new side arcs and short stories on the side – as B-plots to the main stories A-plot (for example). These can be in the shape of additional progressions tied to another feature, or in the shape of time-limited or live events. Thus, you can offer several tracks of story in each season (for the season or as a permanent addition). They can each have different **weight, story focus** (groups, characters, events, locations, etc.) **and length**, as well as **permanence** (just available for the season or a new permanent addition) and how they are **triggered** (beginning of the season, throughout the season, as a live event).

- **Main Arc(s)/A-plot:** The season's central story (or stories) focusing on the main characters and main conflict, where the player is either the main character or at least a central participant, comparable to a TV season or its A-plot. It's a dramatic story progression that is ideally tied to the **main progression of the game**, such as the core gameplay, main missions or general player XP – since we want to give it more weight and attention, we should tie it to the gameplay that will get the most weight and attention from players anyway. Alternatively, it can be tied to the **progression of real time**, rather than player progression. Main arcs can be tied to players progressing through a series of content by playing the game (launched at the start of the season), or the passage of time *plus* players unlocking the content (where episodes are launched throughout the season), or simply the passage of time (with live events or other scheduled content drops or game changes). A live game's main arc can, just as well, be the thematic and gameplay shift from season to season, whereas the rest is expressed through side arcs and additional narrative content (in that case, the comparison to TV shows is mostly limited to key moments in a season). Note that toward the end of the season, players get fewer time to consume the content (if it is exclusive to the season), which may make a time-based episodic scheduling more complicated toward the end. This could be reflected in the size of the packages (getting smaller toward the end), or in the last release happening early enough, giving players plenty of time before the season ends.

–   **Side Arcs/B-plot:** Self-contained side arcs focused on a smaller part of the game world, like individual groups, characters, locations, events, etc. This can be compared to a TV show's B-plot, or a spin-off series, and will usually take up less time than the main arc, if it exists – at least individually. Side Arcs may be longer than main arcs if there is no cinematic story progression attached to the main arc, and it's only expressed through game changes (themes, gameplay, map, etc.). Ideally, side arcs should relate to the topics and ongoings of the main arc and provide a spin-off or additional perspective. They can be tied to **progressions of specific features of the game**, such as a game mode, playable character, NPC, location, or collection, as well as progressions of **time-limited or live events**.

–   **Additional Narrative Content:** Additional content that isn't tied to a narrative *progression*, but expresses narrative nonetheless. These are the changes in the game world that are an expression of its implied dramatic evolution and can be tied to the events in the main arcs and side arcs (either in the current season or the previous season). Additional narrative content can be new lore documents to unlock, new small talk with NPCs, new barks, new map changes, new game modes, new character skins, new visual direction, new sound design, and more. These changes can either happen from one season to the next, scheduled events in the game or based on player actions. The latter raises the question of synchronous worlds between different players, and if you give them the power to have a unique world, compared to another player, and if you intend to equalize it with the start of the next season.

•   **Narrative Tools?** Games offer a large variety of ways how to convey a story, and not each story arc needs to do it in the same way. Whereas television shows have one structure of telling their story (a sequence of cinematic scenes that build up to an episode), you have the freedom to use different storytelling formats for your different seasonal progressions. They could be a series of unlockable animated cutscenes, a sequence of playable missions with contextual narrative, Visual Novel-style dialogues in text boxes, a series of illustrations or comic pages, a collection of documents, or something else. The choice is yours and depends on what would match your game.

•   **Pacing and Length?** Not each arc needs to be the same length. In fact, main and various types of side arcs are likely to hold different narrative weight. Your story will be influenced by how many steps each arc gets, how long each narrative unit is, and how long the overall experience is intended to be, based on how quickly players can play through the progression. Some arcs may be tied to real time, such as the beginning of a new season, key moments of a season, or game changes that tell an implicit dramatic story, while others are tied to player actions, and therefore, players need time to actually complete them. Related to that, it's worth thinking about the pacing of each arc across the season. When are they going to be released (in the beginning, later, or in chapters throughout the season), and are there dependencies between them? Do players have enough time to play through them all, and how will that experience differ for casual and highly invested players? Is this a reasonable amount of content, and a reasonable unlocking pacing, for the time the players get to do it? Is it a satisfying pacing, or will players have a long dry spell – or perhaps get overwhelmed? A lot of this is estimation work and may need adjustment across live service operations.

WRITING TIME-LIMITED AND LIVE EVENTS

While seasonal progressions can provide a story similar to television shows, live games have the opportunity to layer an additional, even more time-limited way of storytelling on top of them. This is likely to boost downloads, engagement, and revenue[4] – it might draw lapsed players back in, make active players invest more time and money, and keep players around longer in the long term. As mentioned in the previous chapter (*Chapter 12*), Time-Limited Events and Live Events can cater to those short-term and social player motivations, and narratively, create a more social, community-based story experience. They allow us to tell short stories nested within the game's world or mark special moments of the season that every player is meant to experience, independent from their progression on the other arcs. Since we have smaller space (just based on their time-limited availability), they need to be short stories or short scenes, self-contained and bite-sized, and would usually focus on individual aspects of the game world or mark specific moments in time (in real world or the game's season).

Uses for Time-Limited and Live Events

Highlighting Key Moments

If you want to mark special moments of your season and make sure that every player is motivated to experience them (no matter where they are on their main or side progressions), time-limited and live events can serve that purpose. Even if you don't have a seasonal main progression so to speak of, you can strip it down to a 3-act structure and use time-limited or live events to take the role of that main progression instead. They can be a framing device for your content, and introduce the changes and new content in the game. You can also only do one or two of them, like just a season premiere, just a season finale, or just both of them (without the mid-season twist).

- **Season Intro:** The intro to the season, right at launch. This would be a moment to introduce what the season is about, including the central conflict, themes, characters, and player activities.
- **Mid-Season Twist(s):** This would be a possible event (or events) between the beginning and the end of a season, logically somewhere in the middle. The conflict of the set-up may take a surprising turn here, or simply escalate the conflict.
- **Season Finale:** The season finale would serve as the resolution of the main conflict, introduced in the intro, and likely add a cliffhanger for the next season so that players can anticipate what comes next and can't wait to play when the next season begins. If you didn't have a season premiere, it might also simply refer to the season's themes, or whatever was narratively set-up in in-game or marketing materials.

They don't need to have the same format either. They can also be exchanged with narrative content drops, instead of a playable event, such as a video trailer for the season intro.

Collaborations with External Brands

Collaboration events are time-limited events where characters or elements of another property cross over into your game world, such as other videogames, entertainment, or brands. Since they're only going to be available for a limited time, you can take more freedom regarding the creative integrity of your game's vision, writing *what if* scenarios that will disappear after the event ends (perhaps even considered as non-canon). For example: Shin Megami Tensei Liberation Dx2 had a collaboration event with Devil May Cry 6, adding a crossover story progression with characters from both games. Here, the DMC characters came through a dimension portal into the world of SMT, and they had to work together to solve a demon invasion at hand and close up the portal again. These collaboration events are usually a marketing strategy for both involved parties, to attract audiences from the other collaboration partner. Ideally, your collaboration partner is a brand fit for your own project, when it comes to tone, genre, audience or simply story potential (the more playful your game, the more freedom you can likely take). Ideally, collaboration events allow you to create crossover spin-off short stories that allow players to see beloved characters interact with each other in an entertaining way.

Tying into Current Events

Due to the time-specific scheduling of time-limited events, they can refer to something that happens during its period of availability. These events can put characters into topical scenarios, referring to the time of year or other current events, such as seasons of the year (spring, summer, fall, winter), holidays (Valentine's Day, Christmas, Halloween, etc.), your game's anniversary, sport tournaments, a character's fictional birthday, etc. In regard to holidays, it's always important to consider your target audience and their diversity in culture and religion. A Japanese audience might expect a Golden Week or White Day event, while Western audiences might not know what that is (which might require additional explanations, if you choose to add it). Also, since different cultures might celebrate different things at the same time, you may also want to consider more belief-agnostic events, such as a winter celebration, instead of Christmas. This doesn't mean you can't get culturally specific, of course, especially for very commercial holidays – you could even tie them to your in-game characters and thus express their culture this way.

Showcasing Game Elements

Time-limited events can also be used to focus on a specific aspect of your game world, such as individual characters and their conflicts, groups of people, regions of your world, or the narrative connected to other game features. These stories can take place in the present tense of the season, or even jump into other time periods, such as the past, the present, or an undefined point in time. They can serve as spin-offs about elements of your world that either stand on their own, relate directly to your current season's plot or theme (as a side story), or can be combined with current events. For example, a time-limited event could be about a specific character, and what they do during Valentine's Day.

Thematic Expansion

Lastly, time-limited events can also be used for stories that enhance the main story, either by serving as a side story that provides information that enriches the player's perspective on the main plot (by changing their perspective or granting a deeper insight into it) or by expanding on the season's themes.

Structuring Time-Limited and Live Events

Part of writing a time-limited event is deciding on their narrative structure, as it will influence the delivery and perception of the story you're telling. Before you start writing, decide on the following aspects:

- **Time-Limited or Live (aka Asynchronous or Synchronous)?**
  A *time-limited* event indicates that players have a limited time to unlock steps in a progression to complete a story. They can do it in their own time, and have a certain freedom and agency to choose when and how fast they progress through it. It's therefore asynchronous.
     A *live* event, on the other hand, is scheduled for a specific time slot, like a live broadcast happening in real time. It's therefore synchronous. Players do not have agency over when and how fast they consume it, they just have to be there for it. This results in a social experience with an even greater sense of exclusivity. A live event is usually much shorter, too.
- **Online or Solo?**
  This question is especially relevant for synchronous live events. When an experience is shared, the question is whether players share a server/map with many others at the same time (all players or on several separate servers), or whether players get their own solo experience. These can be combined, as well, making part of the experience online (for multiplayer moments) and the other solo (for an individual story progression). Anything synchronous and online will take some agency from the players, as the event will progress

without their individual input, but gives greater potential for a social experience, connecting story progression to a group's collective input. The question of server capabilities and technical limitations comes into play here too, of course, and might require you to do some cheating by adding bots in a synchronous live solo experience, instead of real players.

- **Gameplay and Reward?**
  The actions of the players should ideally be an aspect of the story you're telling. What they do drives the story forward, or even downright tells it – or they at least get to be an active observer of something, and be *"in the moment."* The same applies to possible rewards. For example, a Valentine's Day event about a specific character could grant players a special romantic outfit for that character after they complete the event.

- **Story Structure?**
  As with every narrative in your game, you have to decide how you intend to tell the story tied to the time-limited/live event. They can be, for example, a sequence of unlockable dialogues tied to a game feature, a sequence of quests with barks along the way, or just a themed game mode with character representatives, a clever name and a themed reward. Additionally, you have to decide on the number of steps, length of individual narrative units, pacing and thematic focus (see the previous section).

Writing a Time-Limited Event

Keep in mind that these time-limited events can *usually* be played by all players, no matter where they are in the progression of permanent or seasonal stories. That means that they need to function independently, as a self-contained short story that ties into the topics, themes, and world of the game's season (or general story). They can be used to give more details about specific aspects of the world without having to tie into the main or season story and can give the spotlight to specific characters, regions, events, etc.

The potential of time-limited events lies in their time-specific release schedule and their independence from the main story or seasonal arc. So besides being a side story that expands some of your universe, it can also be used to mark important moments within your **season's story** (in-universe events, end of season, transition to next season, etc.), in the **real world** (holidays, annual seasons, real world events), or the **game's lifecycle** (anniversary, collaboration, season ending, etc.). This seasonal relation is a potential, however, that doesn't necessarily need to be fulfilled with every single time-limited event you create. It does make for good marketing material though, and can benefit from a general mood for specific content in the player base.

The story beats themselves should be structured with a 3-act structure, which brings us back to the contextualization of game loops.

1. **Conflict** (Goal, Stakes, Anticipated Consequences)
2. **Action** (Required Steps, Conflicts)
3. **Resolution** (Actual Consequences, Rewards)

If your time-limited event plans to have more than three defined story beats, you can look at 5-step-structures, 12-step-structures or other ones. But keep in mind that giving players context and instructions – and later feedback to their actions – will always remain core-essential to a satisfying narrative wrapper for their actions.

Do not forget that the narrative of a time-limited event is not only in the story beats you apply to it. You can tell a story through the **event's context/set-up, gameplay, player actions, visuals, feedback, reward types,** and even the **naming** of the event. Even if your project has no capacity for dialogue-driven plot progression or anything like that, you should still have the power to make use of the event's individual aspects to portray a narrative experience, through contextualized, themed gameplay and rewards.

Writing a Live Event

Writing a live event actually functions similarly to a time-limited event (as they are a sub-category of the former), but has unique aspects that demand a slightly different approach:

- Firstly, it happens in **real time,** with no player agency for individual pacing.
- Secondly, it's even **shorter,** usually only lasting a few minutes or up to 2 hours.
- Lastly, it's often designed to be a more **social experience,** shared with other players.

This means that writing for a live event must be even tighter, and ideally cater to a sense of being part of a special, spectacular event. Something that happens in the moment and that you wouldn't want to miss. This means that the tools for storytelling might be different than your other time-limited events. For example, the time-limited event could have a sequence of dialogues to unlock, while the live event might throw you into a game scenario with unique animations and live feedback. If you plan to make the live event a **shared synchronous multiplayer experience**, it also makes sense to think of a narrative that puts an **emphasis on a social, collaborative, or competitive aspect**, such as defeating an enemy together, dancing at a concert together, going on a treasure hunt against other teams, etc. Here, again, it's crucial to keep in mind that all players who participate are at a level of information and progression that allows them to understand and enjoy what's going on. I would advice against gatekeeping events behind progressions, just to make sure that the most amount of players get to enjoy what you planned. Depending on your game structure, you may want to offer something for a restricted audience though (like end-of-content players, for example), and that's a choice you can make, too.

The structure should be straightforward, and you'll recognize a traditional 3-act-structure again:

1. **Hook:** Introduce players to the setting and premise of the event, including their role and the goal. They need to be sure what the goal of the event is, and what their next step is going to be. Even if your event is meant to be

mysterious and surprising, inspire the player's curiosity, to motivate them to discover whatever they'll find out by the end of the event.

2. **Engagement:** Let the player engage in the event, actively or passively (gameplay or observation). Make sure they're aware of their possible actions, what's requested of them, and what will help them optimally enjoy the event.

3. **Resolution:** Resolve the event in a satisfying way. If there was a competition, celebrate victories and lament losses. If there was a boss to defeat, show their grandiose death. If this was a concert, let it end with a boom and clarify that it's over. If there was any kind of narrative question raised in the beginning of the event, a mystery or another source of tension, reveal it here (or at least give a partial answer).

The thing to keep in mind when it comes to live events is that they're usually meant to serve as marketing for the game, something that builds social pressure, a fear of missing out and/or a sense of exclusivity. You should probably look into marketing live events outside of the game, push a marketing campaign, or giving at least in-game announcements ahead of time, since they're time-sensitive and can be missed.

SUMMARY

- **TV shows can serve as inspiration** for seasonal plot in live games, as they both have an episodic seasonal structure.
- The difference is that **live game audiences are active participants** interacting with the story – additionally, releases can be permanent or time-limited, and contain several progressions instead of just one.
- **Dramatic structure in games** is created through **gameplay, contextualization and rising challenge levels**.
- The **smallest dramatic element** in a video game is the **game loop**, which is contextualized with a narrative framing.
- A game's **challenge progression** creates a dramatic arc by trying **to evoke flow** – this happens through the rise and fall of difficulty with a persistent upwards tendency.
- The **story themes** of a game should be **reflected** in its **smallest dramatic structures** (game loops) and its **biggest dramatic structures** (the whole game), which is called **micro and macro narrative**.
- TV shows have different types of continuity: **Episodic, Serial, and Anthology**.
- **Episodic series** have an episodic reset, and are watchable in any order, with little character growth.
- **Serials** have a sequential narrative, need to be watched in order, and focus on character growth.
- **Anthologies** have self-contained stories with shared themes, and are watchable in any order, with episode-contained character growth.

- Any of these structures can be **applied to seasonal live games**.
- **TV episodes** consist of **A-plots** (main stories), **B-plots** (side stories), and **C-plots** (references to previous episodes).
- If an episode is written in a **3-Act Structure** (usually 30-minute comedy), it consists of a cold open, act I (conflict), act II (action), act III (resolution), and a tag (standalone joke or epilogue).
- If an episode is written in a **5-Act Structure** (usually 60-minute drama), it consists of a cold open, act I (exposition), act II (rising action), act III (climax), act IV (falling action), act V (resolution) and a tag (standalone joke or epilogue).
- Those dramatic structures **can be applied to live games**, whereas several narrative units might be grouped into one act.
- A character's **seasonal character development** can be **vertical** (they go through changes) or **horizontal** (we discover new sides of them).
- A season can be dramatically separated into Story Beat I (Season Premiere), Story Beat II (Mid-Season Twist), and Story Beat III (Season Finale), with possible additional beats in between.
- Live game seasons can have **several dramatic progressions** in parallel (story arcs, story collections, or additional season changes).
- Each seasonal story can be a **main arc** (tied to the main progression or real time), **side arc** (tied to a feature progression), or **additional narrative content** (changes in the game, such as contextual narrative, map changes, visual direction, new narrative-infused content, etc.).
- Each **seasonal story** can be told through a **different narrative tool,** from cutscenes and missions to documents.
- **Different arcs can have different lengths**, which should be in line with their narrative weight – which means you need to balance whether players will be able to complete them in time.
- **Time-limited and live events** can have a variety of purposes in your game:
  - Highlighting key moments
  - Collaborations with external brands
  - Tying into current events
  - Showcasing game elements
  - Thematic expansion
- To write a **time-limited event, use a 3-act structure** (Conflict – Action – Resolution) for a self-contained short story, in addition to its narrative design (context, gameplay, player actions, visuals, feedback, reward types, naming).
- **Live events** require a different approach, as they happen **in real time,** are **even shorter,** and are often designed to be a **social experience** with other players.
- **Live events** can also be structured in a **3-act structure** (Hook – Engagement – Resolution), in addition to narrative design (context, gameplay, player actions, visuals, feedback, reward types, naming).

REFERENCES

1 Evan Skolnick, "The Three-Act Structure," in *Video Game Storytelling: What Every Developer Needs to Know About Narrative Techniques*, Watson-Guptill, December 2, 2014, 12–26.
2 Mihaly Csikszentmihalyi, *Flow: The Psychology of Optimal Experience*, Harper Perennial Modern Classsics, July 1, 2008.
3 Jesse Schell, "The Experience is in the Player's Mind," in *The Art of Game Design: A Book of Lenses*, 1st edition, CRC Press, August 4, 2008, 118–123.
4 GameRefinery Team, "How Mobile Game Developers Boosted Downloads and Revenue with Halloween 2022 Events," GameRefinery, November 22, 2022, https://www.gamerefinery.com/how-mobile-game-developers-boosted-downloads-and-revenue-with-halloween-2022-events/.

BIBLIOGRAPHY

Daniel P. Calvisi, "A Fascinating Protagonist," in *Story Maps: TV Drama: The Structure of the One-Hour Television Pilot*, 1st edition, Act Four Screenplays, March 19, 2016, 11–26.
Daniel P. Calvisi, "The TV Drama Story Map, " in *Story Maps: TV Drama: The Structure of the One-Hour Television Pilot*, 1st edition, Act Four Screenplays, March 19, 2016, 27–37.
Daniel P. Calvisi, "The Beat Sheet, " in *Story Maps: TV Drama: The Structure of the One-Hour Television Pilot*, 1st edition, Act Four Screenplays, March 19, 2016, 40–58.
Martie Cook, "Developing Your Sitcom Story," in *Write to TV: Out of Your Head and onto the Screen*, 2nd edition, Routledge, April 28, 2014, 43–54.
Martie Cook, "Sitcom Structure," in *Write to TV: Out of Your Head and onto the Screen*, 2nd edition, Routledge, April 28, 2014, 55–62.
Pamela Douglas, "How a Classic Script Is Crafted," in *Writing the TV Drama Series: How to Succeed as a Professional Writer in TV*, 3rd edition, Michael Wiese Productions, November 1, 2011,83–136.
Ken Miyamoto, "How to Structure and Format Your Television Scripts," The Script Lab, accessed April 24, 2023, https://thescriptlab.com/features/screenwriting-101/8930-how-to-structure-and-format-your-television-scripts/.
Lee Sheldon, "Bringing the Story to Life," in *Character Development and Storytelling for Games*, Course Technology, 2nd edition, April 3, 2013, 207–226.

14 Keeping a Long-Running Story Interesting

One of the greatest challenges of long-running narratives is not necessarily how to get it started, but how to keep it going – and make it work for the audience too. Nowadays, audiences have access to a constant stream of new exciting releases, and keeping their attention and building brand loyalty is an important key to long-term success of live narratives. If you're working on a live game, chances are that one of the business goals of the project is to have high player retention and keep players in the game's ecosystem for many months – or even years – to come. This means that you, as a narrative designer, have to make sure the narrative keeps on making sense and being fun for a very long time to come.

There are some brands that have managed to stay relevant for decades, always evolving, changing, and building transmedia empires. Star Wars, for instance, is an ongoing decade-spanning interplanetary epic that has been explored in 12 movies (and counting), several TV shows, countless novels, comics, and videogames. With the first movie being released in 1977, the narrative has been expanding over the course of several real-time decades, ever-expanding what was already there. And the fanbase is notoriously loyal, curious to find out what comes next. Other examples with similar staying power would be the Pokémon franchise, Disney, Marvel, and DC comics. It's also worth looking at long-running scripted television shows, like the Simpsons or South Park, which both have been airing for over 30 and 25 years respectively (at the time of me writing this).

Examples like that (and experience from existing live games) help us learn how to apply some of that to our own live narratives – even though booming popularity and success often depend on some unpredictable factors (like social zeitgeist or getting attention from the right people at the right time). We can only plan for creating the best possible long-term narrative experience and see where it goes. In the past chapters, we've established ways how to build a live narrative that can go on for a long time, so let's now take a look how we can make it *engaging* for this amount of time, too.

MAKE USE OF THE LOVABILITY OF YOUR WORLD AND CHARACTERS

While not every long-running narrative is character-driven, it's often a common denominator between any narrative that keeps on going for a long time. Lovable, in this case, doesn't mean that the world needs to be cozy (though it can be), or that the characters need to be nice people (though some can be)."Lovability" means inspiring an emotional engagement with the world and its characters, no matter if you're witnessing the mistakes of flawed people, or the struggle of heroes, and no matter if

DOI: 10.1201/9781003297628-18

you'd actually like to live in that world, or rather prefer to fantasize about it from the safety of your home.

When you've created your strong core cast (or plans for a strong changing cast) and figured out pillars of engaging worldbuilding, keep in mind to *leverage* them in your stories. With new content releases, give your players the opportunity to dive deeper into an aspect of the world or to get to know the characters better. This can mean revealing more of their backstories or putting characters into new situations or constellations, which allows them to show a new side of themselves or to grow as a person. If a player has fallen in love with a character or setting, they will likely want to consume more stories about them. This doesn't mean that you're only allowed to focus on the same characters and locations all the time – you can of course introduce new ones, which strike similar emotional chords or expand the cast meaningfully, and let players fall in love with those as well. But remember to expand upon what makes your game engaging and lovable in the first place, rather than change its very core.

If possible, try to involve your players, too. Consider data and audience sentiments regarding what they love your game for, and which characters are their favorites. But don't mistake a vocal minority on social media for representatives of the entire fanbase, and don't chase after every single feedback and suggestion – it's a balancing act to keep your game's vision and integrity but also be aware of how it's actually perceived by the players.

KEEP CONSISTENCY, BUT ALLOW FRESH IDEAS

Your audience falls in love with your narrative world for a reason: The way it makes them feel and the kind of experience they get from interacting with it. Based on what you give them, they develop expectations when it comes to tone, themes, and characterizations. If they love a character, they want to be sure that the character is still recognizable when they pick up another story featuring them. If they love the game world, they want to understand its history and how it works and have a reliable emotional experience when they interact with it. They might expect a gorgeous awe-inspiring world they love to explore in peace, or tense and intimidating battlefields that they need to navigate – or a mix of both or something else entirely.

Keeping consistency across a project that has many writers can be a challenge, but this can be navigated with the help of lore bibles, narrative documentation and with narrative leads, directors, or any other such comparable role that serves as a narrative authority. The last title sounds like a big word, but sometimes this simply indicates the most senior narrative specialist of your team, or the creative lead of the project – somebody to keep an eye on all the narrative content and its consistency with existing lore, to make sure everyone is provided with the right information and a sense of coherency is secured. Sometimes this role simply falls into the hands of the only narrative designer or game writer on the team. There are countless projects with indie or AA-sized teams where this is going to be the case.

On the other hand, staying too conservative with your ideas and characterizations can make narratives seem rigid and conservative. Over time, stories, characters, and worlds are bound to change, either because things would get boring to long-time players, or in reaction to the evolving media landscape or a shift in brand strategy. It could also be necessary due to a bigger shift in your game, like its core gameplay, target audience, or monetization structure. Being flexible without losing your game's core vision is important. Don't betray your worlds and characters while chasing a trend, but be open to new things to mix things up after a while.

Sometimes this needed change simply originates from the amount of time your game has been running – and to draw in new players, and keep old players around, something new needs to happen. This can be solved by shifting the focus of your stories, characters, and worlds and introduce new conflicts or elements into your game, but it can also be more extreme. If you consider the strategy of branching out and allow for various tones, focuses, and target audiences in separate iterations of the game – for example, in another game mode, specific mission types, a spin-off game, or transmedia content – it's important to mark a separation between these parts of the game (or make it another tie-in game entirely). The more clearly you mark that a set of content is different from another set, and the more coherent these sets remain within themselves, and the easier it will be for your audiences to curate what they enjoy without being frustrated, confused, or disappointed.

KNOW WHEN TO WRAP THINGS UP, AND WHEN TO INTRODUCE SOMETHING NEW

The longer a story keeps on going, the bigger the risk of players churning or losing interest in it. You can only milk a topic for so long until it goes dry. This can be easily solved by knowing when to wrap something up, and when to move on to new ventures. This doesn't mean that your game should end, mind you, but only that story arcs need to end to make way for something new that comes after.

Picture this: Your story arc has been consistently going on for a year, with no reso-lution in sight and the big bad antagonist still undefeated. By now, it just feels like a string of unrelated action scenes, with no connection to the bigger picture. The tension is gone and players aren't really that curious to see where things are heading anymore – it has become entirely unpredictable how far into the future this may be. Maybe this would be a good time to actually face that final battle (in fact, it might already be long overdue), have a big grandiose climax, and start a new story arc. A new enemy, a new world, maybe even a new main cast – or at least a new phase in a bigger con-flict. This is related to creating motivation with short-term and long-term goals, too. Leading a player from short-term goal to short-term goal without an end in sight runs the risk of feeling meaningless. Leading a player toward a long-term goal without any resolutions in between runs the risk of feeling daunting. So combine them.

While there are no universally applicable time schedules to tell you when these moments come, it helps to look at the roadmaps of similar games, collect feedback and data from your players, and to simply put yourself into their shoes. How long would you remain patient, if you were a player of your own game?

Live games sometimes contain a story arc within each current season, which is often 2–6months long. Other games put a whole self-contained arc into each game progression that is released, independent from real-time schedules (giving players a resolution after maybe 1 hour or 5 hours of content). This deeply depends on the structure of your project, and the pacing of the experience – usually, it's a mix of research of competitors, educated guesses, and adjusting your plans with observation of actual player feedback.

DON'T RESOLVE ALL CONFLICTS – CLIFFHANGERS & KEEPING TENSION

Never fully resolve all and every tension and open conflict of your story. This doesn't only apply to every episode, chapter, and mission individually, but also when you wrap up a season or story arc. If players arrive at a point in the story where all open conflicts have been neatly wrapped up, they have less motivation to keep going. There is nothing left that keeps them curious. You can do this by adding cliffhangers at the end of episodes, but also by introducing new conflicts along the way of solving the current conflict. While characters solve one issue, let their choices create one or several new ones along the way, which they have to deal with later. It feels more natural if these new conflicts don't all get dumped on the audience in the very last chapter, but they *should* be reminded of what might come next at the end of each arc. This is a way to set expectations, make players curious, and keep a base level of tension throughout a long-running story.

KEEP PLAYERS MOTIVATED – SHORT-TERM VS. LONG-TERM GOALS

You want your players to keep playing the game for as long as possible, therefore, you need to uphold their motivation to play. There are actually two sides to motivation when we're talking about narrative design: Player motivation and narrative motivation. **Player motivation** is the player's desire to continue playing the game, willfully and enthusiastically (or sometimes spitefully), as themselves, outside of the game's diagesis. On the other hand, **narrative motivation** is the provided reason for the player's avatar to pursue their goals inside the game world, and therefore, giving players an emotional and narrative reason for their actions inside of the game's diagesis. These are two motivation types that exist on different layers of reality. But if my avatar is fighting their way through waves of enemies *to rescue their friend,* that's also likely going to become part of my motivation to continue: I want to see them reunite, and care about my avatar, their friend, and their relationship. Narrative motivation therefore provides a context that feeds the emotional engagement of the player, their curiosity, and thus, *their motivation.* Player motivation is usually driven by a mix of both, game goals and narrative goals.

Also, in order to string players along in the long run, the game needs to establish long-term and short-term goals. This applies to player motivations beyond the game world and the narrative motivations inside of the game world. When regarding narrative motivations, players need to know the bigger meaning of their actions, and what they do it for (long-term motivation), such as defeating a big bad, saving the world, winning the war, etc. On the other hand, they need to have an idea of their moment-to-moment goals in order to know what to do and feel rewarded when they've done it. It's crucial to have a mix of both, long-term goals (the bigger picture) and short-term goals (current objectives). Always clarify the final goal (or at least a bigger sub-goal, if you want to add some plot twists), and what the player has to do next to reach it – ideally with more narrative context than just the game objectives. Players should be regularly reminded of the long-term motivation for this season or several seasons, so they don't forget what their current actions promise to amount to, in the end of that arc.

In some types of live games, the question of motivation can become a little trickier, since players can enter the game at various times and states of the story. But the same rule applies. Clarify to each and every player where they are now, where they need to go next, and which point they want to reach eventually.

As already mentioned in the previous section (*Know When to Wrap Things Up, And When to Introduce Something New*), a game which only has short-time motivations can appear meaningless, repetitive and lose the player's emotional involvement after some time. But a game which has only long-time motivations can appear tiring, where the players don't have enough energy to go on when they have no release of tension in between. So you need both.

Another aspect to motivation design in live games is the ability to play with the **fleeting nature of content**. Content that is only temporarily available creates a more urgent short-term motivation, like for example, time-limited events that players can only complete within a given timeframe. On the other hand, seasonal content could provide motivation for the duration of the season, and therefore, mid- to long-term motivation. The motivation is as urgent as the timer counting down your remaining time to complete a given piece of content.

SUSPENSEFUL AND SURPRISING CONTENT IN A PREDICTABLE STRUCTURE

There's often a seeming contradiction between what audiences want in an established brand. On the one hand, they want something new and surprising, on the other hand, they don't want it to be too different. After all, they're consuming new content because they do want *more of the same thing*. So finding a balance is key.

Usually, this can be done by releasing suspenseful and surprising stories in a predictable structure, while adhering to some key pillars of the story universe. Maybe audiences expect heroic adventures, or clever puns, or a romantic subplot, and expect to encounter these things while being surprised with an all new story, conflicts and maybe even characters.

So, a strategy to maximize player retention would be a predictable structure with surprising content, which is built on these pillars:

- **A predictable narrative structure** that is structurally consistent within itself. The structure is defined by length, amount of plot beats, conflict structure, and persistence of change. This doesn't mean you have to structure all your narrative units the exact same way. In games, you have the option to structure different types of narrative units individually. A main story mission can have a different structure and tone from a side story mission, or a progression attached to a time-limited event. As long as the structure remains predictable within these different narrative features, you successfully set player expectations.

- **Maintaining core characteristics** that audiences expect and enjoy in your universe, when it comes to content and emotional experience. This is shaped by genre, style, tone, core fantasy, conflicts, themes, running gags, and recurring types of scenes, which the audiences came to enjoy and want to see more of.
- **New and exciting story content** within your established structure. Work with suspense, cliffhangers and open conflicts to get them invested in the drama of your story, so they always want to see what happens next. Highlighting unexplored aspects of the world, its characters and their dynamics, as well as switching up their relationships, can keep things interesting, too. The start of a new season is always a good point to introduce a new season conflict, new characters, new enemies, new main themes, new aesthetics, and new relationships – while the end of a season is a good point to remind players of open conflicts that hint at what might come next.
- **A public release roadmap** that helps manage expectations for the frequency and size of new releases.

In general, try to find a balance between suspense and surprise in a predictable structure – without losing sight of your game's original vision. There is such a thing as straying too far from the source material (also called jumping the shark in TV), so tread carefully.

PLANNING YOUR ONBOARDING

One of the big challenges in live games is that players might enter your game at entirely different points of the story, particularly when you want to have a story progress over time, such as time-limited seasonal stories. Some players join you on the release date, others do it in season 5. You need to think of the first-time-user-experience for every single one of them: Where do they enter the story and how can you help them to hit the ground running? Imagine you create a game that evolves a story in every season but doesn't attempt to give any kind of onboarding: Players would be confused as to who your characters are, what their motivation is, or even what kind of role their character has played up until then. This is a very versatile question depending on your game, your structure, and your story. Is the player playing as a new character, joining a living world that has existed before them? Or do they take over a role that has already done some things without them beforehand? But no matter what you choose, good onboarding will mitigate this issue.

Some **options for onboarding** are the following:

- **Option 1:** An **onboarding campaign or tutorial** that introduces the player to the game world, the conflict, and the key characters, including their own role and motivation in all of this. This can be single-player experience, but doesn't have to be. They are then thrown into the live story/game where it is now, or a more open narrative experience (with many activities and/or progressions to choose from). It's important to consider whether this would serve as enough of a background for players to understand the current state of the live game or not. This can either be obligatory onboarding, or encouraged permanent content that is available in parallel to live content. Consider the following: When does that onboarding campaign take place, in the story's chronology? What's the context? How will it tie into your live narrative? Is there a timeskip or a relocation, and is it compatible with everything you intend to do during the lifecycle of the game? Are players playing the same avatar as in the live segment, or somebody else, in a prequel of sorts? Are you planning to change your onboarding over the seasons, to make sure it gets the players up to speed at the point that they enter the game, or is it the same for everyone at all times?

Onboarding doesn't have to be a big campaign, mind you, it can be as simple as a narrative layer to your tutorial. If you have a tutorial for your gameplay, it makes sense to provide an introduction to your story world at the same time. The challenge lies in valuing the player's time though: Tutorials can easily get annoying if there's too much reading of instructions and not enough learning through actions (perhaps even trial and error). So try to avoid interrupting the flow of the gameplay too much, just to add mountains of lore. Give the players just as much as they *need* (to understand the setup and to be emotionally hooked), and postpone in-depth information to a later point in the game. It's become almost a meme that text-heavy tutorials are notoriously unpleasant, and there are plenty of examples where you "learn by doing" nowadays. Depending on your target audiences, expectations differ on how a tutorial may look. Also, not everything needs to be explained in the beginning, even if it's important for onboarding: You can also split up your narrative onboarding to appear at different points of the game, usually when players first encounter a new type of gameplay, location, or character. If onboarding is separated into smaller bits, players are much more likely to pay attention and remember them. *(Examples:* DC Universe Online and Red Dead Online*)*

- **Option 2: All main story campaigns are permanent,** and live content only provides side stories, side branches, or tie-in stories. Alternatively, your live content may not have an explicit plot, but is more focused on implicit narrative conveyed through themes, gameplay, and visuals. This way, when a player starts up your game, they get the exact same main story campaign as the other players, no matter when they joined the game, with no explicit story progression tied to the passage of real-time and seasonal evolution. This means that all players get the same main story at different points in time, on their own terms.

  So, when you make your main story progressions permanent, there would be two ways of approaching it:
  - **New content releases only continue the main story chronologically** (adding more at the end of it), **and/or add side stories**. New progressions are being added permanently, which means there is **no narratively significant time-limited content**. Time-limited content is narrative-infused, but does not contain plot progressions. *(Examples:* Chapters and Episode*)*

- – Alternatively, in addition to new permanent expansions to existing progressions, all **time-limited content is a self-contained narrative addition** to the permanent main story, such as side stories, alternative routes, tie-ins, spin-offs, character-focused stories, event stories, etc. Here, temporary content would be missable and not needed to understand the main story. *(Examples:* Star Wars: Knight of the Old Republic and World of Warcraft*)*

- **Option 3: Onboarding is non-interactive**, such as an intro cutscene or written summaries that are already available when a player starts up the game for the first time. The most engaging type of onboarding is to have an interactive campaign, something that doesn't only tell the story but lets the player experience it. But depending on your game format, an intro cutscene might be the quickest way to get to the experience you're providing. This can also be a matter of budget.

  Here are a few options:

  - An Intro Cutscene
  - Other Videos (in-game or shared on social media)
  - Summaries of individual previous seasons
  - Summaries of the general state of the conflict
  - Online Wikis or Websites

REMINDERS AND ARCHIVES

When a story goes on for an extended time, even players who have been around since the beginning might lose track of some information. And not knowing what's going on can be detrimental to motivation and enjoyment, which might make players churn. Especially when some content is temporary, you need to make sure that players are reminded of key information as it becomes relevant again. This can either be inside of the ongoing plot (dialogues or texts repeating past information) or in the form of archives, summaries, or other reminders. Depending on how important the information is, you may choose to put it out of the player's way, as an optional resource, or remind them of key information at specific moments, with no way to miss it. Ideally, a player can jump right into any given activity without being lost. Don't require them to do homework to understand what's going on.

GIVE PLAYERS A SENSE OF AGENCY

A sense of agency is important in every kind of game: A player's sense that they have control over their actions, and that these actions have consequences. This can be as simple as controller input translating into avatar action, which causes a feedback from the game. But it also applies to the layer of story. This doesn't mean that a player needs to have the feeling that they have full control over the plot development of a story, but they need to feel like their role and actions in the story matter, somehow. If they don't *make* the hero rescue their friend, the game's events wouldn't happen, and the friend would be doomed. If they see that they can choose what actions to take, see these actions executed, and that they have an effect on the game (its gameplay, world, characters, etc), they feel a greater sense of agency.

And in a long-running live game, this agency needs to be secured, too. Depending on the type of story you're telling, this might get a little complicated. If your live game doesn't have a plot progression, for example, but just implicit scenarios and changing themes across the season – where's the agency in that? Well, the agency can be through the role that the player takes in these scenarios, for example, by playing as a capable soldier who protects an area against another special forces team. Here the agency would come from the general narrative scenario, in combination with gameplay – the enacted story, rather than the told story.

There are, however, more ways you might increase a player's sense of agency. And that could be by actually giving them the power to have an impact of the story they're playing. As previously mentioned in *Chapter 4*, impactful player choices can be a powerful tool in interactive storytelling, giving players a personal involvement in the story evolution.

There are many different ways how **player choices** could be included **in a long-term story**.

- When all story campaigns are **functionally permanent single-player experiences**, you can add as many choices as you want. But the longer a story gets, the tougher it will get to keep them all contained. Simply apply the same rules as for single-player videogames. Also, even if players can play a campaign with others – the question of individual choices can be solved by letting them play on one player's instance, while the others only play support without influencing their own personal story progression.
- When you add branching stories or other **narrative impacts**, they **could be contained to a single season, chapter, or mission**. They don't carry over and therefore don't influence future releases, don't have to be accounted for, and don't have to be recalled. The challenge is to make them so self-contained that future content doesn't contradict either of the options that the player might have pursued.
- **Decisions could be reflected in alternate scenes, individual lines, or other small things** in future seasons, with a default (or random) choice for everyone who wasn't around to make that choice. The **effects should be limited**, both in how big they are and for how long they will keep on being referred to, and the **number of choices should be limited,** too. Since this easily adds tons of extra content to develop that only few will see, it always makes sense to try and limit choices to a specific place or time of a story – we don't want to create a giant branching tree for each individual player for years to come.
- Choices could influence **permanent player variables** which in turn influence how the world and the story react to their avatar, personally, and these variables may stay relevant across seasons. An example would be to have a **personality, affiliation, or morality variable** for all players, and each choice influences their alignment on that scale. Alternatively, players could purposefully make this choice during the onboarding section of the game.

This limits how many versions of any given moment need to be created, no matter how many choices players make. This reduces your writing effort to just creating alternatives for the limited amounts of affinity alignments (good or evil, for example), and **not create new branches for each and every decision that the player has made.** This can be a simple variable, an alignment on a scale, or a set of several variables – as simple or complex as makes sense for your story. Having a simple system that then determines if players see scenes A, B, or C can be an easily implemented and engaging way to give them agency over a story.

- **A player voting system** could decide the trajectory of the story, which will then be the same for everyone. Voting doesn't necessarily mean that it's a decision that pops up on screen, directly asking players to push a button, but could be based on player behavior in-game. For example: Two factions fight for points, and the winning faction is the dominant force in the upcoming season, which is reflected in the narrative. You need to plan your production around these choices though, and either make their effects so simple that they can be quickly produced, give yourself enough time to produce the content for that choice, or pre-produce part of both choices, and then simply complete the one that's chosen.

- Choices can also be reflected in a **purely cosmetic** way, such as skins, outfits, map changes, or other game elements.

SUMMARY

- **To keep a long-running story interesting**, you should...
  - Make use of the **lovability of your world and characters**.
  - **Keep consistency** but allow **fresh ideas**.
  - **Know when to end arcs** and when to introduce new elements.
  - **Don't resolve all tensions** at the end of an arc, but add new conflicts and cliffhangers along the way.
  - Include **long-term and short-term goals** to keep players motivated.
  - Offer **suspenseful content** in a **predictable structure**.
  - Plan your **onboarding in a way that accommodates all players, no matter when they join the game**.
  - Offer **reminders and archives** of important missable information.
  - Give players a **sense of agency**, for example, with choices that influence the game.

15 Best Practices

We've discussed many different topics in the past few chapters, since writing stories for live games is a complex endeavour. When you work on your project, feel free to continue using this book as a reference, and go back to any of the individual points to refresh your memory. Each single element of live narrative design could warrant its own book – but at some point, practical experiences becomes more central to growth than reading textbooks. Therefore, before we wrap up these chapters about the creation of live game narratives, I'd like to summarize the key takeaways of the past chapters.

- Start pre-production by **creating a strong world & cast** that can serve as a solid foundation for many stories to come, and think about which key conflicts, topics, and themes you will explore with them in the future.
- **Set and satisfy player expectations** with **reliable narrative structures, schedules releases** and **a strong game identity** that keeps true to itself over time, while still **listening to your audience (within reason)**.
- Plan ahead! Design your **narrative framework** and make plans for your game's **live roadmap** before it releases. Outline a few seasons ahead of production to know where you're going and tell a coherent story.
- **Write nested story arcs,** which support short- and long-term dramatic tension and motivation. Write a sequence of arcs rather than one single never-ending arc to offer players tension *and* satisfaction. If you have a seasonal plot progression, or sequential plot progressions, take dramatic inspiration from TV shows.
- **Design onboarding** that considers that players join at different times of your seasonal progression and **gives them access to important information** as they need it, may that be in the form of contextual reminders, archives, summaries, websites, videos, or however you see fit.
- Make use of your **medium's unique strengths**! A live videogame is different from videogames without live support, but it isn't a TV show either. It combines elements of both. A game's seasonal narrative can be expressed through *all* content releases and *all* in-game changes, from new plot progressions to gameplay modes or cosmetics. Think of your games's interactive and non-linear aspects, like narrative systems, player stories and emergent narrative. You can structure your narrative in multiple progressions and self-contained side stories, and give players an active role in the pacing and progression. A story can be told explicitly (through plot), implicitly (through changes) and just serve as an expansion of the game world's lore, rather than driving the plot forward.

DOI: 10.1201/9781003297628-19

- Use **all methods of narrative design** to surface your game's narrative everywhere, and don't only focus on explicit story and plot. Even without a seasonal plot progression that is driven by cutscenes or dialogues, you can make use of evolving themes, visuals, environments and other topics of narrative design, and still suggest a narrative development in your game's world. Ideally, you make use of all opportunities that you can, to tell a coherent whole that is brimming with narrative everywhere.
- And lastly, **document everything** in an easily accessible way, to be able to keep your story coherent over a long period of time, even if your team's composition changes over the years.

Part IV

Beyond a Game's Story

16 Transmedia Storytelling

OUTSOURCING NARRATIVE

The most successful media franchises of all times often seem to have one thing in common: They have extended transmedia universes. Transmedia storytelling, sometimes also called multiplatform storytelling, is the approach of designing a cohesive story experience across multiple media formats and platforms, both digital and traditional. They tell various stories (or retellings of stories) set within the same narrative context of a story or franchise while using the unique strengths of different media formats for each entry.

Pokémon is a masterclass of transmedia storytelling that started off with videogames and still keeps them at the center of their release line-up. It isn't just a videogame series but also spawned several anime series, movies, mangas, collectible trading cards, merchandise, toys, stationary, branded snacks, online videos, music CDs, and much more. There are entire Pokémon stores selling exclusive merchandise and even cafés in Tokyo and Osaka, dedicated to serving Pokémon-inspired foods on Pokémon-branded sets in a venue decorated to match. If you wanted a fully Pokémon-branded life, it would probably be possible to live it.

Just because you're a narrative designer or writer on a videogame, it doesn't mean your creative input has to end there, depending on the structure of your company. Thinking about ways how to expand your game beyond your game can be just as much part of the narrative core strategy – no matter if you yourself end up creating this content or not. You don't need to confine yourself to the game itself to reveal all the lore you've developed, and transmedia storytelling can provide an interesting way to set yourself apart from competing products.

Many videogames make use of transmedia content nowadays, especially live games, to create more immersive marketing or to expand the franchise meaningfully. Later in this chapter, we will shed some light on different types of media, but before that, let's consider what kind of content we can cover in transmedia projects.

There are several ways **how transmedia stories can relate to your videogame's narrative**[1]:

- **Retelling the game's story** in another medium, making use of its unique strengths. An example could be a novelization, expanding on details of the story, and providing more insight into the character's inner lives.
- **Expanding the game's story**, or telling it in the first place. This is especially helpful for games that don't have plot or dialogue, and surface narrative through themes, visual storytelling, and game design.
- A **story that runs parallel to the game's story**, to highlight certain characters, events, or locations. This can provide a new perspective on your story and give more depth to those who weren't your protagonists.
- A **new story, set within the same universe**. This can be a spin-off story to highlight certain characters, events, or locations. Stories like that can

expand your fictional world, and give more meaning and depth to elements that weren't the focus of your game.

- A **prequel or sequel** to the game's story, providing new context, backstories and future stories that give more meaning and depth to the story itself.
- A **crossover story with another franchise**, usually in a "what if" scenario that throws known characters into new scenarios and is meant to attract fans of both properties.
- An **alternate universe** that puts the characters into another setting, or changes the setting so drastically that it provides new conflicts and themes to work with.
- **Micro entertainment** set within the game world, making use of its characters. This can reveal lore, but doesn't have to. An example would be fictional Twitter accounts of in-game characters.
- **Lore revealing content**, which simply provides background information. For example: Character biographies, item descriptions, trailers, etc. This can also be used to tease something upcoming before it happens in the game.

WHY DO IT?

There are many good reasons why you might want to consider expanding your game's narrative with transmedia projects. When creating a live game, you want to keep it relevant for a long time to come, and transmedia projects can give you one more tool to do so. They can provide new, unexpected ways to present your game's narrative to your players, and reel them right back into the game's world. It is always a matter of budget and resources when it comes to what you can do, but you don't need to have an established multi-million-dollar franchise to consider it. Not every transmedia project needs to be movie or high-budget TV series – some options can be pretty thrifty and achievable, even for indie developers on a budget, such as social media accounts, websites, or webcomics.

These are some reasons for considering transmedia projects for your game[2]:

- **Expanding the Opportunities of Your Narrative:** The great thing about transmedia storytelling is that you can expand the game's narrative world with the unique strength of the medium you're planning to use. The medium is the message, and this initial choice deeply influences how a narrative is perceived and how it can portray its story. Like every medium, video-games can do *specific* kinds of storytelling very well. They can convey narrative through action, systems, and interactive experiences, including player choices, environmental exploration, and emergent storytelling. But other media have *other* strengths that can be taken advantage of – this expands what you can do with the whole narrative experience of all transmedia projects combined.
- **Marketing for Your Game:** Any additional projects connected to your game increase audience awareness beyond the usual marketing channels. The more often audiences see or hear of a game, the more likely they will perceive it as an impactful game that people seem to care about (may that be positive or negative). Frequent reminders increase the chances of audiences actually taking the step to check it out or to get back in after they churned. Also, they

might find an entry point into the game's universe that they are more easily hooked into (such as a webcomic) and then get so curious that they want to play the game, even though they might otherwise not have chosen to.

- **Strengthening the Brand:** In a similar effect, transmedia projects give players the opportunity to spend more time within the universe of the game. By being immersed in the game's world more often, even when they're not playing the game, they are more likely to develop a deeper emotional bond with the game, and therefore, brand loyalty. There's also the *mere-exposure effect* of believing that a brand that you see more often is culturally more impactful, and therefore, more preferable over other competitors.
- **An Additional Source of Revenue:** Depending on your intended form of release, a transmedia project can mean an additional revenue stream for your company.

If any of this sounds attractive to you, read on, and we'll dive more into transmedia project development, and a few of the options you might want to consider.

IN-HOUSE VS. EXTERNAL PRODUCTION

Many transmedia projects are going to involve external partners who specialize in whatever you intend to produce – may those be part of the company structure or another company altogether. Animation studios, filmmakers, novelists, comic artists, marketing specialists, event organizers, and so on.

No matter if you plan to produce within your own in-house team or join up with an external partner, a project like this should ideally have some involvement from the game's narrative team. Depending on the project and your resources, this may be more or less involved, but even if you take a hands-off approach where you give a lot of freedom to the partner, offering the right support is key to an effective transmedia project.

The more involved the narrative team is, the more resources it will take from them actually working on the game itself. But perhaps you can find a production phase where this wouldn't be an issue or build your narrative team around that workload. Or you expand your team to have narrative specialists focusing on transmedia projects.

A collaboration can be **hands-on**, where the narrative team develops the idea, writes vision documents, provides resources, and completes scripts that the external partner then produces – with the narrative team providing feedback during production to align the product with their vision. For a short film, for example, the narrative team might as well develop everything from the idea stage to the storyboard cinematic and 3D models, whereas the animation studio then only produces the animation with those resources.

But it can also be as **hands-off** as taking an advisor role which gives more creative freedom to the partner. There are a few helpful things to keep in mind when **developing transmedia projects externally** though.

- A **project pitch** should provide all the necessary key elements that you have in mind, no matter how much you want the external partner to expand on these ideas. You know the project inside out, while the partner possibly knows nothing when they start out. So in a transmedia project pitch, it's important to clarify: What is the game? What is the purpose of this transmedia project? What is the tone and content you want to explore? These concepts can emerge from collaborative brainstorming too, but even if the external partner pitches ideas, they need to start from something. They need the resources they require to make well-informed suggestions (to save everyone's nerves and make the collaboration a pleasant one).

- **Providing the right documents** is key. Even if the game's narrative team doesn't end up writing the scripts, they need to feed the external partner with what they need to create this intended addition to the game's world. This probably includes an overview of the game's story, intended tone and relevant characters, as well as the project's general intention, creative freedoms, and limitations. This can be about which lore details you want or *don't* want to reveal in it (because they're meant to be revealed later, for instance) or questions of brand identity. Depending on what the partner needs to know, provide the required lore documentation.

- Being available as a **narrative advisor** to guide the external team is also crucial. Communication is key, and regular check-ups and feedback along the way make sure that the project goes in the right direction. While this responsibility could be taken by a creative director, the marketing team, or even a transmedia team, there's a good chance that narrative designers might find this responsibility on their plate, too. It's all a matter of team setup, the team's resources, and who would be best equipped to serve as the lore master in this collaboration.

- And lastly, keep in mind that you're probably an expert for *game narratives* specifically and therefore should **respect the professional opinion of other specialists**. A transmedia project is going to step outside of your own circle of knowledge as soon as you cross over into another medium and the best results usually come from allowing that other medium to shine with its own strengths. If you let the specialists of the other medium give their professional input, while you guide production with your knowledge of the game and the intended purpose of the project, it can become something awesome through *collaboration*.

WHICH FORMAT TO CHOOSE?

There are no hard rules regarding what medium can be used for transmedia projects as long as it gets to the intended audience. The sky (and the budget) is the limit. Here is a list of a few options that can serve as inspiration.

WEBSITES

A cheap and easy option is to create websites to expand the game's story.

On the one hand, they can be **extra-diagetic** (= outside of your game's narrative) documents like websites or wikis filled with information, such as lore and character biographies. These websites can contain hyperlink narratives, videos, or even browser games. League of Legends, for example, allows you to browse a website full of statistics and biographies of the playable champions, as well as several short stories, comics, videos, and songs about them. Champions are presented as game characters, rather than real people, and the site always makes it clear that League of Legends is a videogame.

But websites can go a more immersive route as **intra-diagetic** (= inside of your game's narrative) documents too, often as part of an ARG (= Alternate Reality Game, an interactive networked narrative that uses the real world as its setting, whereas players can explore a story through transmedia content and often influence its development through investigation and collaboration).

Websites can present narrative in a fully immersive way, providing players with websites that implicitly come from within the game world itself and treating the game's events as if real, rather than a videogame. This could come in the shape of blogs of fictional characters or websites of fictional institutions or locations, presented as genuine. One example for these immersive websites would be the Starrpark.biz website of Brawlstars. Without mentioning the game by name, it takes the shape of a late 90s to early 2000s website of a fictional theme park, Starr Park, collecting photos of memorabilia and an investor video. This Starr Park was later revealed as the setting of Brawlstars season 3 (and offered hints at a deeper lore that implies that the game always takes place in this very park). The website came to player's attention as part of a bigger ARG connected to the game.

Strengths of the Medium
Hyperlinks, hypertextual information, wikis, collecting various media in one place, information structured by categories (sub-sites), and blog-like storytelling.

Potential Use
Game wikis, collections of various media or, fictional websites from the game's universe.

SOCIAL MEDIA

Smartphone and internet users spend a rampant amount of time on micro-blogging platforms, checking their feeds for updates on all the things they're invested in and all the people they want to hear about. Using these popular platforms as a way to tell a story can be an interesting way to get player's attention and expand your narrative world in unusual ways.

Popular platforms (by the time of writing this) are:

- **Twitter**, for text, image, and video-based micro-blogging, which encourages discussions and continuous threads
- **Instagram**, for images and short videos, which centers around posting and sharing engaging visuals
- **TikTok**, for short videos, which encourage remixing and reusing other user's content, creating trends and memes (especially younger audiences)
- …and **Facebook**, for text, image, and video-based blogging (especially older or casual gamer audiences)

A social media account can also reveal lore in an extra-diagetic way, by acknowledging the game as a game, but still providing micro-narrative in the shape of engaging posts.

But we can also approach this intra-diagetically. Fictional characters can come alive with social media accounts, micro-blogging micro-narrative, giving insights into the game's world from the eyes of an in-game character. League of Legends tried this one with Twitter and Instagram accounts for the playable champion Seraphine,[3] who for six months posted about her days with texts and images, giving followers insights into her personality, dreams, and life. This was started even before she was added to the game, and ran until about a week after her release, functioning as an immersive roleplaying marketing campaign for the new character.

Strengths of the Medium
Potential for widespread sharing and virality, micro-narrative, regular updates delivered straight to where people are already spending time, blog-like storytelling, and possibility for interaction and immersive roleplay.

Potential Use
Roleplaying characters or organizations from the game, or micro entertainment.

VIDEOS AND MOVIES

Audiovisual media can take various forms, from movies released in theaters over series on streaming services to short videos uploaded on YouTube.

Big movies are a very ambitious and large-scale undertaking when it comes to transmedia storytelling, but once a brand is established enough, it can become possible. World of Warcraft and Angry Birds are both live games that have seen adaptations on the big screen.

Recently, there has also been a range of Netflix series adaptation that gave us some interesting depictions and expansions of game universes, like the League of Legends' *Arcane* series.

When it comes to shorter formats, short films and videos can both serve as a way to tell short stories and to announce new content. Keep in mind that you can express a story in something more fragmented than a short film, too. Your video content can simply portray a character, a mood, a conflict, a setting, or a joke.

A narrative trailer for content can, for instance, announce a new season, a new game feature, a new playable character, but place it inside an engaging short narrative. May that take the form of a themed showcase (such as Brawlstars' season announcements 1–7) or the shape of a short story (like in the trailer for Fortnite Chapter 2 Season 5: Zero Point). This format can also be presented as a music video, like League of Legends has done multiple times. It started with the "Get Jinxed" music video, which serves as a catchy study of the character Jinx, and more recently, K/DA's POP/STARS music video, which showed off new K-Pop themed skins for a group of Champions that came with a whole alternate universe story around them.

Producing short videos that can be easily shared has great potential for viral marketing and can hype players up for new content or gives them a deeper insight into the existing game world.

Strengths of the Medium

Audiovisual and cinematic storytelling, mood and atmosphere, self-contained or epi-sodic short stories, showcases, potential for sharing and virality.

Potential Use

Content announcements, character or skin showcase, or full cinematic stories (short or feature length).

NOVELS AND SEQUENTIAL ART

Novels are a fundamentally different experience from the interactive, action-driven, and visual format of the videogame, so they can offer a very different approach to the game's narrative. They can be more introspective and detailed when it comes to dialogue and plot, since they don't depend on a budget to produce it all. You only need words on the page, and there are no limits to dialogue length (as there are no voice actors and no animation), extravagant settings, or action sequences. They can therefore expand the game's story and world where the videogame was potentially limited by budget (or a pleasant *game flow,* as players want to play after all).

Numerous game franchises have released tie-in novels during their time – includ-ing live games. World of Warcraft can occupy entire shelves with their series of novels set in the game's universe, and also Minecraft has seen several releases fol-lowing the same pattern. What is remarkable is the difference between those two games when it comes to in-game lore, illustrating that an engaging setting is enough to kick off novel tie-ins, which then expand what the game already offers. Google videogame novels. You'd be surprised just how many have been released over the years – some of which are direct novelizations of the events inside the game, while others are tie-ins that offer new stories set in the same universe.

Those books can also be gamified by being written as choose-your-own-adven-ture novels, where readers can take choices that lead them to designated pages with a new story branch and often multiple endings. The Temple Run tie-in novels have taken that form, for example.

Sequential art, meaning graphic novels, comics, mangas, and webcomics, is another interesting format for adaptations and tie-in stories. With the visual aspect, they are often quicker reads and have a higher chance of appealing to a similar audi-ence as the videogame. Even though they have completely unique strengths and sto-rytelling methods, they can be used for a similar purposes as novels – as adaptations or as tie-ins with new stories. One example would be Far Cry: Esperanza's Tears, a tie-in graphic novel for the game Far Cry 6, telling a prequel story which casts an NPC from the game, Juan Cortez, as the main character. If these stories are released as comic issues (such as the Batman/Fornite crossover comics) or webcomics (such as the Mystic Messenger tie-in webcomic), they can go the route of episodic story-telling as well. Just as novels, sequential art can give a deeper insight into events of the game, and take more time to go into details that the game might have left out. They can expand the world with new tie-in stories and grant insights into characters' minds. Showing locations or characters that might have been cut from the game becomes much easier in this format too, because they remain in two dimensions, and don't need to be fully modeled and textured as an in-game asset.

Strengths of the Medium (Novels)

Longer prose, more detailed events, and internal narrative can describe elements that the game didn't show without budget restraints, insights into the character's minds

Strengths of the Medium (Sequential Art)

Sequential storytelling, visual storytelling, can depict elements that the game didn't show without budget restraints.

Potential Use

Revealing the game's backstory (in case it's a game with little plot), adaptations, prequels, sequels, tie-ins, or new stories set inside the game universe, focusing on specific characters or parts of the world.

AUDIOBOOKS AND PODCASTS

In a similar vein to novels and comics, using audio formats can be another interesting medium for tie-ins and adaptations. They can take the form of a one-time audiobook release for a large self-contained story (such as Assassin's Creed Gold), or episodic releases as podcasts, such as the Marvel Wastelanders series. While this podcast isn't directly related to a game, Marvel has seen many videogame released over the years, so they are all part of the same transmedia universe. The Marvel Wastelanders podcast series each focus on a specific character, such as Star-Lord, who then experiences an adventure told through a series of podcast episodes.

Compared to novels, the unique strength of audiobooks and podcasts is that they tell a story through the use of audio (naturally), creating soundscapes through sounds, music, character voices, and possibly narration. They can be more easily consumed on the side, while the listener does other things (such as cleaning, working out, or even gaming), and might open up longer stories to audiences who otherwise don't find the time to read.

Strengths of the Medium

Can be consumed while doing other things, longer prose, more detailed events, internal narrative, insights into the character's minds, episodic storytelling, can depict elements that the game didn't show without budget restraints.

Potential Use

Revealing the game's backstory, adaptations, prequels, sequels, tie-ins, and new stories set inside the game universe, focusing on specific characters or parts of the world.

ARGs

An alternate reality game (ARG for short) is an interactive networked narrative that employs various media to tell a story, marked by deep audience involvement and a tendency to blur the lines between reality and fiction. When a player first stumbles upon a piece of an ARG, it might not be obvious what the ARG relates to, or that it is a fictional experience at all. An ARG involves audiences as active parts of the narrative, often putting them in the role of detective trying to unravel a mystery, and sometimes even allowing them to influence the development of events. While other media are often available for an extended period of time, an ARG takes place in real time, over a specific period of time, in an event unfolding over the course of multiple content releases. It is usually a multimedia transmedia narrative that can make use of just about anything, like websites, forums or social media posts, videos, e-mails, physical mail, telephone calls or even real world objects, locations, or performances. Instead of relying on AI, such as a videogame would, an ARG might employ real-world actors to play the part of a character in the narrative – on the phone, on the internet, or wherever they might interact with the audience.

The gameplay of an ARG is usually that players gather media, analyze the story, solve puzzles, and coordinate online activity with others to influence the story and/ or reveal the mystery of the ARG, reaching some kind of conclusion. No matter how complex an ARGs challenges are, in the end, players patch together a narrative from various sources.

Collaboration between players, and a creation of a hive mind, is central to the experience. As a narrative without one single platform, online forums, fan websites, or discord channels become the participant-created hubs for other members. It is worth mentioning that ARGs are often treated as if they aren't a game (without trying to mislead or spread misinformation, of course) – with audiences becoming part of a shared roleplay.

Throughout history, several videogames have used ARGs as a means to promote their game – sometimes saving the reveal of the connection for the ultimate end. An early example would be the I love Bees ARG that marketed Halo 2.[4] It was kicked off with a secret message in the Halo 2 trailer, which led players to a website (Ilovebees.co) about beekeeping that seemed to have been hacked. By solving puzzles and audiologs posted to the site, players would gradually uncover more about the backstory of the game, involving an AI stranded on Earth, trying to put itself back together.

A more recent example is the Starr Park ARG of Brawlstars, which I already mentioned for their intra-diagetic website. Prior to the announcement of the theme of season 3 (Welcome to Starr Park!), some videogame influencers had received mystery boxes in the mail. Those contained several pieces of merchandise of the aforementioned fictional theme park, such as a fan t-shirt of a rollercoaster. The name of the park was dropped on several pieces of goodies as well, such as a wooden toy penguin. When googling the name of the theme park, players could find a website that was dedicated to the park as if it was real, including an "investor video" that starts as an informative clip about the park, but slowly turns darker, eventually revealing that things have gone very wrong there. In addition to that, the so-called WKBRL stream started streaming on YouTube, as an online radio, which sometimes aired fictional emergency messages from within the park.

Through clues given during the radio livestream, the investor video and the website, it seems implied that the game takes place in a theme park that closed down in the early 1970s, where obscure experiments with toxic chemicals and mind control went out of hand. This rather dark backstory was a new addition to the game's ingame lore and captivated players who were eager to find out more about the backstory of their favorite game.

ARGs are often less accessible to mainstream audiences, but ARG players tend to be extremely dedicated and passionate – which can sometimes lead to the hunt making waves in wider circles than just the actual participants. Especially nowadays, with video content creators specializing in gathering and revealing secret lore of videogames (like the YouTube channel Game Theory), ARGs can be an intriguing narrative experience even to those who don't actively participate in the interactive aspect of it.

Strengths of the Medium
Immersive lore reveal, audience participation, collaboration between audience members, viral marketing, and content creators might make videos about it.

Potential Use
Revealing lore from the game universe, making audiences part of the story, or creating an immersive side story, either as a preview or an expansion of narrative elements in the game.

PHYSICAL GOODS AND MERCHANDISING

Using physical goods as a means of narrative expression can take the form of purchasable merchandise, marketing goods at conventions, or exclusive goodies for content creators or premium players.

For a start, your game's purchasable **merchandise** should ideally stem from the game's lore. Figurines express the personality and look of characters, with little blurbs on the back of the box. Trading card games explore the game world by categorizing its elements in another game format, or even expanding its lore with new things. Stationary graphics can express their personalities through visual storytelling. But physical items that players can buy aren't the only physical items that can be used for storytelling.

Another interesting narrative potential lies in the goods used for marketing. If you've ever been to videogame conventions, you've likely seen how developers hand out **marketing goodies** at their booths to advertise their game. These can be as simple as handouts, but the chance of players wanting and keeping a cool goodie is much higher than a mere piece of paper. This can be anything from in-universe drinks or candies branded with in-universe companies to entrance bracelets to in-universe events. These goods can draw from in-universe lore, or even reveal additional hitherto unknown narrative or tease things that are yet to come. These objects can be part of an ARG (mentioned previously) or stand on their own. If anything, they at least serve as narrative-infused marketing materials that players are likely to find engaging.

Another way to distribute physical goods comes in the form of **packages sent to content creators**, who then might unpack them on camera as part of their video or livestream on the game or its new feature. The Sims 4, for example, hosted an in-game music festival called Sims Sessions in June/July 2021. In that context, they sent out a package to influencers that contained a lanyard, a baseball cap, some pins, and a VIP access invitation to the music festival – basically treating it like a real music festival.

These packages could also go to premium players, who have bought a subscription, a premium package, or something similar. The F2P otome game Mystic Messenger, for example, offers a physical VIP package that contains business cards of the in-game characters, as well as a membership lanyard of the RFA (a fictional party planning association from the game), additional soundtracks and audio dramas on CDs, guidebooks and more – in addition to in-game credits.

Strengths of the Medium
Marketing objects are more likely to be kept than handouts, desirable for collectors, and content creators might make videos about it, serving as great marketing.

Potential Use
Storytelling through objects, making fictional objects real, revealing game lore immersively, as part of an ARG story, or content creator marketing collaborations.

REAL-WORLD EVENTS

Lastly, real world events can be used as a form of narrative expression, as well. These can be performances, such as stageplays, escape rooms, get-togethers, "experiences" and concerts, but might take other forms as well. A live game that has done this is the augmented reality app Pokémon Go, where in-game time-limited events would be tied to real world locations (such as big parks) and encourage players to meet there for a special gameplay experience.

Strengths of the Medium
In-person, highly immersive, takes audience's full attention.

Potential Use
Performances, collaborations, or local events.

OTHER MEDIA

For the sake of completion, I'd like to end this chapter on the reminder that there is no limit to what can be used for a transmedia project, as long as it gets to the intended audience. It makes sense to consider whether your target audience has interest in interacting with the medium chosen for a transmedia project, or whether you are planning to expand your target audience this way. Each project should be treated in accordance to its own audience and narrative potential.

SUMMARY

- A transmedia project can **retell the game's story** in another medium, **expand the game's story**, create a **new parallel story**, create a **new story set within the same universe**, serve as a **prequel or sequel**, be a **crossover with another franchise**, explore an **alternate universe**, provide **micro entertainment** and reveal **more lore**.
- Transmedia storytelling can expand the **opportunities of your narrative**, serve as **marketing** for your game, **strengthen the brand**, and provide an additional **source of revenue**.
- Such projects can be done **in-house or external.**
- When done with an **external partner**, it's important to **provide the right documents**, have **a pitch**, be there as a **narrative advisor**, but also **respect the professional opinion** of other specialists.
- Transmedia projects can take **many different forms**, such as:
  - Websites
  - Social media
  - Videos and movies
  - Novels and sequential art
  - Audiobooks and podcasts
  - ARGs
  - Physical goods and merchandising
  - Events
  - Other media
- All these mediums have **different strengths and potential uses**.

REFERENCES

1 Ross Berger, "Transmedia," in *Dramatic Storytelling & Narrative Design: A Writer's Guide to Video Games and Transmedia*, CRC Press, August 27, 2020, 149–154.
2 Ross Berger, "Transmedia," in *Dramatic Storytelling & Narrative Design: A Writer's Guide to Video Games and Transmedia*, CRC Press, August 27, 2020, 131–149.
3 Twitter User "Seraphine," accessed April 22, 2023, https://twitter.com/seradotwav.
4 "i love bees," Halopedia: The Halo Wiki, accessed April 22, 2023, https://www.halopedia.org/I_love_bees.

17 Narrative Monetization

Chances are you're either a developer passionate about monetization strategies, or a developer who sighs at the demands of the stakeholders or company leadership. Either way, it is quite the investment to keep a game live, therefore it needs to make some money in return. Even if you're not a *passionately* monetization-driven narrative designer, being aware of the ways that narrative can support your monetization strategies can be helpful for seeing your project succeed. Or perhaps you need some arguments to convince stakeholders of your narrative feature ideas, and some monetization suggestions could help out on that front.

Live games monetize with an **upfront payment** (paying for the app), a **subscription**, **paid DLCs** and/or **in-game purchases**. Besides that, **in-app advertisement** can be a source of income as well – either automatic (after a certain number of play sessions) or as a voluntary option to gain additional game resources ("*watch ad to get 1 more life*"). Many live games are free-to-play, but even premium live games (which you have to purchase to play) usually offer in-game purchases and new DLCs over time. The *subscription* model between a premium live game and a free-to-play live game is often defined slightly differently – one is a subscription for access to the game or a certain part of the game (e.g., after onboarding, or for additional character slots), while the other is access to additional rewards that can be unlocked by playing the game (a season pass, trophy road, etc.), while yet another subscription service can be for permanent advantages like more XP gain, regular free items, and so on.

This chapter focuses on the role of narrative design in additional purchase options that come with the field of live games.

KPIs

Although key performance indicators (KPIs) aren't something that can be purchased, they usually relate to a game's income in some way. There are a variety of KPIs[1] which are commonly used to measure the success of a game – and the more successful a game is, the higher its chances of making money. Even though these two elements are separate from each other, you need active players before anybody can buy anything. Therefore, if narrative can boost KPIs, it effectively means increased general and often financial success.

User Engagement

MAU, WAU, and DAU are KPIs that measure engagement over a period of time, namely monthly, weekly, and daily active users. These KPIs describe the amount of players that have opened the game to play it, in a given timeframe. So they don't designate the total number of players, but a changing rate of the *currently active* players – a player who has downloaded the game but never opens it is effectively unimportant for our revenue.

DOI: 10.1201/9781003297628-22

Narrative can work as an incentive to check the game regularly, keeping players coming back for more. This can be based on the game's **general narrative**, a desire to spend more time within the fictional world and its characters because a player has grown to love them. Another alluring factor is **timed narrative**. In a game with an energy system or other timers that pass in real time, players are more likely to open the game regularly, maximizing the speed at which they can see new (possibly narrative) content. A fully charged energy bar may allow them to read a few new chapters, thus driving up regular game activity. This can be tied to push notifications, reminding the player of their new content waiting for them – ideally in a personalized manner that ties into the narrative of the game (instead of coming off as generic and pestering). Another strategy is the **regular release** of new narrative content that keeps players coming back. With a new season, time-limited events, live events, or new DLCs, they have reason to return yet again. These content updates should always have an element of narrative to them, may that be in an overall theme, actual story, or the narrative inside the announcements. Sometimes a trailer showing off your new season skins can be all the more shareable if it tells a little story.

Retention

Another important KPI is the player retention rate, which describes what percentage of players keep on playing the game over a certain amount of time passing. Day one retention is usually a popular metric, but so is one week and one month – or even longer periods of time. If a player stops playing entirely and moves on, perhaps even deleting the app, that's means they've *churned*. The lower the churn rate, the better – you want to keep them around. In order to be able to monetize your game, you need players to be active in it – so this too doesn't directly refer to financial gain, but more players equal more potential buyers of in-app products.

Retention is often tied to **emotional attachment** to the game. The more attached a player is to game's world and its characters, the more likely they will keep on coming back. Game and brand loyalty is only made possible by creating an emotional attachment, which happens through storytelling of some kind (may that be inside of the product or the narrative *around* the product). And when a live game keeps on adding **new content** for that world, in the form of new seasons, live events, and/or new DLCs, players who are emotionally attached to the game's world are more likely to be curious what happens to their favorites next – and log back in. If the game offers some kind of long-term promise of narrative, like seasonal storytelling with arcs over arcs, it can be much like a TV series that draws players back in with every new release.

Revenue

And lastly, of course, there is direct money made through in-app purchases and subscriptions. Revenue is often tracked as total revenue (over the game's lifetime), yearly revenue, monthly revenue, weekly revenue, and daily revenue. Another popular KPI is also how much one user spends on average, the average revenue per user (ARPU) – or how much a paying user spends on average, the average revenue per paying user (ARPPU). The latter cuts out all players who don't spend any money in game and therefore gives a better idea of how much an average payer spends, once they do decide that they're willing to spend money. Let's look at the way narrative design can influence total revenue, too.

NARRATIVE AS A PURCHASE INCENTIVE

The advertisement industry is all about storytelling. Ads are rarely an objective list of the uses for a product – advertisers craft a scenario that is meant to intrigue, amuse, or speak to basic human needs. Coca-Cola isn't only a sugary bubbly drink with caffeine, it's a lifestyle choice of action, badassery, and explosions (as in the "Life as it should be" Coca-Cola Zero commercials of the 2000s[2]) or a symbol of nostalgia, warmth, and family (as in the countless Christmas Coca-Cola commercials that feature a bright-eyed Santa Claus dressed in red and cozy polar bear families). Storytelling in ads tugs at people's heartstrings, giving lofty promises of fulfillment of an emotional need, and simply stick in their memory for longer. If anything, knowing about a brand makes you more likely to trust a brand, which makes you more likely to buy a brand – whether the advertised promise resonated with you or not. This is the mere-exposure effect – the more often you see something, the more likely you will gravitate toward it.

The same applies to in-game purchases: **Narrative can make a product more attractive** for potential buyers.

EMOTIONAL APPEAL

One influencing factor is the **emotional appeal** of a product. It's the promise of an emotional fulfillment if you buy it. This weapon will make you cooler, this avatar will make you funnier, completing this hardcore DLC will make you badass, and so on. This isn't only about an actual video ad for a product, although you might choose to have announcement trailers for new purchasable content, but the entire narrative presentation inside and outside of the game. This can also take the shape of in-game ad pop-ups, highlighted sales offers in the in-game shop, the general description and presentation of the product, the story told by or inside of the product, or other marketing strategies. The narrative lies is the exact wording, the visual presentation, and the implied emotional reward for buying the product. Popular emotions to appeal to would be the desire for power and potential, a fear of missing out, a sense of adventure, desire for popularity and inclusion, a solution for frustration/pain, the attractiveness of scarcity, self-expression, status and pride, expression of values, celebrity endorsement, general gratification, or even a promise for romance (usually fictional). These emotional appeals can be created through clever visual, textual, and general narrative design – or actual storytelling.

EMOTIONAL ATTACHMENT

Another factor lies in the **emotional attachment** to the game world and its characters. The more a player cares about the world as an emotionally real place, the more strongly they feel about the things that happen inside of it. A playable hero character becomes more interesting if they have a backstory and personality, and thus become a more well-rounded product, even if it's "only" reflected in, for example, their name, outfit, attack moves, and in-game barks. If such a vivid character is tied to gacha or lootbox mechanics, players might be more tempted to invest more to pull them, as opposed to purely aesthetic collections. Players can become so attached to individual characters that there are several terms to describe the phenomenon. They might become their *main* (a character they play as most often) or their *waifu or husbando* (a character they like the most, likening the intensity of their emotions to a humorously "romantic" sentiment). Also, if players are emotionally attached to a playable character, they're more likely to invest in them, may that be in upgrades, weapons, skins, or emotes. There is no inherent obligation for deep narrative to achieve this attachment, but it makes it all the more likely – after all, it's harder (but not impossible) to develop an emotional bond to a cardboard cutout. Emotional attachment can also be toward avatars that don't have an extensive written backstory, but serve as roleplay avatars of the player. Here, the emotional attachment comes from the character being the player's vessel in the virtual world and their subjective interpretation they project onto them during all their playtime together.

CURIOSITY AND IMPATIENCE

Lastly, there is the aspect of **curiosity and impatience**, mainly focused on the progression of a plot or the revelation of information. A game might have a system where you have to unlock or wait for new story content to be available, may that because it's tied to a mission progression, time-management features, or an energy system. Player curiosity about the continuation of a story, and the subsequent impatience, can also be a motivating factor for making a purchase. An episodic interactive fiction game might sell new episodes in bulk (as in Paris: City of Love), so that players can binge them instead of having to play in moderation over an extended period of time. Another example for curiosity-driven narrative purchases are premium options for alternative story developments, which are otherwise unavailable or take a long time to earn in-game (like flirtatious options in Love Island).

NARRATIVE AS A PRODUCT

Narrative can do more than serve as an incentive for players to keep on playing and spend money. It can be a product[3] in itself.

This can take the shape of purchasable **story content**, such as:

- A completely new **storyline,** such as a new season with the same characters, a new series with new characters, or a DLC with a new story.
- Access to new **episodes** or the **ability to skip a waiting period** or other gates to access these episodes (like required progress or achievements). For example, if your season has a story, and players have a limited time to unlock this story, you can offer a purchase that unlocks the whole story at once, or stories you missed in previous seasons.
- New **story routes**, such as romance routes that let you woo a character from a story you already know.
- New self-contained **spinoff stories or game missions** that give more insight into the world's individual characters, locations, or events.
- **Premium choices** in interactive fiction, such as being able to flirt with a character you like.

- Additional **side content**, such as personal chats, phone calls, documents, or going on dates with characters.

Besides the story content itself, there is also **narrative-infused content** – game elements that aren't a plot-driven story, but contain meaningful narrative elements. They are an expansion of the game's universe through new elements that tell a story through their design, function and perhaps descriptions and advertisement.

- **Game packages or items**, such as weapons, characters, skins, or other narrative-infused content.
- **Expansions/DLCs** that provide new themed game content that expands the game with new locations, characters, weapons, gameplay, missions, or other things (as in GTA Online).

Lastly, there is also **micro narrative** in the form of in-game products that have a narrative nature, but not necessarily story in the traditional sense. Narrative content doesn't need to be a whole plot line to hold value. **Emotes**, for example, can express a lot about a character – especially if they're tied to specific ones. Another example would be the variety of **audio products** some games offer, usually in multiplayer environments. There are usually two audio products on offer, if games choose to sell audio products: Voice line emotes and announcer packs.

- **Voice line emotes** are a cosmetic feature that allow players to trigger a voice line on command, or during a specific event (such as kills or during a character intro in Apex Legends). These voice lines are usually hero specific, matching their voice and personality. They serve both as a form of self-expression for players, much like regular emotes, but add restrictions that fit within the character's personality, expressing them further (as in Overwatch).
- Meanwhile, **announcer packs** unlock a new announcer voice, the voice-over that informs the player about current events in a game match (such as teammates needing help, a player achieving a killstreak, a team having destroyed an enemy tower, time running out, etc.). When initially, the announcer may be neutral in nature, a new announcer pack could express their distinct attitude and personality within their role as announcers. These could either be original personalities or already existing in-game characters. The otherwise informative tone could then become grumpy, extra excited, seductive, etc. The new announcer might also take the form of a cameo, by being a popular (voice) actor, eSports commentator, content creator, general celebrity, or a guest role from another videogame character (as in Dota 2 or SMITE). The possibilities are endless.

FREE VS. PREMIUM CONTENT

Every F2P game has to answer the question how a non-paying player and a paying player each experience the game. Some games purely focus on cosmetics and optional extra content nowadays, rather than game advantages. Implementing *soft level caps* (when the game experience slows down over time, coming almost to a stand-still if players don't invest money) and so-called *pay-to-win* mechanics (paying for game advantages over other players, making it less about time investment and game skills, but a pure matter of money) have been often met with disdain from audiences and critics. The common ground for these critiques of monetization strategies is when non-paying players feel like the game experience has been made worse on purpose, just to pressure them into paying money. It feels manipulative and anti-consumer.

Transferring this to the narrative perspective, it would mean that players feel like the narrative experience was made worse in order to provoke purchases. And if non-paying players experience the game narrative as lacking, they probably don't get hooked and churn – not to mention the negative perception of the game. So, in order to fully make use of your narrative in a context of monetization, it is crucial to design your narrative content for both non-paying and paying players in mind. Both should have great experiences, and don't feel like not paying (or paying) ruined the story for them.

There are several options to navigate designing a **narrative for** both, **non-paying and paying players**:

- Monetize **side stories or additional narrative** that only expands the core narrative experience, while the main story is free for everyone. This can be in the form of DLCs, extra missions, additional story scenes that expand the main story, additional story paths, story-driven gacha, and more. This extra content can be independent from the main progression, like character-focused stories, vignettes, or spin-offs, or interwoven with the main story. It can be tied to an external purchase, in-game purchases, or a season pass. For example: MMOs like to offer DLCs with a whole new story, setting, and gameplay package at an additional cost, but these DLCs are just a new story within that world, rather than the base story (as in GTA Online or World of Warcraft).
- Monetize **speeding up the rate** at which narrative can be consumed, or **grant early access** while trying to not frustrate non-paying users too much. This speed can be tied to an energy system or gameplay progression. The right balance is a question of estimations and playtesting, depending on the length of daily possible play sessions. Based on personal experience, we can assume that once per day, for at least a few minutes, is probably the bare minimum amount of narrative content players would want. You may also want to consider if players can stack their energy for longer play sessions with less frequency, or if they can only have these short play sessions with high frequency. Of course, you'd want daily active users, but it's always important to keep the players' *actual* enjoyment in mind, rather than just trying to optimize numbers. Making frustratingly short episodes risks a low opinion of your game's quality. You can, however, also decide that this method of limiting daily narrative progression won't be included in your game at all – as it creates an artificial scarcity that can be perceived as pressuring players to spend money by some.
- These strategies can also be combined, when you offer side stories that can be unlocked with both, a **hard currency** (bought with real money) **or a soft currency** (acquired through playing the game). The choice, therefore,

is between time investment and money investment (therefore skipping the process). This way, hardcore non-paying players might happily choose to invest the time and effort and feel happy about this option, while other players might bite the bullet and just spend a few bucks for immediate access instead (as in Mystic Messenger).

- Monetize **additional items or cosmetics** (with narrative meaning) which are not necessary for an enjoyable core experience. Here, it is important that they don't give the players unfair gameplay advantages (often negatively called *pay-to-win*). Items like this can hold narrative meaning in the sense of exploring a side of a character, or using it for self-expression, which influences the player's perception and experience of the game. For example: Defeating your opponents in a cute maid outfit has another narrative meaning than defeating them in full military gear.

ETHICAL MONETIZATION DESIGN

Throughout this chapter, we already touched upon some good practices when it comes to **monetization design for narrative features**. But to wrap this topic up, it can be enlightening to take a closer look at the ethics of monetization design, seen through the lens of narrative design. After all, monetization isn't only about making profit and not alienating your audience, but also about avoiding exploitative methods.

There are a few questions you can ask yourself to check if your game accidentally uses **unethical monetization methods:**

- Is your narrative design reinforcing the **exploitation of addictive behavior**? Is it consciously misleading about products, reinforcing gambling and creating parasocial relationships with the game characters, pressuring players into choices they didn't actually want?
- Are you using **dark patterns**[4] to misguide and manipulate players? Some of these relate to UI and UX design, where narrative design comes into play. Examples for this would be **misleading** players about the product by text or visuals (e.g., showing a picture of rare and common objects that suggest other chance ratios than the actual chance ratios inside the lootbox) **confirmshaming** (guilting the player into opting into something by phrasing the decline option in a way that makes it seem like a worse choice), or **appealing to emotion in a manipulative way** (as in "*your favorite character will hate you if you don't buy this!*"). Depending on your country, some of these dark patterns may be regulated by law. Misleading players about the chances in randomized purchases, and not giving access to actual numbers, is penalized in some countries already.
- Is the game's story unplayable and **unenjoyable for non-paying players**? Is it impossible to have a coherent and pleasing story experience without paying, and therefore, either unengaging or putting them under extreme pressure to buy something? Is the game's story gated behind such enormous time and effort investment that it results in a soft cap, making it unenjoyable for non-paying players?

If you answered yes to any of it, it's time to reconsider your design. *Do not do these things.* Not only is it a question of ethical design, but it also poses a risk of gaining a bad reputation among players.

Games are a product in a highly competitive space, so it is important to have an edge over competition. But this makes it all the more crucial to design monetization methods with an *ethical mindset.* The goal is to make everyone happy, the developer *and* the players, and to create great experiences no matter if players are payers or non-payers.

SUMMARY

- Financial success is tracked through **KPIs**, like user engagement, retention, and revenue.
- Narrative can **improve financial performance** of a product in several ways:
  - As a **purchase incentive** (emotional appeal, emotional attachment and curiosity)
  - As a **product** (story packs, episodes, routes, spinoff stories, side content, premium choices and skipping waiting periods)
- It's important to plan your **free and premium content** in a way that is financially viable, but still allows enjoyable experiences for non-paying players. This can be done by...
  - Providing core content for free, but locking optional stories behind a paywall.
  - Monetizing time, by speeding up processes or granting early access.
  - Offering additional side content for both hard currency (paying players) and soft currency (non-paying players who prefer time investment).
  - Monetizing items and cosmetics only, which only influence the narrative experience by changing its context.
- **Monetization** should always be **done ethically**:
  - Don't exploit addictive tendencies.
  - Don't use dark patterns.
  - Don't make the game unenjoyable for non-paying players.

REFERENCES

1 Oscar Clark, "Counting on Data, " in *Games as a Service: How Free to Play Design Can Make Better Games*, Routledge, August 10, 2018, 190–191.
2 YouTube Video "Coke Zero Life As It Should Be, " accessed April 22, 2023, https://youtu.be/ITY9RIVrI8k.
3 Toiya Kristen Finley (Editor), Eddy Webb, "Buy Gems to Woo Your Lover: Free-to-Play Narratives," in *Narrative Tactics for Mobile and Social Games: Pocket-Sized Storytelling*, 1st edition, CRC Press, July 19, 2018, 227–242.
4 Harry Brignull, "Types of deceptive pattern," Deceptive Design, accessed April 22, 2023, https://www.deceptive.design/types.

Part V

Conclusion

Conclusion

While live games have arguably emerged for commercial reasons, this doesn't mean that they aren't a fascinating storytelling medium with their own unique methods and opportunities. Throughout the course of this book, we've looked into what live games are, how they work, and how to tell stories with them – may that be plot-driven, and similar to a television series, or without seasonal plot, and rather driven by gameplay, creative direction, and general narrative design.

Videogames are unique in how they can express a story through interactivity, creative direction, and contextual narrative. Live games add a whole range of other tools to this, giving us the possibility to create stories that continue to engage players for a long time to come. Even if a live game is kickstarted due to financial reasons (games are a product after all), this doesn't mean that we don't have the creative and artistic responsibility to create meaningful experiences for players and further develop the medium to reach its full potential. We can build huge words that are ever-expanding, develop characters for a much longer time, and give audiences an ever-expanding fictional world to get lost and find meaning.

It's as if videogames and television shows made a baby, and that's an exciting new way to tell stories.

I hope this book will help you craft awesome stories for games and live games alike, and that it provides you with that additional spark of inspiration needed to see the medium's true potential. We've got a long way to go to actualize all the things we can do with this new way of storytelling. And like a live game itself, this discovery journey is bound to continue for a long while to come.

DOI: 10.1201/9781003297628-24

Index

Note: **Bold** page numbers refer to tables.

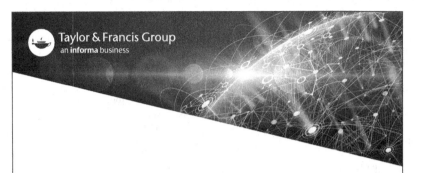